NEWMAN

The Contemplation
of Mind

NEWMAN

The Contemplation of Mind

BY

THOMAS VARGISH

OXFORD
AT THE CLARENDON PRESS
1970

Oxford University Press, Ely House, London W. 1

GLASGOW NEW YORK TORONTO MELBOURNE WELLINGTON
CAPE TOWN SALISBURY IBADAN NAIROBI DAR ES SALAAM LUSAKA ADDIS ABABA
BOMBAY CALCUTTA MADRAS KARACHI LAHORE DACCA
KUALA LUMPUR SINGAPORE HONG KONG TOKYO

PRINTED IN GREAT BRITAIN

TO MY
FATHER AND MOTHER

PREFACE

By the time of his conversion to Roman Catholicism in 1845, Newman had developed what he and his contemporaries comprehensively termed a 'philosophy of mind'. The phrase suggests an interest in mind in the broadest sense of the word and Newman's speculative range includes such wide and difficult subjects as the reality of external phenomena, the relation of perceiver to object, the presence of spirit in matter, the evidence for design in the physical universe, sequence and causality, order and volition. This range of speculation creates a problem of approach when we try to interpret the major works of his Roman Catholic career, each of which contains applications of his philosophy of mind. An examination limited to Newman's psychological insights proves too limited because psychology deals primarily with internal psychic activity, the subjective life of the individual human mind, and there exists scarcely a sentence in Newman's writings which is not informed by his awareness of what he took to be the momentous objective facts of his religion. This original psychologist was first of all a firmly orthodox Christian. His impulse is always to employ psychological discoveries as evidence for the truth of Christian doctrine. In his contemplation of mind he may best be seen as an independent but superbly acute epistemologist, moving with unusual delicacy and power from the human fascination with the human unconscious to the human aspiration to know the will of God.

In examining Newman's generous philosophy of mind I have not attempted to relate it to modern schools of psychology, philosophy, or theology with anything approaching technical definition. Although his descriptions of mind are sufficiently precise and consistent to be related by specialists to the terminology of their particular fields, little of Newman's writing, almost none of his epistemology, is technical in a scientific or narrowly philosophic sense. I am interested here in suggesting a central and flexible approach to the interpretation of his major works for their own sake and not in relating them to specific academic disciplines. He addressed his most important books to educated general readers and in this I have tried to follow him.

Newman knew that such readers are not necessarily Christians. He foresaw that greater numbers of the educated lay world would find his 'solution', as Matthew Arnold called it, 'impossible'. Newman is separated from most of us by an immense gap in sensibility, in what he calls 'first principles', a rift which the twentieth century bridges only with a considerable intellectual effort. This book is intended to reach what was once called a mixed congregation, but its author's special hope is to help make Newman more accessible to those who have less difficulty with, for example, Arnold.

The studies of Newman's theories of mind which have previously appeared try variously to use his ideas to defend faith in Christian doctrine, to support the authority of the Roman Catholic Church, to relate his psychology to traditional schools of thought such as Thomism or empiricism, or to interpret his ideas of development or his *Grammar of Assent*. My own attempt is to outline his epistemology as directly and clearly as its complexity permits and then to demonstrate its relevance to the interpretation of those of his works which are most widely read and taught.

In my first chapter I sketch the influence of the two most important traditional sources for Newman's early interest in the mind and its powers, Evangelical Christianity and English empiricism. Chapter Two sets forth at greater length his philosophy of mind as developed in his Anglican sermons and the *Essay on Development* and as finally formulated in the *Grammar of Assent*. This discussion provides the background for the following three chapters wherein I try to indicate the relevance of Newman's psychology and epistemology to his attacks on liberalism, his theories of education, and his dramatic representations of the religious development of individual minds in the novels and the *Apologia*. Each chapter, though containing references to what has been said earlier and closely related to the others, may be read independently. Readers who plunge directly into one of the last three chapters and then find a particular assertion abrupt, presumptive, or unpleasantly dogmatic are invited to consult Chapter Two in order to discover whether the point in question is explained or elaborated there. A brief summary concludes each chapter.

G. M. Young observes that one does not feel disposed to restate what Newman has said already. The caution is a sage one and I quote frequently and at length. Care has been taken to keep the terms employed exact, consistent, and faithful to the meanings they bore for Newman. I have used the standard editions of Newman's works as published by Longmans except where more attractive and easily available ones exist. Among the latter are those prepared by C. F. Harrold and the new and comprehensive Oxford *Apologia* edited by Martin J. Svaglic.

My thanks are due to Princeton University for fellowship assistance and to Dartmouth College for a Dartmouth Faculty Fellowship of two terms' leave of absence. The Reverend Doctor Thomas Parker of University College, Oxford, kindly watched over my preliminary research and Professor E. D. H. Johnson of Princeton gave precise criticism and general encouragement throughout the composition of the work in its original form as a doctoral dissertation. The Reverend C. S. Dessain, whose recent short Life offers the best biographical introduction to Newman, generously provided access to the wealth of material still to be published at the Birmingham Oratory. Professor John Finch of Dartmouth College made valuable suggestions for the final revision of the manuscript. I would like to thank the staff of the Clarendon Press for thoughtful help and advice in preparing this book for publication. My wife Linden gave many hours to the checking of notes and quotations and chiefly to her I owe the omission of those stylistic vagaries no longer to be found within.

CONTENTS

CONTENTS

CHRONOLOGY OF NEWMAN'S LIFE
AND MAJOR WORKS

1801 Born in London

1808 Enters Ealing School

1817 Takes up residence at Trinity College, Oxford

1818 Wins Trinity College Scholarship

1820 Awarded B.A. degree

1822 Becomes Fellow of Oriel College

1825 Appointed Vice-Principal of Alban Hall under Whately. Ordained priest

1828 Vicar of St. Mary's Church, Oxford

1832–3 Trip to Sicily with Hurrell Froude and his father

1833 Keble preaches sermon on 'National Apostasy' which Newman takes as the beginning of the Tractarian Movement. Newman publishes *The Arians of the Fourth Century*

1833–41 *Tracts for the Times*, of which Newman writes thirty

1836 *Lyra Apostolica* (Newman main contributor)

1837 *Lectures on the Prophetical Office of the Church*

1838 *Lectures on Justification*

1841 *Tract XC*

1843 *Sermons bearing on Subjects of the Day*
Sermons preached before the University of Oxford
Gives up St. Mary's. Preaches last Anglican sermon

1845 *An Essay on the Development of Christian Doctrine*
Gives up Oriel Fellowship. Received into the Roman Catholic Church

1847 Ordained priest in the Roman Catholic Church

1848 Founds the English Oratory. *Loss and Gain*

1849 *Discourses addressed to Mixed Congregations*

1850 *Lectures on Certain Difficulties felt by Anglicans*. Awarded Doctorate of Divinity

1851 *Lectures on the Present Position of Catholics*. Appointed Rector of the Catholic University of Ireland

1852 *Discourses on the Scope and Nature of University Education*, later published as *The Idea of a University*

1856 *Callista: a Tale of the Third Century*
The Office and Work of the Universities

xiv *Chronology*

CHAPTER ONE

Early Influences on Newman's Philosophy of Mind

How shall I seek the origin? where find
Faith in the marvellous things which then I felt?
Oft in these moments such a holy calm
Would overspread my soul, that bodily eyes
Were utterly forgotten, and what I saw
Appeared like something in myself, a dream,
A prospect in the mind.

(WORDSWORTH, *The Prelude*, II. 346–52)

IN his *Apologia pro Vita Sua* Newman recalls that during his childhood he sometimes found it difficult to think of the world as possessing a reality separate from himself. He thought life might be a dream, he an angel, and 'all this world a deception, my fellow-angels by a playful device concealing themselves from me, and deceiving me with the semblance of a material world'.[1] The loss of external reality in fantasy is not unusual among children. The experience, at any rate, was shared by Tolstoy,[2] and—what is of greater importance to the study of Newman—byWordsworth, who late in life, speaking in relation to the *Immortality Ode*, confessed an early distrust of the independent existence of the external world:

But it was not so much from feeling of animal vivacity that *my* difficulty came as from a sense of the indomitableness of the Spirit within me. I used to brood over the stories of Enoch and Elijah, and almost to persuade myself that, whatever might become of others, I should be translated, in something of the same way, to heaven. With a feeling congenial to this, I was often unable to think of external things as

[1] *Apologia pro Vita Sua*, ed. Martin J. Svaglic (Oxford, 1967), p. 16.
[2] See Aylmer Maude, *The Life of Tolstoy* (London, 1908), i. 32.

having external existence, and I communed with all that I saw as some-thing not apart from, but inherent in, my own immaterial nature.[1]

As part of a similar egocentric experience, which in its fullness must be seen as theocentric as well, the young Newman also believed for a time in the certainty of his own salvation. It was, in fact, the doctrine of final perseverance which assisted in isolating him from surrounding objects, which confirmed him in his 'mistrust of material phenomena', and which permitted him to rest in the thought of 'two and two only absolute and luminously self-evident beings', himself and his Creator.[2] Even in his first serious work, *The Arians of the Fourth Century*, New-man can speak of a connection between a belief in Christ's divinity and 'an emancipation from the tyranny of the visible world'.[3]

The source of Wordsworth's experience is beyond the scope of this chapter, but the significance of the comparison lies in the intensity of his recollection and that of Newman's. The parallel strikes the proper introductory note to a chapter which proposes to indicate how Newman's 'childish imaginings' were exploited and developed by two very different schools of thought, Evan-gelical Christianity and English empiricism.

EARLY RELIGIOUS INFLUENCES

The Evangelical writers, whose works the young Newman admired, characteristically emphasized the importance of a healthy and lively inner spiritual life. They urged the necessity of maintaining a personal sense of guilt, of exercising the con-science lest this conviction of personal guilt should fade, and, emphatically, of properly distinguishing between transient sentiment and genuine religious conviction.[4] They thought of the glories of the Creation with gratitude, but in their

---

[1] *Poetical Works*, ed. Ernest de Selincourt and Helen Darbishire (Oxford, 1947), iv. 463.
[2] *Apologia*, p. 18   [3] *Arians* (London, 1897), p. 273.
[4] See, for example, Philip Doddridge, *The Rise and Progress of Religion in the Soul*, seventh edition (London, 1753), pp. 126 ff.

intense preoccupation with the inner state they tended to dismiss the material world, at least in their theological and devotional literature, as a scene of trial and temptation in which spiritual realities were obscured. Ford K. Brown discusses at length what struck more radical contemporaries as the Evangelical indifference to broad domestic institutional reform, an indifference resulting from the belief that the important reality dwelt within:

To do away with the irreligion that is the cause of vice and sin was the whole Evangelical purpose. . . . Human institutions that seemed to other people to create sin, vice and depravity had no immediate or primary interest. They were not even *second causes*. In so far as they were bad—that is, were not divinely ordered—they did not produce but came from the depravity of the human heart.[1]

About the time of his conversion to serious Christianity at the age of fifteen, Newman fell under the influence of an Evangelical divine, the Reverend Walter Mayers. Mayers urged him to read Doddridge's *The Rise and Progress of Religion in the Soul*.[2] The Christian, Doddridge argued, must be *'spiritually minded'* for *'to be carnally minded is death'*. The Christian attends to his interests in the world merely as a matter of duty, but his thoughts, affections, and pursuits will be spiritual. He *'will walk by Faith, and not by Sight'*. Invisible and even 'incomprehensible' objects will occupy his mind. His faith will act upon the apprehension of Christ, whom without having seen he will love and honour. His mind will be drawn to the unseen world which he knows to be eternal and therefore infinitely more worthy of his 'affectionate regard' than any of *'those Things which are seen'*.[3]

These sentiments exemplify the passionate commonplaces of Evangelical devotional literature, but Newman did not receive them as platitudes. His early sense of the unreality of material phenomena led him to accept this form of Evangelical spirituality as the most forceful and necessary of emotional attitudes.

---

[1] *Fathers of the Victorians* (Cambridge, England, 1961), p. 28. In quotations, any italics are the original author's, not mine.

[2] R. D. Middleton, *Newman at Oxford* (London, 1950), p. 12.

[3] *Rise and Progress*, p. 129.

Even the more intellectually rigorous Joseph Butler, in his idea of an analogy between the separate works of God, leading to a belief in the sacramental connection between the material and spiritual worlds, could strengthen Newman's youthful impression of 'the unreality of material phenomena'.[1] Again, according to C. F. Harrold, the works of the Calvinist William Romaine not only led Newman to the doctrine of final perseverance but also fostered his sense of isolation from the material world.[2]

If the sources of sin and the keys to salvation lie in the mind and heart, then among the most significant of Christian activities must be intense self-examination. Evangelicals exercised constant watchfulness over their feelings as the indices of their spiritual readiness. Many of them, and the young Newman, kept journals in which they recorded their spiritual progress and their lapses.[3] This watchfulness, Romaine observed with somber psychological perspicacity, is the more anxious because the believer, certain of Christ's coming, is ignorant of the time.[4] Although Newman soon came to distrust intense self-examination as reducing religion to a mere exercise in introspection, his letters at the age of seventeen show him examining his heart as he prepares to compete for the Trinity scholarship. Perhaps he wants the scholarship too much? Let God refuse it if he desires it in vanity.[5] At nineteen he believes that Christ's *inward* suffering in the garden was His 'greatest agony'.[6]

From the constant self-examination and keeping of journals fostered by Evangelicalism, Newman learned what might be called autobiographical habits early in life. Indeed, the 'lives' of good men were approved Evangelical reading, and perhaps the most celebrated of these was Thomas Scott's *The Force of Truth*. Newman called Scott the man 'to whom (humanly

---

    [1] *Apologia*, p. 23. Newman credits Keble with precisely the same influence, a knowledge that 'material phenomena are both the types and instruments of real things unseen' (*Apologia*, p. 29).
    [2] *John Henry Newman* (London, 1945), p. 4.
    [3] See *John Henry Newman: Autobiographical Writings*, ed. H. Tristram (New York, 1957), p. 144.
    [4] William Romaine, *Whole Works* (London, 1837), pp. 882-3.
    [5] *Autobiographical Writings*, pp. 157-9.   [6] Ibid., p. 164.

speaking) I almost owe my soul',[1] and admired his proverb, 'Growth the only evidence of life'. Scott's own religious growth provides the subject of *The Force of Truth*, subtitled 'An Authentic Narrative'. He excuses himself for writing it on the grounds that it presents an account of a man being led to embrace a system of doctrine which once he heartily despised.[2] Scott spends most of his time, as Newman was to do in the *Apologia*, discussing the process of his conversion.

In addition to intensifying his concern with the reality of the visible world, arousing his interest, at first passive and personal, with the psychology of belief, and confirming him in certain autobiographical tendencies, Evangelicalism probably established in Newman's thought certain crucial assumptions about the nature of the mind, assumptions which he later modified but never lost.

One traditional idea most alien to twentieth-century readers is that the mind, its thoughts and impulses and reactions, can be carefully controlled by the believer. William Beveridge, whose *Private Thoughts upon Religion* was given to Newman at sixteen by the Reverend Mr. Mayers, resolved not only to be always exercising his thoughts upon good objects, but also to 'stop every Thought at its first entering my Heart, and to examine it whence it comes and whither it tends'. He plans as well so to order his thoughts, 'that they may not one justle out another, nor any of them prejudice the business I am about'. He will take care not to let fancy or imagination impose upon him, but

---

[1] *Apologia*, p. 18. Newman's gratitude to these Evangelical writers suggests that he remained sympathetic to many of their emphases. It has been convincingly argued, however, that the term 'Evangelical' can be applied to Newman's youth only with considerable qualification. His first conversion lacked the violence or passion of conviction, though perhaps not the assurance, considered characteristic of Evangelicalism. See Stephen Dessain, 'Newman's First Conversion', *Newman Studien*, iii (1957), 37–53.

[2] *The Force of Truth* (Philadelphia, 1793), p. 89. This work was first published in 1779. Scott's maxim, 'Growth the only evidence of life' is echoed in Newman's *Essay on the Development of Christian Doctrine:* 'Thus, a power of development is a proof of life, not only in its essay, but especially in its success; for a mere formula either does not expand or is shattered in expanding. A living idea becomes many, yet remains one' (ed. C. F. Harrold, New York, 1949, p. 173).

to make his affections subservient to the dictates of his understanding.[1] Doddridge shares these resolutions with Beveridge,[2]
but the goal of complete self-control of mental processes finds
a still more powerful exponent in William Law.

Law influenced both Evangelicals and Tractarians. His major
work, *A Serious Call to a Devout and Holy Life*, is a classic of
doctrine as well as of introspective devotion. The Christian,
Law urges, must maintain a temper which enables him to perform worldly tasks with a spiritual mind. Devotion is no mere
form of words, but a spiritual state, a 'state of the heart'. It should
grow and increase as an 'improvable talent of the mind', as
'a temper that is to grow and increase like our reason and
judgment, and to be formed in us by such a regular, diligent
use of proper means, as are necessary to form any otherwise
habit of mind'.[3] Newman echoes these ideas in his early sermons.
It is the Christian's duty not merely to examine, but to control
the mind's activity. In 'The Religious Use of Excited Feeling'
(1831), he views faith as a 'calm, deliberate, rational principle'.[4]
In a sermon on 'Religious Emotion' (1831), the religious principle is 'calm, sober, and deliberate'; indeed, the more religious
men become, the calmer they become; they form 'habits' of
faith.[5] 'Moral truth', writes Newman to his mother in 1829,
'is gained by patient study, by calm reflection, silently as the
dew falls'.[6] A year later he tells a friend that moral truth is
discovered 'not by reasoning, but by habituation'.[7] And although
the chief point here is in the disciplining of the mind, it is worth
noticing in passing that Newman already sees the habit of faith
as a perceptive as well as a regulatory power.

[1] *Private Thoughts* (London, 1709), pp. 176, 185, 189–90.
[2] Doddridge, *Rise and Progress*, pp. 126 ff.
[3] William Law, *A Serious Call to a Devout and Holy Life* (London, 1906),
p. 183.
[4] *Parochial and Plain Sermons* (London, 1901), i. 123.
[5] Ibid., i. 181.
[6] *Letters and Correspondence of John Henry Newman during His Life in the English
Church*, ed. Anne Mozley (London, 1891), i. 206. This work will hereafter be
designated 'Mozley'.
[7] Ibid., i. 231. The significance of Newman's idea that the mind gains truth by
growing *habituated* to it will be discussed in the following chapters.

Newman's theories on the duty of the Christian to control his thoughts and beliefs and on the power of the will to direct them will be analysed in the next chapter. But as a preliminary indication of the significance of these principles to Newman's later writings we may take three of his 'propositions of liberalism', each of which he 'earnestly denounced and abjured' and which he felt, in 1865, had been held by the forces opposing Tractarianism:

2. No one can believe what he does not understand.
4. It is dishonest in a man to make an act of faith in what he has not had brought home to him by actual proof.
5. It is immoral in a man to believe more than he can spontaneously receive as being congenial to his moral and mental nature.[1]

'Indeed,' asks G. M. Young, 'why should he? Or indeed, how can he?' Young observes that we here approach a chasm which the twentieth-century mind cannot easily cross. 'Somewhere about 1860 a rift opens in the English intelligence.'[2] It is Newman's almost prophetic anticipation of this rift and his realization of it as it opened which helped drive him to his life-long endeavour to construct a psychology of assent, a psychological and a metaphysical basis for assent to the mysterious, the unproved, and the uncongenial, and which led to his creation of a 'grammar' for the expression and defence of the assenting mind.

To the Evangelicals who influenced him Newman's later subtle intellectual handling of assent would have seemed a darkening and confusing of the obvious. In their sphere the rift had yet to open and most Christians had yet to feel publicly the tremors caused by the popularization of late eighteenth- and early nineteenth-century scepticism. And besides, belief, in the Evangelical opinion, derived more from a right state of heart than of head. John Newton, one of whose titles, *Cardiphonia or, The Utterance of the Heart*, recalls Newman's motto as Cardinal, *Cor ad cor loquitur*, speaks slightingly of a 'moonlight

[1] *Apologia*, p. 260.
[2] G. M. Young, *Daylight and Champaign* (London, 1948), p. 100.

head-knowledge, derived from a system of sentiments'.[1] Newman echoes this Evangelical assumption in a letter of 1825
to his brother Charles, who was experimenting with various
forms of freethinking: 'I wish it to be distinctly understood
that I consider the rejection of Christianity to arise from a fault
of the *heart*, not of the intellect; that unbelief arises, not from
mere error of reasoning, but either from pride or from sensuality'.[2]
These assertions are also characteristic of the brilliant eighteenth-
century Calvinist, Joseph Milner, whose church history Newman
read simultaneously with the works of Thomas Newton. Plain
men of little skill in argument are 'most susceptible of assent
in all questions of a religious and moral nature'. In a being so
corrupt as man, the most rigorous exercises of reason in religion
do little more than confound and mislead. 'The intellectual
faculty, the more solid and piercing it is, sinks only the deeper
in absurdity, while it mixes itself with the mire and dirt of human
depravity.'[3]

It was Locke, said Milner, who 'led the fashion in introducing
a pompous parade of *reasoning* into religion'. Reason was once
the submissive handmaid of Christianity; now she usurps its
function. The train of influence moves from Locke to Hume,
'a gradual melancholy declension from evangelical simplicity'.
Reason has indeed benefited mankind, but anyone possessed of
'spiritual understanding' will lament that reason 'impertinently
intermeddled with the Gospel', and bewail the increase in moral
misery which, 'since Mr. Locke's time, has pervaded these
kingdoms'. The 'intrusions of reason', argues Milner in anticipation of Newman's 1831 University Sermon entitled 'The
Usurpations of Reason', 'have been a most powerful cause of
our national depravity'.[4]

---

[1] John Newton, *Cardiphonia or, The Utterance of the Heart* (Philadelphia, undated), pp. 289–90.

[2] Unpublished letter at the Birmingham Oratory, dated 24 March 1825. The
materials at the Oratory will henceforth be designated 'Birmingham Papers'.

[3] Joseph Milner, *Gibbon's Account of Christianity Considered with some Strictures
on Hume's Dialogues Concerning Natural Religion* (Lincoln, 1808), pp. 218–19.
This work will hereafter be designated 'Milner'.

[4] Ibid., pp. 172, 173–4.

Other than this similarity in terminology and content, there is no conclusive evidence that Newman read Milner's attack on Gibbon and Hume as he had read his church history. But Milner's book shows how acute an Evangelical could be in attacking the sceptical use of reason against Christianity. Joseph Butler, of course, had effectually weakened the rational attack on religious faith in his *Analogy* and *Sermons* by demonstrating that most of our conclusions are based at best upon 'probability', an idea which ultimately led Newman to the question of the logical cogency of faith. Indeed, Newman ultimately became so alive to this question that even Keble's *The Christian Year* stimulated his interest in the rationality and firmness of religious assent.[1]

Some time before the appearance of *The Christian Year*, Newman's early spontaneous questioning of the reality of the material universe, supported by Evangelical distrust of reasoning in religion, had confirmed him in his search for some extra-rational approach to the discovery of religious and moral truth. A memorandum dated 1 June 1821 indicates the depth of the young Newman's involvement with the question:

About a week ago I dreamed a spirit came to me and discoursed about the other world. I had several meetings with it. Dreams address themselves so immediately to the mind, that to express in any form of words the feelings produced by the speeches themselves of my mysterious visitant, were a fruitless endeavor. Among other things it said that it was absolutely impossible for the reason of man to understand the mystery of the Holy Trinity, and in vain to argue about it; but that everything in another world was so very, very plain that there was not the slightest difficulty about it. I cannot put into any sufficiently strong form of words the ideas that were conveyed to me. I thought I instantly fell on my knees overcome with gratitude to God for so kind a message.[2]

Newman's insistence on the strength of his feelings, the reassurance provided by the spirit in actually dismissing reason as inadequate to comprehend this primary mystery of Christianity, and the profusion of the dreamer's gratitude for such a message should all impress us with the extraordinary importance

---

[1] *Apologia*, pp. 23, 30.   [2] Mozley, i. 54–5.

this epistemological difficulty had for him. What may be considered the great question of Newman's intellectual life came to
him early: If reason as generally exercised is earth-bound, how
can the human mind reach religious truth?

We have seen that John Newton and Joseph Milner thought
men of simple intellectual natures more susceptible to assent.
Milner, making a point which Newman was to employ in
various writings throughout his career, argued that the apprehension of the Gospel is the same kind of apprehension as that
suggested by Locke's 'simple ideas'. In his *Essay Concerning
Human Understanding*, Locke maintained that the basic sources of
reasoning are the simple ideas formed directly from sensory
perceptions. Milner states that in a similar way the virtuous man,
the Christian, responds directly to the biblical narrative because
it is in his mental nature to do so.[1]

The true Christian responds positively to biblical and moral
truth because of a natural but divinely implanted capacity for
response and judgement closely associated with conscience.
Like Newman, Milner believed that conscience is an innate
quality, rather like one aspect of the Renaissance concept of Right
Reason, a voice of the Moral Governor present in man from
birth. It cannot be implanted or utterly eradicated by education.
It has no connection with any elaborate process of reasoning.
'Its voice is plain and strong, not inimical to, but far superior
to the voice of reason.' And 'the very *intuitive* nature of this
moral sense is no contemptible proof that it is from God'.[2] With
similar arguments Newman praises the virtues of self-examination
in his earliest sermons. Neither books nor sermons can profit us
unless we examine our hearts, not merely for a sense of our own
sin, but for that sense of guilt for sin which informs us that our
conscience is an agent of the Moral Governor. Only by developing this self-awareness can we respond properly to doctrine.[3]

In both Milner and Newman, however, the faculty which
apprehends religious truth is not precisely the conscience. Despite
the sanctity of its origins, the conscience remains primarily a

[1] Milner, pp. 175–6.   [2] Ibid. 215–17.
[3] 'Secret Faults' (1825), *Parochial and Plain Sermons*, i. 42–3.

monitor. But the idea of a perceptive faculty was also inherent in Right Reason. When I discussed the assumption that extensive control could be exercised over the activities of the mind, its beliefs and impulses, I quoted William Law as urging that devotion be considered 'as an improvable talent of the mind, as a temper that is to grow and increase like our reason and judgement, and to be formed in us by such a regular, diligent use of the proper means, as are necessary to form any other wise habit of mind'.[1] On the same theme, Milner argued that 'this divine taste, and all the knowledge deduced from it, may be strengthened by exercise, and impaired by sloth'. Thus '*He that is spiritual judgeth all things*'; but because such a faculty is a mystery to the wicked, '*he himself is judged of no man*' (1 Cor. 2).[2] Perhaps these arguments from Law and Milner help explain the meaning of Newman's conviction that moral truth is gained 'silently, as the dew falls', and 'not by reasoning, but by habituation'.[3] In an early sermon Newman urges that if we obey God strictly, in time 'faith will become like sight; we shall have no more difficulty in finding what will please God than in moving our limbs, or in understanding the conversation of our familiar friends. This is the blessedness of confirmed obedience'.[4] This 'improvable talent of the mind', this 'divine taste', this 'habituation'—to group concepts whose distinctions are at most minor—in being natural to the mind, in requiring cultivation to become perfect, and in passing judgement upon its own apprehensions, bears a distinct resemblance to the faculty which a half-century later Newman christened the Illative Sense.

Thus Evangelical writers such as Newton, Scott, Beveridge, Doddridge, and Milner, and other more catholic religious thinkers, like Law, Butler, and Keble, exercised a strong influence on Newman's early interest in the nature of the mind and the origins, methods, and limits of knowledge. The Evangelical emphasis upon self-examination and the right state of heart contributed to Newman's doubts about the religious importance

---

[1] *A Serious Call*, pp. 183–4.   [2] Milner, pp. 175–6.
[3] Mozley, i. 206, 231.
[4] 'Religious Faith Rational' (1929), *Parochial and Plain Sermons*, i. 202.

of external phenomena and directed his attention within himself. He formed certain autobiographical habits, preserving letters and keeping a journal in which he questioned his motives and recorded his aspirations. At the same time he accepted certain assumptions about mental activity, such as the personal ability to exercise rigid control over beliefs, impulses, and reactions. He grew suspicious of the efficacy of reason in religious matters and became concerned with its 'usurpations'. He began to seek a more accurate psychological vocabulary, a more precise means of describing the processes by which the mind judges the truth and virtue of religious influences.

RATIONALIST AND EMPIRICIST INFLUENCES: WHATELY

Writing the *Apologia* in 1864, Newman tried to explain why he had broken with the man who had been his guide during the first years of his Oriel fellowship and why he thought that Richard Whately had joined those forces of liberalism which he saw as disrupting the organization of the Anglican Church and undermining the faith of her congregation. Newman's attitude toward Whately's liberalism will be discussed in a later chapter. For my present purpose, that of examining early influences on Newman's theories of the mind and of the 'reasonableness' of religious belief, it is not as Archbishop but as Oxford don that Whately is important.

In the *Apologia* Newman cites Butler's notion that 'probability is the guide of life' as a source of his own preoccupation with the logical cogency of faith.[1] Three years before Newman was elected Fellow of Oriel College, Whately had published an interesting pamphlet entitled *Historic Doubts Relative to Napoleon Bonaparte*. Following Butler's method, Whately observes that sceptics accuse believers of taking the premises of doctrine for granted. But is this habit of assumption not equally true of sceptics themselves? Many who never actually saw Napoleon believe accounts of his actions. There is perhaps as much logical or rational difficulty in accepting these representations as in

[1] *Apologia*, p. 23.

receiving the narratives of the Old Testament. Whately illustrates his point with an account of Napoleon in biblical style.
We are forced, he maintains, to conclude that 'this case is much
more open to sceptical doubts than some miraculous histories'.
Not quite ingenuously, Whately calls upon those who profess
to be advocates of free inquiry, who disdain to be carried along
with the stream of popular opinion, and who will listen to no
testimony that runs counter to experience, to follow their own
principles fairly and consistently: 'Let, them, in short, shew themselves ready to detect the cheats, and despise the fables, of poli-
ticians as of priests.' In a polemic style which anticipates that
of Newman's *Tamworth Reading Room*, Whately concludes by
urging those who, after all that he has said, cannot doubt the
existence and achievements of Napoleon, honestly to confess
that they do not apply the same sceptical demand for proofs
to Napoleon as to Moses. They are therefore bound to renounce
this plan of reasoning altogether, and allow that probability
can legitimately induce certitude. If a man accepts nothing but
what is perfectly authenticated, he is compelled to doubt the
existence of any event which he has not personally witnessed.[1]

'We shall never have done beginning', writes Newman in
1841, 'if we determine to begin with proof.... Resolve to
believe nothing, and you must prove your proofs and analyse
your elements.'[2] Newman, like Whately, enjoys demonstrating
that most of our certitudes rest ultimately on convergences of
probabilities, and that religious convictions are therefore as
'reasonable' as most assumptions held by sceptics. This risky
argument implies that the Christian has the right to maintain
with inner certitude convictions which are logically only probable. Newman's favourite example, which he employs instead
of the existence of Napoleon, is the proposition that 'Great
Britain is an Island'.[3] Most of us, he observes, though we have

---

[1] *Historic Doubts Relative to Napoleon Bonaparte* (London, 1819), pp. 42, 47, 18.
[2] 'The Tamworth Reading Room', *Essays and Sketches*, ed. C. F. Harrold
(New York, 1948), ii. 206.
[3] See, for example, *An Essay in Aid of a Grammar of Assent*, ed. C. F. Harrold
(New York, 1947), p. 143.

never circumnavigated Britain, accept this as fact without question. But how do we really know? We accept it on the probability, which is nevertheless sufficient to induce certitude. Whatever one thinks of the validity of this argumentative gambit, it seems likely that though Newman's ultimate source for the argument from probability was Butler, his polemics came from Whately.

But the association between Newman and Whately was closest during the composition of the *Elements of Logic*. Whately acknowledged Newman in the preface as one 'who actually composed a considerable portion of the work as it now stands, from manuscripts not designed for publication, and who is the original author of several pages'.[1]

Whately viewed logic primarily as a science of reasoning. Logic can lay down the principles by which all men must reason, whether they are aware of it or not. The reasoning process is similar in all subjects. Logic relates a great number of small points to one great principle, thus incorporating the method of induction and making logic useful to empirical science, of which it is the expression. Whately qualified this definition by observing that those who have made exaggerated claims for logic have brought it into disrepute by raising impossible expectations. But, as the enemies of the Gospel employ logic, the friends of religion had better not ignore it.

Logic, Whately insisted, is not concerned with discovery, but with forms of expression. It lays down the principles on which reasoning should be conducted and can ascertain the validity or fallaciousness of any apparent argument, 'as far as the form of expression is concerned; that being alone the proper province of logic'.[2]

The qualification is vital, for by defining logic as the guide to 'the form of expression' Whately deprives it of much of its traditional power. Logic is the science of reasoning and

---

[1] *Elements of Logic* (London, 1827), p. vi. In 1852 Newman remembered writing only a few pages on the history of logic in the introduction (*The Letters and Diaries of John Henry Newman*, eds. Charles Stephen Dessain and Vincent Ferrer Blehl, S.J., London, 1964, xv. 176).

[2] *Elements of Logic*, p. 127.

'Reasoning shall be taken in the sense not of *every* exercise of the Reason, but of Argumentation'. Reasoning is only one of the three operations of the mind which are involved in argument. First comes 'Simple Apprehension' (real or notional, as Newman was to observe in the *Grammar of Assent*), then 'Judgment' (forty years later a prerogative of the Illative Sense), then 'Discourse or reasoning'. Discoveries are made 'by means of Reasoning *combined* with other operations'. May a theory be made out concerning these suggestive 'other operations'? To the young Newman the question must have been a stirring one. Whately, if it is he and not Newman writing, observes that some examination of those powers of consciousness which are not logical might be made but 'it would hardly be possible to build up anything like a regular Science respecting these matters, such as logic is, with respect to the theory of reasoning'.[1] Indeed, we can witness the truth of this prediction in the irregularity, the tortuous difficulty, and the explosive suggestiveness of the *Grammar of Assent*.

In a letter of 1826 Newman acknowledges Whately's guidance: 'I know who it was that first gave me heart to look about me after my election and taught me to think correctly, and (strange office for an instructor) to rely upon myself.'[2] The parenthesis seems odd: why should an instructor not teach his pupil to rely upon himself? Probably Newman already wished to stress his independence of Whately. But if the influences I have been suggesting are valid, the acknowledgement is also incomplete. Newman not only derived habits of mind from Whately but also particular ideas and techniques. Specifically, he learned the value to controversy of the argument from probability; and, perhaps, in examining the process by which the mind leaps from probable evidence to intellectual conviction or certitude, he deepened his interest in the psychology of belief. Certainly he was led to consider the ways in which the mind apprehends, judges, and reasons when he assisted Whately on *Elements of Logic*. Possibly, too, this task confirmed him in his view that

---

[1] Ibid., pp. 215, 54, 235, 245.
[2] *Autobiographical Writings*, p. 68.

reasoning by itself is inadequate for the apprehension of spiritual reality and for the discovery of spiritual truth.

<h2 style="text-align:center">RATIONALIST AND EMPIRICIST INFLUENCES:
LOCKE AND HUME</h2>

Locke was perhaps the first English philosopher Newman read carefully.[1] We can say of Locke and Newman, perhaps of Hume as well, what J. S. Mill said of Bentham and Coleridge, that 'They agreed . . . in perceiving that the groundwork of all other philosophy must be laid in the philosophy of the mind'.[2] In chapter 6 of the *Grammar of Assent* Newman acknowledges Locke's epistemological pioneering and expresses his admiration for it. But in the *Grammar*, Newman's chief concern is to correct Locke's assumption that the mind can accord the precise degree of assent warranted by the evidence for each inference. In a letter of 1870 to R. H. Hutton, Newman asserts that this is to judge human nature not from facts but from pure imagination, from 'a self-created vision of an optimism by the rule of "what they think it ought to be" '.[3] As we have seen, Newman came to believe that assent is always an absolute mental state, though the evidence which induces it may be merely probable.[4]

But perhaps Newman's earliest quarrel with Locke did not concern his own theory of mental operations, a philosophy of mind which began to assume a pronounced outline only in his thirties. Probably Newman's suspicion of the reality of the material world, his awareness of a universe moved not by physical laws but by spirits, led him to distrust sensory experience as the primary source of knowledge. The senses may perhaps be trusted in what they convey to us, but we should not imagine

[1] Middleton, *Newman at Oxford*, pp. 26–7.

[2] In 'Coleridge' from *John Stuart Mill on Bentham and Coleridge* (New York, 1962), p. 102.

[3] Quoted by Adrian J. Boekraad and Henry Tristram in *The Argument from Conscience to the Existence of God according to J. H. Newman* (Louvain, 1961), p. 189.

[4] As early as 1846 or 1847, Newman directly attacked Locke's equation of certitude with objective proof: 'a conclusion may be more certain than the premises . . . a clear steadfast conviction, may be the legitimate consequence of arguments in themselves but probable' (Birmingham Papers).

that what they convey is the only, or even the important reality. In a sermon on 'The Resurrection of the Body' (1832), Newman observes that we are apt to talk about our bodies as if we knew what they really are, 'whereas we only know what our eyes tell us'. Bodies grow, mature, decay; but we know no more about them than what meets our senses. 'We have no direct cognizance of what may be called the substantive existence of the body, only of its accidents.' We distinguish between body and soul as if we knew much about them, but we use the words, for the most part, without clear or profound meaning. And when by these assertions Newman has sufficiently shaken his audience's trust, not so much in the simple accuracy as in the depth, the very significance, of their perception of matter, he awakens a sense of the sacramental principle with the alarming but orthodox statement, 'The dust around us will one day become animate'.[1]

Newman's sense that a vividly animate spiritual universe lies behind or in the physical one owes much to his reading, in his late twenties, of the Fathers of the Church. The teaching of Clement and Origen struck him 'as if in response to ideas, which, with little external to encourage them, I had cherished so long'. These cherished ideas should now be familiar to us. They concern especially the sacramental principle, the principle that 'the exterior world, physical and historical, was but the manifestation to our senses of realities greater than itself'.[2] The Alexandrian Platonists taught Newman, or confirmed him in his suspicion, that one must see behind the attributes, through the disguises of the material world. They revealed to him the doctrine of the 'economy', that nature and history provide those who can read them with allegorical information on the spiritual world.[3] Thus the more important function of consciousness

---

[1] *Parochial and Plain Sermons*, i. 273, 278.

[2] *Apologia*, p. 36. It has been suggested to me that a link between the Alexandrian Platonists and the Evangelicals could have been provided by the Platonist influence of the Epistle to the Hebrews and the opening of St. John's Gospel.

[3] For an admirably concise account of these influences, see C. F. Harrold, 'Newman and the Alexandrian Platonists', *Modern Philology*, xxxvii (1940), 280–2.

seemed to Newman not to form simple ideas from basic sensory experience but to transcend the world of matter, the world of Lockean intelligence, by treating it as in itself a mere 'economy'.

If Locke's assumptions about the capacity of the senses to perceive material reality with accuracy and his assertion of the authority of reason (a comprehensive term in Locke's writings) were viewed coldly by the Evangelicals who knew of them, Hume's scepticism was abhorred. Milner observes that infidels have not stopped where Mr. Locke did; Locke, at least, was a 'speculative believer'. From Locke down to Hume, 'that is to say, from a cold historical assent down to atheism itself, or to what is much the same, there has been a gradual declension from evangelical simplicity'. Hume had the sagacity to perceive the argumentative or apparent advantage Locke gave reason over religion; and Hume has so displayed reason's triumph, 'that she seems in his hands to be, what Grecian vanity feigned of Alexander, at a loss for more work, and groaning because she has no more enemies to conquer'.[1]

Newman tells us that at the age of fifteen he gave his father to understand that he read 'some of Hume's Essays; and perhaps that on Miracles'. 'But', he adds, 'perhaps it was a brag.' What influence Hume could have had on him at that age, it is impossible to say. The verses from Voltaire denying the immortality of the soul gave rise to religious doubts.[2] Perhaps Hume's essays had the same effect. We know that at twenty Newman could still question the security of his religious convictions: 'But I principally wish to attain a strength of faith, of which at present I feel the want very much. Every now and then momentary clouds of doubt cross my mind.'[3]

Whether Hume was behind the clouds is a matter for only the most tenuous speculation, but Newman read the great sceptic with some sympathy. He refers to Hume in his first essay on miracles, composed in 1825–6: Hume supplies us with an observation 'so just, when taken in its full extent, that

---

[1] Milner, pp. 173–4.   [2] Apologia, p. 17.
[3] From his Private Journal, entry for August 1821, Autobiographical Writings, p. 174.

I shall make it the groundwork of the inquiry on which I am entering'. Hume observes that the Deity discovers himself to us by his works, so that we have no rational grounds for ascribing to him attributes or actions inconsistent with those which His works in nature convey. Hume, of course, employs this argument ironically to discredit miraculous accounts in general. Newman, however, employs the criterion that a miracle be a recognizable work of the Creator of the natural order in the interests of Christianity, contending that 'this reasonable demand is satisfied in the Jewish and Christian Scriptures'.[1] His audience must have been compelled to admire the intellectual daring which would take an argument for the authenticity of scriptural miracles from the writings of their most brilliant sceptic.

Such tactics are typical of Newman as controversialist, and nowhere more striking than in his use of Hume's epistemology. It is here that G. M. Young's appraisal most justly applies: 'He is always skimming along the verge of a logical catastrophe, and always relying on his dialectic agility to save himself from falling: always exposing what seems to be an unguarded spot, and always revealing a new line of defence when the unwary assailant has reached it. I am not sure it is not a general characteristic of Oxford.'[2] The risks of such a method are obvious, and Newman perhaps needed all his dialectical skill to prevent his admiration for Hume from affecting religious convictions.

As J. M. Cameron points out, the philosophical affinities of Newman with Hume are very pronounced. Indeed, Newman's intellectual sympathies are, in philosophical matters. often with the empiricist school:

It is not accidental that we find in the unpublished material at the Birmingham Oratory appreciative notes, written in 1857, on Mill's *Logic*; or that in this material we find such remarks as: 'The logical evolutions of science (induction &c.), are a rule of the game, not in the nature of things' (note of 16th November 1861); '... the soul would

---

[1] 'The Miracles of Scripture', *Two Essays on Biblical and Ecclesiastical Miracles* (London, 1892), pp. 15–16.
[2] *Daylight and Champaign*, p. 57.

C

not think without some external stimulus (but) our experience is not so much of external things, but of our own minds' (24th February 1859); 'In most departments of writing to speak of self is egotistical: not so in metaphysics. In it the writer cannot propose to do more than record his own opinions, the phenomena to which he appeals and the principles which he assumes being within his own breast. . . . His hermit spirit dwells in his own sphere' (1st December 1859). There is no mistaking the company these remarks keep.[1]

Nor can there be any doubt that these notes relate back to the prevailing impression of Newman's childhood that the material world is unreal, that they demonstrate a continued interest in our 'emancipation from the tyranny of the visible world'.

Cameron points out that one of the philosophical questions Hume discusses is whether we can reasonably believe in the existence of bodies external to ourselves. Hume concludes that there are no convincing arguments for this belief. Still, we persist in believing and acting as if such bodies do exist, and no philosophical arguments to the contrary produce any lasting impression. Nature, not reason, observes Cameron, 'gives sentence against scepticism', or, in Hume's words, Nature 'has doubtless esteemed it an affair of too great importance, to be entrusted to our uncertain reasonings and speculations'.[2] Newman, Cameron continues, makes a similar point when he desires to show the 'reasonableness' (rather than the 'rationality') of faith. We trust our senses though they occasionally deceive us, but even if they were always consistent, Newman observes, 'their fidelity would not be thereby proved'. We think that the antecedent probability that they are faithful is so strong that we dispense with proof. 'We take the point for granted; or, if we have grounds for it, these either lie in our secret belief in the stability of nature, or in the preserving presence and uniformity of Divine Providence—which, again, are points assumed'.[3] In the same way, as

---

[1] J. M. Cameron, 'Newman and Empiricism', *The Night Battle* (London, 1962), pp. 220–1.

[2] Quoted by Cameron, 'The Logic of the Heart', ibid., p. 210.

[3] 'The Nature of Faith in Relation to Reason' (1839), *Fifteen Sermons Preached Before the University of Oxford* (London, 1887), p. 213. Hereafter cited as '*University Sermons*'.

another assumption which Newman considers naturally congenial to the mind, Christians trust to the fidelity of testimony
offered for a revelation.

Thus we can see that the same early questions about external
reality, and the sense of separation from the visible world which
so intensified Newman's participation in Evangelical doctrine
and devotion, prepared him to be responsive to the explorations of English empirical philosophy. Newman himself makes
the connection in a letter to his sister Jemima in 1834 in which
he confesses his ignorance of Berkeley, but gives his opinion
that to a man who holds the moral governance of God as *existing in and through his conscience* it does not matter whether he
believes his senses. For he will in either case hold what he apprehends as the external world to be a scene of trial, whether a
separate reality or not, 'just as a child's game may be a trial'.
Newman himself does not mean to deny the existence of matter,
but—he echoes what he said in 'The Resurrection of the Body'—
'I should deny that *what we saw* was more than accidents of it,
and say that space perhaps is but a condition of the objects of
sense, not a reality'.[1]

Indeed, as Newman observes in an early sermon called 'Religious Faith Rational' (1829), when we examine the subject carefully we find that 'we know little more than that we exist, and
that there is an Unseen Power whom we are bound to obey'.
Beyond this we *trust*, 'so that, in fact, almost all we do, every
day of our lives, is on trust'. It may be said that we act on faith

---

[1] Mozley, ii. 40–1. This letter suggests a necessary modification of Cameron's
thesis that in both Hume and Newman 'a destructive philosophical analysis is a
moment in an argument designed to show that we have no alternative to putting
our trust in "nature". But as to what putting our trust in "nature" commits us to,
here the two men could scarcely be more different' (*The Night Battle*, p. 223).
Newman generally seems content to put his trust in nature, and certainly his
commitment is radically opposed to Hume's. But, as this letter to his sister
proves, he did have an alternative: if the 'hermit spirit dwells in his own sphere'
and what we perceive are merely images projected within our minds by a Divine
Examiner, we still have the Christian duty to face this internal trial. And as we
remain conscious of our own being, the necessary objective existence of the
Creator is not questioned. As we shall see in a discussion of the *Apologia*, Newman
later speculated at greater length on this alternative.

all the time; and when faith is designated a religious principle, it is 'the thing believed', not the act of believing, which is peculiar to religion. The example of Abraham shows us what this sort of 'trust' can be when extended into religious matters.[1] But faith itself means any sort of confidence in or reliance upon the knowledge we possess. Or, as Newman put it in 1859, 'I would draw a broad line between what is within us and without us, and apply the word "faith" to our reliance or certainty of things without and not within us.'[2]

Hume's sceptical approach to sensory perception may have led Newman to distrust the arguments with which many Christians met the attacks of sceptics generally.[3] In his sermon on 'The Usurpations of Reason', preached in 1831, Newman quotes Hume as saying that those who undertake to defend religion by the principles of human reason are either disguised enemies or dangerous friends. Hume had drily observed that 'Our most holy Religion is founded on Faith, not on Reason'. Newman recognizes the irony in the statement, but characteristically appropriates it as 'true as far as every important question in Revelation is concerned'. He wishes to show the dangers of such rational defences of Christianity as inferring its truths from Nature, commonly called the 'argument from design', and considered throughout the eighteenth century as a powerful supporting argument for the basic claims of Christianity. Evidences drawn from Nature, says Newman, enable those already of a devotional temper to admire the wisdom of the Creator, but do comparatively little to keep men from infidelity. When men have not already recognized the echoes of God's voice in their own consciences, the argument from design is ineffective, 'possibly from some unsoundness in the intellectual basis of the argument'.[4] Newman had recognized this unsoundness in his first essay on miracles where, as we have seen, he tries to apply Hume's demands for divine consistency to a defence

[1] Parochial and Plain Sermons, i. 193, 196–7.
[2] Boekraad and Tristram, The Argument from Conscience, p. 123.
[3] Cameron, The Night Battle, p. 207.
[4] 'The Usurpations of Reason' (1831), University Sermons, pp. 60, 70.

of scriptural miracles. If a being from a world of chaos, Newman speculates, were transported into our orderly universe, he would have an infinitely more powerful argument for the existence of a Designing Mind than miraculous interruptions of the system can afford. 'A Miracle is no argument to one who is deliberately, and on principle, an atheist.'[1] Thus we see that neither the design nor its interruptions, in Newman's opinion, can provide a secure philosophical argument for Christianity. And Newman's distrust of the argument from design grew stronger and his utterances of it bolder. In 1839 he writes: 'It is indeed a great question whether Atheism is not as philosophically consistent with the phenomena of the physical world, taken by themselves, as the doctrine of a creative and governing Power.'[2]

Locke stimulated Newman's interest in epistemology and probably equipped him with its terminology and methods of argument. Whately taught Newman the controversial force of Butler's idea that we reach certitude in matters for which we have no absolute proof. In a similar argument, Hume pointed out that we trust our senses because it is our nature to trust them, not because we have any logical proof of their fidelity. Both Hume and Whately must have weakened Locke's position in Newman's mind: Hume challenged the bases of Locke's reasoning by speculating upon the accuracy of sensory perception and the ability of reason to control the will. Whately demonstrated that we do not employ strict reasoning in reaching the majority of our conclusions, that logic provides primarily the argumentative expression of reasoning, and that certain suggestive 'other operations' of the mind are necessary for the discovery and judgement of truth.

---

[1] *Two Essays on . . . Miracles*, p. 11.

[2] 'Faith and Reason Contrasted as Habits of Mind' (1839), *University Sermons*, p. 194. One later important connection between Newman and Hume may exist. Hume's dictum that reason can never oppose passion in the direction of the will, his rejection of the Lockean recommendation that we decide everything by referring it to reason, probably influenced Newman when, in *The Tamworth Reading Room*, he wished to disparage the power of human reason to control the passions (see Cameron, *The Night Battle*, pp. 174–5). This question will be taken up in Chapter Three, as it relates to problems of liberalism.

Such influences combined forcefully with Newman's Evangelical propensities—with the personal or autobiographical as distinguished from the traditional or historical, with the precedence of spiritual over material reality, with the intuitive rather than the rational, and with an interest less alive to the material world than to the world of the mind.

CHAPTER TWO

Newman's Philosophy of Mind

Le coeur a son ordre, l'esprit a le sien qui est par principe et démonstration.
Le coeur en a un autre. On ne prouve pas qu'on doit être aimé en exposant
d'ordre les causes de l'amour; cela serait ridicule.

(PASCAL, *Pensées*)

IN the preceding chapter I have tried to indicate in brief the
most important early influences upon Newman's interest in
the mind. In so doing, I have used such words as reason, faith,
conscience, and belief in their broader and more common
meanings. I have tried not to employ such terms in any way
which might distort the significances which my author understood them to bear. But Newman developed precise uses for
each of the words he used to describe the operations of the
mind, creating for his particular purposes—purposes of controversy as well as of investigation—a personal religious and psychological vocabulary.[1] The subtleties of Newman's language,
as is well known, brought him not only fame but distrust,
distrust not only among his contemporaries but among ours.
G. M. Young, masquerading as John Bull, protests against the
delicate distinctions of the *Apologia*:

But if the public, or the modern reader, said 'Never mind all that:
what we want to know is, when Dr. Newman or one of his pupils tells
us a thing, can we believe it as we should believe it if the old-fashioned
parson said it?' I am afraid the upshot of the *Apologia* and its appen-
dices is No. And what is one to make of a man, especially of a preacher,
whose every sentence must be put under a logical microscope if its full
sense is to be revealed?[2]

[1] The rhetorical effectiveness of Newman's personal vocabulary has been
treated in passing as part of his 'integrated view of things' by John Holloway in
The Victorian Sage (London, 1953).
[2] *Daylight and Champaign*, p. 103. The criticism, from such a source, seems
disingenuous. To expect Newman to speak like the 'old-fashioned parson' is like

I hope in this chapter to put Newman's language, his psychological and epistemological vocabulary in particular, 'under the microscope'. As Henry Tristram remarks, 'it is always well to observe precisely his nuances of expression'.[1] A *logical* microscope, however, would not be our most suitable instrument. We have already seen that, for Newman, logic deals primarily with forms of expression in argument, whereas I shall now be concerned with the entire range of his theories about the origins, nature, methods, and limits of awareness, chiefly as expressed before his conversion to Roman Catholicism in 1845.

He was, indeed, almost indifferent to systematic philosophers and theologians. As Abbé Nédoncelle puts it:

Indifférent à la construction technique des idées, maladroit quand il veut l'entreprendre, il nous offre la plus riche des spectacles philosophiques et nous laisse le moins explicite des systèmes...C'est un penseur sans dénomination. Et par conséquent, lorsqu'il est philosophe, c'est sans le savoir![2]

Newman's language is precise and distinct, but his definitions are his own, not directly derived from any single, homogeneous philosophical or theological school. And here we have the cause of much misunderstanding and distrust. If, as I believe, the most complex and troublesome part of his vocabulary deals with the operations of the mind, then an investigation of his writings during the period when he was forming his epistemological theories—from his first university sermon in 1826 through the completion of his *Essay on Development* in 1845—should provide us with an appropriate basis for examining the great works of his Roman Catholic career. At least Newman will have defined his own terms and indicated the direction of his own ideas.

expecting the Day of Judgement to fall on Sunday. In this study, certain inconsistencies and developments in Newman's theories are discussed, but I have found nothing in letters, journals, or other writings which justifies Mr. Young's insinuation.

[1] *Newman, The Idea of a Liberal Education*, ed. H. Tristram (London, 1952), p. 8.
[2] Quoted by Boekraad and Tristram, *The Argument from Conscience*, p. 47.

In a letter to his sister in 1843, Newman admits his ignorance of metaphysics and observes that his *University Sermons* are neither theological nor ecclesiastical, 'though they bear immediately upon the most intimate and practical religious questions'. The sermons are difficult, Newman agrees, and they are not held together by a particular system; nevertheless he thinks that they have a common aim: 'I have for twelve years now been working out a theory, and whether it is true or not it has this recommendation, that it is consistent.'[1] The theory was his defence of religious belief, and the *University Sermons* constitute Newman's most complete single statement of it before he wrote the *Grammar of Assent*. In his preface to the third edition of the sermons (1871), Newman in fact recognizes their connection with the *Grammar:* 'The Author has lately pursued this whole subject at considerable length in his "Essay in Aid of a Grammar of Assent".'[2]

The connection between the *Grammar of Assent* and the theories Newman had developed by 1845 is important. Except for *The Tamworth Reading Room*, the other masterworks of his career were written after his last university sermon and before the *Grammar*. Of these, the *Essay on Development, Loss and Gain, The Idea of a University*, and the *Apologia pro Vita Sua* were most affected by Newman's theory of the mind. To gloss these works with the *Grammar of Assent* would be patently unhistorical, but if we can show that the opinions Newman held about reason, or logic, or faith in 1845 he held still in 1870, then we have the right to infer that he held them when he wrote *Loss and Gain*, or *The Idea of a University*, or the *Apologia*. The *Grammar of Assent* is the summation of Newman's ideas on

[1] Mozley, ii. 406.

[2] *University Sermons*, p. xvii. After the *Grammar* was published, Newman wrote in an autobiographical memoir: 'The book itself I have aimed at writing this twenty years;—& now that it is written I do not quite recognize it for what it was meant to be, though I suppose it is such. I have made more attempts at writing it, than I can enumerate. However I actually have MS remaining, to prove the following distinct separate beginnings' (*Autobiographical Writings*, p. 269). He then lists eighteen dates with notes, the first on 17 June 1846, and the last on 11 August 1865. Newman, then, 'began' to write the *Grammar* shortly after his conversion and but three years after his last university sermon.

psychology and epistemology. Provided we do not neglect the hundreds of amplifications he left along the way in the form of journals, letters, and sermons, we may use the *Grammar's* explicit definitions to clarify our understanding of his other major works.

In discussing early influences upon his interest in the mind, I suggested that during his Evangelical period Newman adopted the assumption that the thoughts, impulses, and reactions of the mind could be controlled with some rigour by the believer. And the believer was capable not only of controlling his own faculties, but also perhaps of accurately perceiving external phenomena as well. Like Hume, Newman ultimately finds it necessary, in the absence of a practical alternative, to assume that the evidences of the senses are trustworthy:

We have an instinct within us, impelling us, we have external necessity forcing us, to trust our senses, and we may leave the question of their substantial truth for another world, 'till the day break, and the shadows flee away'. And what is true of reliance on our senses, is true of all the information which it has pleased God to vouchsafe to us, whether in nature or in grace.[1]

I have also pointed out that the value of sensory perception to spiritual well-being is qualified by Newman's recurring assertion that what we apprehend through the senses, however accurate in itself, is not the most significant of realities. Nevertheless, these two premises, that the mind can control itself and that we perceive accurately, may strike us, with our fixed twentieth-century pessimism about the mind, as naïvely optimistic. We suspect that the peculiar psychological pressures on each individual colour his perceptions and predetermine such matters as his

---

[1] 'The Theory of Developments in Religious Doctrine' (1843), *University Sermons*, p. 349. In the *Grammar*, Newman argues that we have no option in the matter. We cannot act or speculate without accepting sensory evidence as a first principle. 'My first elementary lesson of duty is that of resignation to the laws of my nature, whatever they are; my first disobedience is to be impatient of what I am, and to indulge in an ambitious aspiration after what I cannot be, to cherish a distrust of my powers, and to desire to change laws which are identical with myself' (*Grammar of Assent*, p. 264).

affirmation of a religious creed as one congenial to his mental and moral nature. We know about illusion and delusion. And even if we were to find an objective basis for its action, could the will really master the complexes of guilt and desire formed early in childhood and which, we suspect, retain the power to snatch the reins and perhaps the responsibility from our control?

Newman did confront these problems. We have seen how the doubts raised by idealism haunted him and how he learned to strip away common prejudices and assumptions. But a difficulty lies still closer to the bases of Newman's thought than the suspicions aroused by empiricism. The Christian doctrine of the fall of man raises a crucial epistemological question: what objective value can the perceptions of an inherently flawed being possess?

In an early sermon called 'Promising without Doing' (1831), Newman tells his congregation that he wishes to lead them 'to some true notion of the depths and deceitfulness of the heart, which we do not really know'. Christians tend to speak piously of human corruption and then gladly drop the subject. But we cannot really apprehend our inherent limitations 'till we view the structure of our minds, part by part; and dwell upon and draw out the signs of our weakness, inconsistency, and ungodliness, which are such as can arise from nothing else than some strange original defect in our moral nature'. Such introspection, leading to self-distrust, should make us more dependent upon God, because 'We are in the dark about ourselves', and when we act 'We are groping in the dark, and may meet with a fall at any moment'. We see a little truth now and then, Newman continues, but 'in our attempts to influence and move our minds, we are making experiments (as it were) with some delicate and dangerous instrument, which works we do not know how, and may produce unexpected and disastrous effects. The management of our hearts is quite above us'.[1] One wonders in passing how the young preacher would have reconciled these remarks with the doctrines of free will and Christian responsibility which he could also propound with force. But I wish chiefly to call attention to Newman's emphasis upon the untrustworthiness

[1] *Parochial and Plain Sermons*, i. 172–3.

of the mind, its inconsistency, its darkness, delicacy, and danger-
ousness, its suddenness, its liability to disastrous effects.

Newman's recognition of the inconsistent and stealthy character
of the mind does not appear again in the sermons, at least not
so acutely stated. Not that Newman lost his fear of it: he hints
unmistakably at a dread of madness in a letter written late in
his life.[1] But after the first volume of *Parochial and Plain Sermons*,
Newman does not say that the management of our hearts is
above us. Instead, he recognizes how difficult it is to command
oneself, how weak the 'governing principle' of the mind is,
how hard it is for the Christian to command his feelings of
grief, anger, impatience, joy, and fear:

how difficult to govern his tongue, to say just what he would; how
difficult to rouse himself to do what he would, at this time or that; how
difficult to rise in the morning; how difficult to go about his duties and
not be idle; how difficult to eat and drink just what he should; how difficult to fix his mind on his prayers; how difficult to regulate his thoughts
through the day; how difficult to keep out of his mind what should be
kept out of it.[2]

Not only is our control of our thoughts and impulses at times
tenuous, but we find it nearly impossible to account for the
memories which often give rise to them. Our recollections
themselves may seem clear to us. We may remember that this
man was bent upon a certain object, that another was displeased,
or suspicious, happy or unhappy. But our impressions depend
upon manner, voice, accent and gesture—'all the many subtle
symptoms which are felt by the mind, but cannot be contemplated'. Newman preaches in 1840 that 'No analysis is subtle
and delicate enough to represent adequately the state of mind
under which we believe, or the subjects of belief, as they are
presented to our thoughts'. In painting, a minute defect spoils
the likeness of the portrait. We recognize the man whom the artist

---

[1] Regarding the composition of the *Grammar*: 'I have at times been quite
frightened lest the labour of thought might inflict on me some terrible retribution
at my age' (quoted by Wilfred Ward, *The Life of John Henry Cardinal Newman*,
London, 1913, ii. 266).

[2] 'Sins of Infirmity' (1838), *Parochial and Plain Sermons*, v, 214.

intended to represent, but we do not believe the representation to be successful. From this analogy we can understand the difficulty, 'or rather the impossibility, of representing the outline and character, the hues and shades, and in which any intellectual view really exists in the mind'. Indeed, any given opinion held by individuals even of the most congenial views is probably 'as distinct from itself as are their faces. . . . Is it not hopeless, then, to expect that the most diligent and anxious investigation can end in more than giving some very rude description of the living mind, and its feelings, thoughts, and reasonings?'[1]

If Newman had retained his conviction that a subtle analysis of the 'state of mind under which we believe' is impossible, he would perhaps never have written the *Grammar of Assent*. Later I shall discuss some of the experiences in education, autobiography, and the study of the 'principle of dogma' which led Newman to his formal attempt to explore the psychology of assent. At present, I wish to point out that he did not lose his appreciation of the mind's complexity, of our almost paralysing sense of infinity when we begin to examine consciousness by means of consciousness: 'The mind is like a double mirror, in which reflections of self within self multiply themselves till they are indistinguishable, and the first reflection contains all the rest.'[2]

Before the *Grammar of Assent*, Newman writes, his efforts to investigate the psychology of belief 'were like attempts to get into a labyrinth, or to find a weak point in the defences of a fortified place. I could not get on, and found myself turned back, utterly baffled'. These metaphors, like Newman's apprehension of the treacherous nature of the mind, are strikingly Freudian. Like Freud as well, and perhaps like every original psychologist, Newman's breakthrough came with his creation of a vocabulary capable of describing psychic activity with greater precision than before: 'At last, when I was up at Glion over the Lake of Geneva, it struck me "You are wrong in

[1] 'Implicit and Explicit Reason,' *University Sermons*, pp. 274, 267–8.
[2] *Grammar of Assent*, p. 147.

beginning with certitude—certitude is only a kind of assent—
you should begin with contrasting assent and inference". On that
hint I spoke, finding it a key to my own ideas.'[1] Long before
he received this 'hint', Newman had seen that the ratiocinative
faculty was really a collection of faculties—reason, will, instinct,
intuition, faith—grouped under one name. In the *Grammar*
he lays out a kind of ideal mental landscape or kingdom ruled
by the Illative Sense. But in Newman's writings before his conversion the different faculties or departments of the mind had
already begun to collect appropriate moral connotations which
prepared them for their places in the hierarchy of the *Grammar*.
In interpreting the great works written between the *University
Sermons* and the *Grammar of Assent*, we must attend to these
moral overtones if we wish to understand the direction and
force of Newman's language.

Freud also saturated his own more allegorical divisions of the
mind with moral or social values. Both Newman and Freud
distorted the common meanings of the traditional terms they
employed. Both were remarkably precise in their definitions.
But, perhaps because Newman, unlike Freud, was primarily
a psychologist of the *conscious* mind, he selected his terms from
the vocabularies of theology and classical and empirical philosophy, vocabularies already freighted with a wealth of implication
and suggestion. Sometimes Newman tells just how much he
means by a word and how much he does not mean. We can
usually discover precisely what he means by 'reason'. The
definition of other terms, like 'will', or 'intuition', we must
determine from contexts.

Thus the problems of investigating the workings of the mind
were recognized by Newman. He knew that his readers would
feel them. The difficulty and the occasional awkwardness of the
University Sermons and the *Grammar of Assent* pained him. But
when we have apprehended the difficulties and suitably modified
our expectations of success, Newman's admonition from the
Grammar seems appropriate: 'We must take the constitution
of the human mind as we find it, and not as we may judge it

[1] *Autobiographical Writings*, p. 270.

ought to be'.[1] Despite the deceitfulness of the heart, the treach-
erousness and obscurity of the mind—which must rely upon its
own faculties for its self-examination—despite the complexity
and diffuseness of the terms employed, and the disparate connotations they suggest to different individuals, we still retain
the power to attack the facts of our own experience.

What follows in this chapter represents an attempt to clarify
and make accessible Newman's psychological vocabulary.
Each section deals with terms or concepts which have caused
difficulty and misunderstanding in the interpretation of his
most widely read works. In discussing Newman's terminology
I have aimed for simple clarity and accuracy and, as these are
qualities characteristic of most of Newman's writing, I have
generally allowed him to supply his own definitions. Like him,
I address the general critical reader. The trained theologian,
philosopher, or psychologist will make his own applications
and relate Newman's vocabulary to that of his own discipline.
My broad intention is to show how Newman carefully developed
and explored and tested those ideas and attitudes which so often
strike his readers as arbitrary or unpleasantly dogmatic. This
general outline of his psychology, and what is an untechnical
sense may be called his epistemology, will provide the bases
for subsequent chapters on Newman's attacks on nineteenth-
century liberalism, his theories of education, and his fictional
and autobiographical representations of the process of conversion.

REASON

Essential to an understanding of all Newman's thought, but
obviously relevant in particular to his antagonism to rationalism,
is a knowledge of what he means by the term 'reason'. The
word, as we all know, has had a most varied career in our intellectual history. It came to Newman with its burden of meanings
and values and he made perhaps hundreds of attempts throughout his life to explain what he meant by it. These were not

[1] *Grammar of Assent*, p. 164.

always successful. But we can move around or through the confusion by asking a question which I believe leads to a general clarification of his meaning: At what point and in what areas do those mental processes grouped under the term 'reason' become irrelevant or improper? Or, in other words, precisely in which contexts in Newman's writings is he apt to attach a derogatory meaning to it?

'Reason, according to the simplest view of it, is the faculty of gaining knowledge without direct perception, or of ascertaining one thing by means of another.' In this sense, to reason means simply to draw conclusions from premises. This is a natural activity of the mind, 'a living spontaneous energy within us, not an art'. This natural, or what Newman calls 'unconscious', mental activity does not take place according to formal rules of organization and procedure, such as those of logic. But when the mind reflects on its own activity, and especially when it becomes necessary to explain the processes by which a particular conclusion has been reached, some sort of formal representation or analysis seems desirable. Thus we create a form of explanation, a pattern. The pattern serves as a communication and analysis of the 'steps' leading to a conclusion. 'Here, then, are two processes, distinct from each other—the original process of reasoning, and next, the process of investigating our reasonings.' Newman thus distinguishes between spontaneous unreflexive or 'unconscious' mental activity and formal analysis, calling the two types 'Implicit and Explicit Reason'.[1]

He asserts that it is of the greatest importance to maintain the distinction. Clarity in formal argument has no direct bearing upon the accuracy of the conclusion reached. 'The exercise of analysis is not necessary to the integrity of the process analyzed.' The analysis is merely an account of the processes by which we have reached a conclusion, and an incomplete account at best. Therefore, 'it does not make the conclusion correct'.[2] When we confuse the formal description with the actual events that take place in the mind, we risk making psychic activity sub-

---

[1] 'Implicit and Explicit Reason' (1840), *University Sermons*, pp. 256–9.
[2] Ibid., p. 259.

servient to verbal representation. We take as our authority not
the mind's actual operations, but our verbal simplification of
them. We become 'rationalists', claiming that no conclusion
can be valid unless it lends itself to formal expression or logic,
unless it can be made 'explicit'.

An act of faith, however, does not generally admit of such
formal expression. It is personal, spontaneous, implicit: 'it will
be of this very character which the world despises and does
not allow to be Reason. The world's reasonings necessarily
must be explicit, because [they are] the reasoning of many,
and implicit reasoning[s] are but the reasonings of individuals.'[1]
The fact that an individual cannot formally explain the process
by which he draws a conclusion, or, as a religious example, by
which he makes an act of faith, ought not to discredit the validity
of the assent. But when the explanation of psychic activity
becomes confused with the activity itself, the ability to explain
or rationalize a conclusion may unfairly be made a criterion
of validity, and the individual subjected to such pressures tends
to suspect those private beliefs which he cannot satisfactorily
communicate or prove. It is this insistence upon explicit reason
or formal expression that Newman attacks when he opposes
reason to faith. And it is in this limited sense that the word is
employed in what follows.

Reason, as opposed to faith, properly serves to assist the senses
in various ways, directing their application and arranging the
evidence which they supply. It collects sensory evidence and
deduces conclusions. It can move from what is known to what
is unknown and it can confirm and prove hypotheses in appropriate subjects. But in other areas of human experience, Newman
maintains, the exercise of reason is inappropriate. In questions
of duty or in the perception of the divine, reason may usurp
the functions of conscience and faith. When reason is used to
criticize the revealed doctrines of Christianity it resembles a 'blind
man who seriously professed to lecture on light and colours'.
Newman characteristically insists upon the prerogatives of each

[1] From a rough draft of the preface to a French translation of *University
Sermons*, dated 1847, in the papers at the Birmingham Oratory.

department of the mind: 'Why should we be surprised that one
faculty of our compound nature should not be able to do that
which is the work of another?'[1]

Newman, perhaps partly in reaction to the Oriel Noetics
but also certainly in Evangelical *and* Tractarian rejection of
eighteenth-century rationalism, came to fear the triumph of
reason over faith. In a sermon on 'The State of Innocence' (1838),
he uses almost Blakean language to suggest that the usurpations
of reason may be seen as continued consequences of original
sin. Since the Fall,

passion and reason have abandoned their due place in man's nature,
which is one of subordination, and conspired together against the
Divine light within him, which is his proper guide. Reason has been
as guilty as passion here. God made man upright, and grace was his
strength; but he has found out many inventions, and his strength is
reason.[2]

But how, in less devotional language, does this usurpation
take place in the minds of individuals? Newman's clearest
explanation comes in the *Grammar of Assent*. Questioning and
reasoning, he argues, exercised on any subject-matter, readily
become habits of thought. They tend 'to substitute exercises
of inference for assent'. When we begin to give *reasons* for
assenting, reasons for doubting are apt to occur to us. Assents
previously and properly spontaneous, 'realities to our imagination', become mere abstract notions. The mind loses what Newman calls its 'elasticity', and its capacity for simple assent or faith.[3]

In his sermon 'Faith and Reason contrasted as Habits of Mind'
(1839), Newman compares reason with the 'art of criticism'
and likens the capacity to perceive religious and moral truth
to 'poetical or similar powers'. Reason 'like a spectator', acknowledges and concurs in what goes on in the devout mind, and
this is its proper function. But we must not mistake 'a critical
for a creative power'.[4] The exercises of reason are 'external'
or at least only 'ministrative' to religious inquiry and knowledge,

---

[1] 'The Usurpations of Reason' (1831), *University Sermons*, p. 61.
[2] *Parochial and Plain Sermons*, v. 114.
[3] *Grammar of Assent*, p. 164.   [4] *University Sermons*, pp. 184, 183.

'useful in their place, but not necessary'.[1] Reason perceives nothing directly. It can only proceed from things which have been perceived to things which have not. The expressions Newman commonly uses to describe reason include 'a process', 'a progress of thought', 'an exercise of mind', 'an investigation', 'an analysis', and it may 'compare, discriminate, judge and decide'. It is 'the faculty of gaining knowledge upon grounds given', not a discoverer of the grounds themselves: 'when its exercise is conducted rightly, it leads to knowledge; when wrongly, to apparent knowledge, to opinion, and error'.[2]

Newman retained his view of reason as a critical rather than creative power. In the *Grammar of Assent*, he writes that 'formal inference', or ratiocination deprived of intuition, common-sense, experience, and what he calls 'nature' and 'genius', determines neither our first principles nor our ultimate judgements. It is 'neither the test of truth nor the adequate basis of assent'.[3]

In fact, during his years as a Tractarian, Newman at times appears to doubt that reason, defined as systematic thought, possesses any really extended power to represent reality. Reason, he wrote in a sermon called 'Wisdom as Contrasted with Faith and Bigotry' (1841), proceeds to new ideas by means of given ones. From scanty data it develops entire systems, consistent and regular within themselves. But the accuracy of its deductions can be ascertained only where a means can be found of comparing them with the reality the system claims to represent.[4] In mathematical science, which Newman, perhaps following Aristotle, uses as a *type* of strict reasoning, we employ various methods or calculi which we hope embody those immutable 'principles and dispositions' with which science deals. The external principles and dispositions, however, really exist independent of these calculi. Newman calls the calculi 'economies', meaning in this context useful symbolic simplifications of the truth. We require economies, however imperfect, in order to apprehend and make

[1] 'The Usurpations of Reason' (1831), ibid., p. 67.
[2] 'The Nature of Faith in Relation to Reason' (1839), ibid., pp. 206–7.
[3] *Grammar of Assent*, p. 218.   [4] *University Sermons*, p. 290.

use of the principles which govern nature. None of our symbolic descriptions actually 'carries out the lines of truth to their limits'. First one system fails, then another. At length our 'instrument of discovery issues in some great impossibility or contradiction, or what we call in religion a mystery'. We become aware that our calculus was merely an approximation of the immutable laws. 'It has never fathomed their depth, because it now fails to measure their course.' An economy is not useless on this account; we employ it within the range in which it functions accurately. But it has proven itself to be only 'a shadow of the unseen'.[1]

The particular failures of our calculi are not given in this last university sermon. But Newman employed a similar argument in the *Grammar of Assent*, and he offers as an example the 'bad fit' of algebra to geometry. Applied to the fifth book of Euclid's *Elements*, algebra enables us to dispense with the cumbrous method of proof in questions of ratio and proportion. But how then is the 'fourth power of *a*' to be translated into geometrical language? It seems to suggest that space has four dimensions. In this case algebra exceeds geometrical limits. Conversely, algebra falls short of geometry when it abortively attempts to express, as the square root of *minus a*, what it is really beyond the power of algebra to express, 'the direction and position of lines in the third dimension of space, as well as their length upon a plane'. Similarly, arithmetic, another economy, must subject all that it deals with to numeration. But this poses the problem of categorization. It would be nonsense to throw together 'Napoleon's brain ambition, hand, soul, smile, height, and age at Marengo, and say that there were seven of them'.[2] Newman thinks well enough of this argument to apply it to the rational difficulty with the doctrine of the Trinity: we cannot know what 'one' and 'three' signify when applied to God. Newman wishes to shake us loose from the assumption that when we employ reason, even as in mathematics, we are working directly with reality.

Many evidences in religion are accessible to reason. The doctrine of the Trinity is not. Since we know that our rational

[1] 'The Theory of Development in Religious Doctrine' (1843), *University Sermons*, pp. 344–6.   [2] *Grammar of Assent*, pp. 37–8.

calculi fail in other areas of investigation, he argues, the doctrine of the Trinity is not suspect merely on the grounds that we cannot give a rational (or mathematical) account of it. In a sermon called 'Faith without Sight' (1834), Newman says of religion, 'Indeed, that it is at all level to the reason, is rather a privilege granted by Almighty God, than a point which may be insisted on by man; and unless received as an unmerited boon, may become hurtful to us'.[1] What becomes 'Formal Inference' in the *Grammar of Assent*, and what in the sermons is usually meant by 'reason', amounts to an argument consistent in itself but closed off from the continuous experience of reality by which we naturally and spontaneously apprehend and judge truth. The fact that certain calculi do to a limited extent apply to areas of experience beyond their own antecedent grounds, as algebra does in geometry or syllogistic logic in religion, may be considered a piece of good fortune, a lucky coincidence, or in Newman's words, a 'privilege', an 'unmerited boon'.

The imperfection of our temporal economies leads Newman to speak of the isolation of rational man from the spiritual universe, a universe which he conceived of as being richly complex. We can apprehend our material surroundings through the senses. But whatever 'direct intercourse' goes on between the soul and immaterial beings, we have no such consciousness of it as our senses give us of the material world. We accept information of the spiritual world, if at all, on the basis of authority, on the testimony of Scripture and the Church. As we shall see, Newman's argument from authority is based in a large measure upon his psychology. My present point, however, is that, for Newman, reason (except occasionally and as if by accident) can do nothing to weaken our spiritual isolation. 'Acquiescence in testimony, or in evidence not stronger than testimony, is the only method, as far as we see, by which the next world can be revealed to us.'[2]

---

[1] *Parochial and Plain Sermons*, ii. 24.
[2] 'The Nature of Faith in Relation to Reason' (1839), *University Sermons*, pp. 205-6, 214. Even what we now think of as 'existential' problems had, for Newman, no connection with reason. 'Thought and being, or sensation and being

As we might expect, much of Newman's epistemology is
anticipated by orthodox Catholic theology, even by that of
a severely rationalist cast. Aquinas, to whom Newman
occasionally refers, held that we can have a 'natural' knowledge
of God only in so far as finite things point beyond themselves,
and manifest the existence of that upon which they depend—
only, that is, in so far as they are genuine economies. Thus the
proofs of God drawn from the material world tell us primarily
about material things. The proofs argue that the things depend
upon something which transcends them. They cannot give
the philosopher an 'intuition of God'. More immediate experience
of God must be supernatural in character and 'the work of God
Himself within the soul; it cannot be obtained by philosophical
analysis and reflection'.[1] As we have seen, Newman agrees
with the substance of this argument. He departs from Thomism,
however, perhaps in the complexity of his qualifications about
our ability to perceive significantly the external world, and
certainly in his distrust of reason—really a more comprehensive
term in Aquinas—as a means of extending religious knowledge.

In his *Essay on the Development of Christian Doctrine*, Newman
as historian finds reason inadequate in two respects. We are
familiar with his argument that for most men it is not the source
of religious truth and must, therefore, be a mere exposer rather
than developer of doctrine. Secondly, reason operating as formal
logic, precisely because it claims to work on infallible and consequently timeless principles, fails to account for the undeniable
historical changes which take place in doctrine. Even in physical
sciences laws are discovered over a period of time by means of
experiments. So, he argues, the Church operates through time,
developing, expanding, clarifying the body of Christian doctrine.
Continuing this important analogy with science, Newman
observes: 'In such a method of proof there is, first, an imperfect,

are brought home to me by one act of the consciousness, prior to any exercise
of ratiocination, though I may afterwards, if I will, survey the complex idea by
means of that exercise.' This passage is quoted by Boekraad and Tristram in *The
Argument from Conscience*, p. 105.
    [1] F. C. Copleston, *Aquinas* (Penguin Books, 1955), p. 44.

secondly, a growing evidence, thirdly, in consequence a delayed inference and judgment, fourthly, reasons producible to account for the delay.'[1] As Owen Chadwick points out, this process admits the possibility of a far more drastic change in dogma than traditional Thomism could allow.[2]

After his conversion Newman was troubled to find that Roman theologians disagreed with his *Essay on Development* primarily because it included sceptical language about the capacity of reason to achieve religious certitude, particularly when the doctrine to be assented to had developed historically. Catholic theologians had for centuries explained doctrinal development by the use of logical inferences. 'Yet', as Chadwick observes, 'the Christian public now associates the idea of development with a thinker whose suspicion of Dr. Hampden or the Reverend Charles Kingsley was as nothing compared with his distrust of the syllogism.' And one cannot help agreeing with Chadwick that in his *Essay on Development* Newman makes one of his strongest arguments against formal inference. In what meaningful sense can the variations and redefinitions in Catholic doctrine be considered as inherent implications which are or can be logically explicated?[3]

Newman stresses his concern over this question in his letters from the College of Propaganda during January and February of 1847. He suspects that the Roman theologians without admitting it really do recognize a distinction between 'demonstrative' (formal) and 'moral' (informal) proof. He acknowledges that reason *can* prove the existence of God, but maintains that this is 'very different from saying that reason is *the mode* by which individuals come at truth'. He attempts to explain his criticism of reason found in the *University Sermons* in such a way as not to offend the Roman theologians and succeeds with a definition of reason as 'reasoning' or reason operating '*not under the guidance of conscience*'. He accuses the divines at the Collegio Romano of jealousy, but wants to agree with them. They take, he writes

[1] *Essay on Development*, p. 114.
[2] *From Bossuet to Newman* (Cambridge, England, 1957), p. 193.
[3] Ibid., pp. 174, 48, 193.

to Dalgairns who is supervising the French translation of the *Essay*, 'a broad *sensible* shrewd view of reason and faith'. A 'great deal', he believes, will depend upon his projected preface to the French edition explaining 'what I mean by reason and faith'.[1] Finally, under these pressures, Newman after 1847 begins to demonstrate a greater readiness to acknowledge the value which reason *can* have in the religion of an intellectual minority. But he has not modified his basic position. In the late 1830s he called reason 'external' to or at least only 'ministrative' to most religious inquiry, useful in its limited sphere, but not necessary. He thinks so still in 1847.

In this section we have seen that human reason, for Newman, is a critical rather than a creative or perceptive faculty. It constructs internally consistent systems upon antecedent grounds, systems which have no necessary connection with realities beyond the grounds upon which they are based. The doctrine of the Holy Trinity, for example, cannot be disproved mathematically because it exists in an entirely different order of reality. But although reasoning is primarily a form of expressing and testing truth in a limited field, it can form habits of mind which usurp the provinces of other faculties. The exercise of reason in religious matters is dangerous for most men because reasons for assenting suggest reasons for not assenting and doubt is the consequence of extending the application of reason beyond its proper sphere. Our attempts at any kind of 'formal inference', such as in mathematics or syllogistic logic, result in 'economies', systems which are highly useful as far as they function effectively, but which eventually collapse when they are applied to some reality alien to their antecedent grounds or their particular laws of operation. Logical inferences, for example, because of their rigid application and necessary claim to immutability, cannot explain certain developments in Christian doctrine. And, what is perhaps the argument most congenial to our twentieth-century sensibilities, the encroachment of reason into religious life tends to isolate the reasoner from what Newman thought to be the richest of human

---

[1] *The Letters and Diaries of John Henry Newman*, ed. Charles Stephen Dessain ondon, 1962), xii. 29–34, 8. Henceforth cited as *Letters and Diaries*.

experiences, the awareness of contact with a world beyond
that reached by the senses.

IDEAS AND WORDS

The source of much of Newman's dissatisfaction with the exercise
of reason in problems of religious belief lies in his suspicion
that language really cannot adequately describe those spontaneous mental processes which lead to assent in the minds of
individuals. We can go beyond this and say that for Newman,
as for several modern epistemologists, the accuracy of any
expression of truth, the description of any reality is highly
suspect. This becomes especially apparent when we attempt
to describe very complicated realities, to discuss what Newman
calls 'ideas'.

In the *Essay on Development* the idea Newman proposes to
examine is nothing less than the process by which the major
teachings of Catholic Christianity are developed in doctrine.
In *The Idea of a University*—to which the present discussion will
be applied in a later chapter—the 'idea' comprehends his entire
theory of liberal education. Ideas, for Newman, are vast, apparently heterogeneous complexes, involving time, place, and
the agency of man. No single aspect or point of view can comprehend the entirety of a real idea. But an idea cannot be apprehended by the mind except through a variety of aspects. The
means by which the mind realizes an idea is analogous to the
process of viewing some material object, perhaps a sculpture,
from different angles in different lights:

Ordinarily an idea is not brought home to the intellect as objective
except through this variety; like bodily substances, which are not
apprehended except under the clothing of their properties and results,
and which admit of being walked round, and surveyed on opposite
sides, and in different prospectives, and in contrary lights, in evidence
of their reality. And, as views of a material object may be taken from
points so remote or so opposed, that they seem at first sight incompa-
tible, and especially as their shadows will be disproportionate, or even
monstrous, and yet all these anomalies will disappear and all these con-
trarieties be adjusted, on ascertaining the point of vision or the surface

of projection in each case; so also all the aspects of an idea are capable of coalition, and of a resolution into the object to which it belongs; and the *primâ facie* dissimilitude of its aspects becomes, when explained, an argument for its substantiveness and integrity, and their multiplicity for its originality and power.

The process by which the aspects of an idea are brought into consistency and form Newman calls its *development*, 'being the germination and maturation of some truth or apparent truth on a large mental field'.[1]

But despite Newman's faith in the transcendent harmony and unity of his idea in the *Essay on Development*, an epistemological problem remains. We perceive only one aspect of the idea, as he says, 'in each case'. No one aspect exhausts the complexity of the entire idea. The 'large mental field' is not immediately personal but historical and institutional. Whereas an individual can reconcile one aspect of Christianity with his general sense of the *comprehensive* idea, it is clearly beyond his power to reconcile it with each of the aspects which constitute the *complex* idea. Our personal conception of the idea falls short of the historical reality, or, if one takes the Roman Catholic Church as containing the living idea of Christianity, of the institutional reality. Our personal conceptions are either general and vague, or specific and confined.

We clothe these conceptions in words, words which are themselves inadequate expressions of the inadequate conceptions. The process has been outlined in this way: We form a conception of an object, which does not contain all the aspects of the object. We express this conception in words which fail not only to express the object but also even to approximate the conception.[2] These limitations inhere whether the object we perceive is

---

[1] *Essay on Development*, pp. 32, 36. The admirable longer passage serves to illustrate not only Newman's apprehension of the complexity of reality and our inability to view it as a whole, but his deep conviction of its transcendent coherence, a point which John Holloway elaborates in *The Victorian Sage*, and which I discuss in my fourth chapter.

[2] Dr. Zeno, O.F.M., *John Henry Newman: Our Way to Certitude* (Leiden, 1957), pp. 38–9. In mathematics, of course, there is no necessary disproportion or even distinction between the symbol and the idea.

material or an aspect of an idea. Language attempts to embody the truth at two removes.

We speak of material objects more freely than of ideas because our senses reveal material reality to us independently of the language used to describe it. But religious knowledge is largely extra-sensory. How, asks Newman in his last university sermon, can temporal analogies convey an idea of the invisible to us? They can suggest no meaning but what is natural and earthly. Words like 'Person', 'Substance', 'Consubstantial', 'Generation', 'Procession', 'Incarnation', 'Taking of the manhood into God' either suggest some 'abject and human meaning, or none at all'. We can have no concrete conception of these doctrines distinct from the dogmatic language which expresses them. The metaphors by which they are represented are not mere symbols of ideas which exist independently of the dogmas themselves: 'Their meaning is coincident and identical with the ideas.' We cannot test them by comparing them with the objects they are designed to express as we can test words describing sensory experiences. Our apprehensions of spiritual realities are 'coextensive with the figures by which we express them, neither more nor less, and without them are not; and when we draw inferences from these figures, we are not illustrating one existing idea, but drawing mere logical inferences'. Many of our controversies in religion, many of our personal struggles and sufferings, are about 'the poor ideas conveyed to us in certain figures of speech'. Our idea of God is an earthly one, and our difficulties of belief often merely verbal.[1]

As we have no sensory experience of spiritual reality sufficient to illuminate the words of Scripture for us, we should remember that our apprehension of it is based largely on mere words. We become like children and we must be taught in a language we can understand. When we speak to children, we adjust our language to their immature faculties, because what is short

---

[1] 'The Theory of Developments in Religious Doctrine' (1843), *University Sermons*, pp. 338–40. Newman, of course, does not deny that the source of Scripture and dogma is divine. He is concerned with our human apprehension of the ideas hidden in dogma.

of actual truth may be to them 'the most perfect truth, that is, the nearest approach to truth, compatible with their condition'. To speak to a blind man of colours and light, Newman observes, would be to mock him. The colour scarlet can be compared to the sound of a trumpet, but the comparison also illustrates the inadequacy of metaphor. Much cannot be expressed in language, which is merely a kind of 'analysis of thought', a 'method definite and limited'. Some foreign languages contain courses of thought absent in others. Some individuals cannot communicate with others, because they have employed different principles in dividing and subdividing the world of ideas. They lack 'a common measure or economy to mediate between them'.[1]

When Newman studied Italian in Rome he wrote in his journal that learning a language is like learning sanctity. One is better one day, worse the next: 'How bad our pronunciation must be to the angels!'[2] Often when we attempt to express religious ideas in words we are struck by apparent contradictions. Christianity, for example, teaches that the soul is throughout the body, but not of the body, an assertion which Newman believes is borne out by our experience of human nature. The contradiction, he argues, is merely verbal.[3]

But because Scripture and Catholic dogma provide our primary sources for religious ideas, we must treat their language with respect. The Church teaches the Ascension of Christ. What is meant by *ascending*? 'Philosophers' have said that there is no difference between down and up, 'as regards the sky'. But 'whatever difficulties the word may occasion, we can hardly take upon us to decide that it is a mere popular expression, consistently with the reverence due to the Sacred Record'.[4]

This discussion of Newman's views on language has set forth his arguments on the coherence of complex historical and institutional 'ideas', such as the body of Christian doctrine or a

---

[1] *University Sermons*, pp. 340–2.
[2] *Letters and Diaries*, xi. 264. Entry for 22 October 1846.
[3] 'The Mysteriousness of Our Present Being' (1836), *Parochial and Plain Sermons*, iv. 286. Tennyson's 'The Higher Pantheism' may be seen as an attempt to express spiritual truths, as Swinburne put it in his parody, 'in a nutshell' by means of 'verbal' contradictions.   [4] 'Mysteries in Religion' (1834), ibid., ii. 208.

theory of liberal education. He believed that we can at best imperfectly perceive at any one time only a single aspect of an idea, an aspect which we then relate to the coherent whole. Words serve but imperfectly to express these limited perceptions, and are thus at two removes from the vast compound reality. Our apprehension of religious truths embodied in Scripture and dogma, however, cannot be separated from the language which expresses them. We have no consistent sensory experience of spiritual reality, so that Scriptural language, divine in source but capable of bewildering us with its apparent contradictions, is nevertheless our primary source of information about that greater universe.

I have been emphasizing Newman's sceptical approach to man's powers of reason and expression. But it is well known that his personal solution was far from being a sceptical or agnostic one. His absolute belief in the authority of the Roman Catholic Church drove some of his contemporaries to question his intellectual integrity and stability. When invited to reply to the *Apologia*, Charles Kingsley wrote angrily to Alexander Macmillan: 'I cannot trust, I can only smile at the autobiography of a man who (beginning with Newman's light, learning and genius) ends in believing that he believes in the Infallibility of one Church, and in the Immaculate Conception. If I am to bandy words it must be with sane persons.'[1] This expresses Kingsley's understandable frustration, and certainly the *Apologia* cannot be refuted by such impassioned assertions. But Kingsley does inadvertently point to a difficulty inherent in any examination of Newman's ideas on mind: How are we to reconcile his brilliant analysis of the mind's limitations with his absolute assent to Roman Catholic dogma? Is it true, as has sometimes been asserted, that his affirmation of orthodoxy represents an arbitrary leap into the assurances of dogmatic certainty, a leap made in reaction to his vivid realization of the sceptical abyss?

The answer, as careful readers of Newman know, is that whatever the hidden personal motives may have been which

---

[1] Quoted by Una Pope-Hennessy, *Canon Charles Kingsley* (London, 1948), pp. 222–3.

led him to embrace his solution, he created a psychology of belief as carefully worked out, as little presumptive, as his critique of reason. I wish therefore to begin a gradual shift of emphasis from Newman's views on the mind's limitations to his analysis of its powers, a shift of emphasis which will lead us ultimately to an examination of that compound faculty of investigation and judgement which he called the Illative Sense. And our turning point will be provided by his conception of the imagination.

IMAGINATION

Aquinas thought that the function of distinguishing and collecting data was performed by general sense, the *sensus communis*. He also postulated an imaginative power which conserves the forms received by the senses. He held that we cannot use the knowledge we have acquired without the employment of images or 'phantasms'. When we try to understand something we form images in our minds by which we can *see* what it is that we are trying to understand.[1]

For Newman, the imagination is like Aquinas's conserver of forms, a reservoir which stores up sense impressions. Closely allied with memory, it is often seen as a passive agent, more acted upon than acting. 'Newman agrees with Addison that the imagination consists of images collected in the mind through the agency of sight.'[2] This collection of images or pictures in the mind may function as a stimulus, but the faculty is not a creative one. Newman usually employs the word to mean approximately what Coleridge meant by 'Fancy', not a shaping spirit of imagination but 'no other than a mode of Memory

---

[1] Copleston, *Aquinas*, p. 44. In a letter of 1851, Newman associates Aquinas with the theory that spiritual reality may be perceived *in* or *through* visible objects: 'I worship the seen as the visible form of what is unseen', that is, the reality existing in the image. Newman had become familiar with Thomas's epistemology (*Letters and Diaries*, xiv. 241).

[2] M. E. Lawlis, 'Newman on the Imagination', *MLN*, lxviii (Feb. 1953), 75. Lawlis unfortunately goes on to argue that Newman subordinated his imagination to 'reason', and as he grew older rejoiced that its influence became less strong, 'giving undisputed supremacy to reason' (p. 78). Of course, Lawlis is using reason in a sense antithetic to the one Newman usually gave it.

emancipated from the order of time and space; . . . the Fancy must receive all its materials ready made from the law of association.'¹

But to conservative eighteenth-century writers, alive to the allegiance of wit and madness, and to Newman, the imagination was not quite so innocuous a faculty as Coleridge's 'fancy.' Samuel Johnson, whose writings Newman knew well, was concerned with the imagination's seductive power. Newman had read the chapter in *Rasselas* on 'The Dangerous Prevalence of Imagination'² where Johnson warns against its excesses. In his sermon on the 'Contest between Faith and Sight' (1832), Newman stresses the dangers to which Christians are exposed from the 'visible course of things', or what St. John calls 'the world':

It assails their *imagination*. The world sweeps by in long procession; —its principalities and powers, its Babel of languages, the astrologers of Chaldaea, the horse and its rider and the chariots of Egypt, Baal and Ashtoreth and their false worship; and those who witness, feel its fascination; they flock over it; with a strange fancy, they ape its gestures, and dote upon its mummeries; and then, should they perchance fall in with the simple solemn services of Christ's Church, and hear her witnesses going the round of Gospel truths as when they left them: 'I am the Way, the Truth, and the Life;' 'Be sober, be vigilant;' 'Strait is the gate, narrow the way;' 'If any man will come after Me, let him deny himself;' 'He is despised and rejected of men, a Man of sorrows and acquainted with grief;'—how utterly unreal do these appear, and the preachers of them, how irrational, how puerile!—how extravagant in their opinions, how weak in their reasoning!—and if they profess to pity and bear with them, how nearly does their compassion border on contempt!³

---

¹ *Biographia Literaria*, ed. J. Shawcross (Oxford, 1962), i. 202. Newman did not read Coleridge until the spring of 1835 and was probably uninfluenced by his use of the word 'imagination'. But, because of the acknowledged importance of Coleridge's definition of it as 'The living Power and prime Agent of all human Perception' (ibid.), it seems proper to relate Newman's definition to his. Wordsworth makes an interesting comparison between 'Imagination', whose meaning he believes has been strained, and 'Taste', a passive faculty. See 'Essay Supplementary to the Preface', published in 1820, *Poetical Works*, ii. 427.

² Lawlis, p. 78.   ³ *University Sermons*, pp. 132–3.

Take the world as it is, preaches Newman in 'The State
of Innocence' (1838), 'with its intelligence, its bustle, its
feverish efforts, its works, its results, the ceaseless ebb and
flow of the great tide of mind', and we see that it is the
fruit of the tree of knowledge of good and evil, not,
perhaps, sinful in itself, but the 'consequence of sin'.[1] Those
who prefer the world and its images to the 'leadings of God's
Spirit within them' learn to lean upon the world as a god.[2]
Saul, in contrast to David, serves as an example of such a person,
dead to all influences and considerations unconnected with the
present world.[3] Nor ought it to surprise us that men of acute
understanding should not be Christians, because 'quickness,
sagacity, depth of thought, strength of mind, power of comprehension, perception of the beautiful, power of language'
are all attributes of quite another order from spiritual excellences.
Newman finds no necessary connection between faith and
ability. Ability is a *'gift'*, faith a *'grace'*.[4] When the world has
captured the imagination and secured it, not even a miracle
can alter one's unbelief. Do the 'startling accidents which happen
to you now produce *any* lasting effect upon you? Do they lead
you to *any* *habits* of religion?'[5]

The world, then, assails our imagination. We must not, however, give up the world on that account. 'It is our duty to change
it into the kingdom of heaven.'[6] Christianity, writes Newman
in his *Essay on Development*, teaches that matter was originally
'very good'. Matter as well as the human spirit was corrupted
by original sin. Christ began its purification along with the
purification of man's spirit by taking a material form when he
assumed human flesh.[7]

Indeed, spiritual realities may be concealed in the physical
world itself. One of Newman's best illustrations of a sacramental

[1] *Parochial and Plain Sermons*, v. 113.
[2] 'Faith without Sight' (1834), ibid., ii. 19.
[3] 'Saul' (1830), and 'Early Years of David' (1830), ibid., iii. 36, 52–3.
[4] 'Truth Hidden When Not Sought After' (1830), ibid., viii. 188.
[5] 'Miracles No Remedy for Unbelief' (1830), ibid., viii. 77–83.
[6] 'Offerings for the Sanctuary' (1839), ibid., vi. 304–5.
[7] *Essay on Development*, pp. 375–6.

view of nature comes in his celebration of music. Out of the simple musical scale a composer can create an entire world: 'Shall we say that all this exuberant inventiveness is a mere ingenuity or trick of art, like some game or fashion of the day, without reality, without meaning?' As there is a divinity in the theology of the Church, 'so there is also in the wonderful creation of sublimity and beauty of which I am speaking'. Can music be mere sound, 'which is gone and perishes'? Newman's prose reveals a rare tendency towards extravagance when he speaks of the effects and sources of music:

Can it be that those mysterious stirrings of heart, and keen emotions, and strange yearnings after we know not what, and awful impressions from we know not whence, should be wrought in us by what is unsubstantial, and comes and goes, and begins and ends in itself? It is not so; it cannot be. No; they have escaped from some higher sphere; they are the outpourings of eternal harmony in the medium of created sound; they are echoes from our Home; they are the voice of Angels, or the Magnificat of Saints, or the living laws of Divine Governance, or the Divine Attributes; something are they besides themselves, which we cannot compass, which we cannot utter,—though mortal man, and he perhaps not otherwise distinguished above his fellows, has the gift of eliciting them.[1]

We must, certainly, make some allowances for the unusual emotion of this sermon. But Newman continued to believe that music bears a special relation to the mind and spirit. Writing to thank Church for a violin in 1865, he recalls that he never wrote more than when he 'played the fiddle', which he did very well. He observes that he always sleeps better after music, perhaps because of some 'electric current passing from the strings through the fingers into the brain and down the spinal marrow. Perhaps', he speculates, 'thought is music.'[2]

[1] 'The Theory of Developments in Religious Doctrine' (1843), *University Sermons*, pp. 346–7.
[2] Quoted by Henry Tristram, *Newman and His Friends* (London, 1933), pp. 188–9. In the first book of the 1805–6 edition of *The Prelude*, Wordsworth writes, 'The mind of man is fram'd even like the breath/And harmony of music.' The 1850 edition reads more piously: 'Dust as we are, the immortal spirit grows/Like

I make much of Newman's attitude towards music because it shows that he conceived of a faculty of mind never precisely labelled by him but which functions like Coleridge's 'Imagination' or Wordsworth's 'mind', half creating, half perceiving. When we listen to music, Newman urges, though the source and explanation for it may be physical, we have a glimpse of something beyond the actual sensations, beyond the mathematical relationships of its separate notes. We respond to the physical sounds as if to a reality beyond the sensory. To take an appropriate line from Wordsworth's 'Tintern Abbey', 'We see into the life of things'. Music, like the natural objects in Wordsworth's poems, is apprehended directly, and its *life*, the spirit which informs it, comes home to us not by any process of inference or reasoning, but as part of the 'real apprehension', the immediate act of perceiving, even though that life or spirit itself is not perceived by the senses.

As we have seen, however, Newman's actual use of the word 'imagination' is traditional, Johnsonian. Closely allied with memory, it functions primarily as a reservoir for images received through the senses. And yet for Newman the imagination possesses a certain security against the errors characteristic of improperly applied reason. In a letter to his sister Harriett in 1835, he explains that 'rationalism' is an attempt to know *how* things operate about which we can know nothing; when we rationalize we impose a relationship upon various facts which really have nothing to do with each other. The imposition of this false order gives us satisfaction, a satisfaction of the 'reason'. When we receive facts as isolated and unaccountable, however, we feel a satisfaction of the 'imagination'. Thus Newman implies that the imagination thrives upon the absence of causal relationships. If we create false causes for phenomena we 'rationalize'.

harmony in music' (*The Prelude, or Growth of a Poet's Mind*, ed. E. de Selincourt and H. Darbishire, Oxford, 1959, pp. 22–3). Carlyle has a passage perhaps closer still to Newman's thought: 'The meaning of song goes deep. Who is there that, in logical words, can express the effect music has on us? A kind of inarticulate unfathomable speech, which leads us to the edge of the Infinite, and lets us for moments gaze into that!' (*On Heroes, Hero-worship, and the Heroic in History*, 2 vols., London, 1926, i. 101).

But 'when we detach and isolate things which we should connect, we are superstitious'.[1]

And this brings us to an important question: how can we protect ourselves against superstition and yet present a mind prepared to accept religious truth on the basis of testimony? Newman's answer is complex and perhaps not quite satisfactory. He was acutely aware that religious men seemed superstitious to the sceptic or the rationalist. In his *Essay on Development* Newman vividly presents Plutarch's notion of superstitions:

it was the imagination of the existence of an unseen ever-present Master; the bondage of a rule of life, of a continual responsibility; obligation to attend to little things, the impossibility of escaping from duty, the inability to choose or change one's religion, an interference with the enjoyment of life, a melancholy view of the world, sense of sin, horror at guilt, apprehension of punishment, dread, self-abasement, depression, anxiety and endeavour to be at peace with heaven, and error and absurdity in the methods chosen for the purpose.[2]

This representation of Plutarch's idea of superstition is really Newman's vision of primitive Christianity, a Christianity un-corrupted by the comforts and attractions of nineteenth-century England. As we shall see in the following chapter on liberalism, Newman likes to argue that England would be better off if she were somewhat more liable to enthusiasm and superstition. The only forbidden subject which Englishmen can imagine, he preaches in a sermon called 'Ignorance of Evil' (1836), is one which is not *true*. They reject no subject of investigation or con-versation because Scripture proscribes it or the Church teaches that it leads to a conflict with faith. False religions everyone

---

[1] Mozley, ii. 137. No doubt Newman's use of 'Imagination' in this letter is in a high degree congenial to Coleridge's definition, 'as a repetition in the finite mind of the eternal act of creation in the infinite I AM' (*Biographia*, i. 202), which seems to preclude causal connections, or at least operate independently of them. There can be no doubt that romantic writers such as Wordsworth, Scott, and Southey influenced his epistemology and psychology. Certainly the satisfaction derived by the imagination from facts received as isolated and unaccountable to the reason describes the satisfaction which, for example, Wordsworth attempted to convey in such poems as 'The Thorn' or Coleridge in 'Christabel'.

[2] *Essay on Development*, p. 211.

knows to be wrong, but wrong not because they contradict
Christian doctrine but simply because they are false. Englishmen have not understood that real knowledge may be denied
us and that we must proceed on faith, risking superstition.[1]
Newman admits in the *Grammar of Assent* that 'Of the two, I
would rather have to maintain that we ought to begin with
believing every thing that is offered to our acceptance, than that
it is our duty to doubt of every thing.'[2]

LOVE AND FEAR AS SOURCES OF KNOWLEDGE: THE CONSCIENCE

In an important university sermon called 'Love the Safeguard
of Faith against Superstition' (1839), Newman recognizes some
of the difficulties in his view of faith. If reason does not protect
the majority of men against religious error—and we have seen
that he believed that reasoning in religious subjects tends towards
doubt—then faith may be made an excuse for every variety
of bigotry and superstition. Antecedent probabilities are equally
available for what is true and for what only pretends to be true.
Why should we not believe the miracles of India as well as those
of Palestine? How are we to manage an argument from 'presumption' in such a way as to prevent it from becoming an
argument against Christianity? Some corrective or critical principle
is clearly necessary.[3]

This corrective principle is none other than the Evangelical
doctrine of a 'right state of heart', the doctrine which Newman
so often preached in his youth. He carried it with him into the
Oxford Movement, and indeed for all Tractarians 'holiness',
or 'dutifulness', or 'love'—rather than reason—prevents faith
from attaching itself to unworthy objects.[4] Newman asserts that
if we give up this world by faith, we reach into the next by love.[5]
When we realize a religious truth 'we have a feeling which they

---

[1] *Parochial and Plain Sermons*, viii. 261.   [2] *Grammar of Assent*, p. 286.

[3] *University Sermons*, p. 232. Faith, according to Newman, need not be much
more than a 'presumption'. 'Presumption' does not mean mere conjecture or
prejudice, but that 'the mind cannot master its own reasons and anticipates in its
conclusions a logical exposition of them' (ibid., p. 234, n. 3).

[4] Owen Chadwick, *The Mind of the Oxford Movement* (London, 1960), p. 44.

[5] 'Faith and Love' (1838), *Parochial and Plain Sermons*, iv. 315.

have not, who take words for things'. Only the contemplation of God is 'capable of accompanying the mind always and everywhere'. If we can find 'that real and most sacred Object on which our heart may fix itself, a fulness of peace will follow, which nothing but it can give'.[1] Love of God protects the Christian against bigotry, credulity, fanaticism. Love quickens and illuminates faith, 'giving it eyes, hands, and feet'. Love forms 'an image of Christ'. ' "My sheep hear My voice, and I know them, and they follow Me".'[2]

The 'Image' of Christ satisfies the Christian's inherent longing for an object for his religious love. In Newman's words, 'The divinely-enlightened mind sees in Christ the very Object whom it desires to love and worship—the Object correlative of its own affections.'[3]

In Newman's second novel, the bishop Caecilius tells the religiously inclined but still sceptical Callista that if she feels 'needs, desires, aims, aspirations' which demand an 'Object', and Christianity professes a message which comes from that Object, then she is bound to inquire into Christian teaching. ' "This is what a slave of mine used to say," Callista responds, "What is your remedy, what your Object, what your love, O Christian teacher?" '[4] Similarly, in the _Apologia_, Newman credits Keble with teaching that the firmness of assent which the devout give to religious doctrine results not from the probabilities which introduced the doctrine but from 'the faith and love which accepted it'. Faith and love are directed towards an Object and they live in the vision of that Object. Love for the Object renders it 'reasonable' to assent absolutely to a probability. 'Thus the argument from Probability, in the matter of religion, became an argument from Personality, which in fact is one form of the argument from Authority.'[5]

---

[1] 'The Thought of God the Stay of the Soul' (1839), ibid., v. 321–2.

[2] 'Love the Safeguard of Faith against Superstition' (1839), _University Sermons_, pp. 234–5.

[3] Ibid., p. 236. It need hardly be pointed out that Newman's 'Object correlative' of the mind's affections bears striking similarities to T. S. Eliot's 'objective correlative'.

[4] _Callista: A Tale of the Third Century_ (London, 1910), ch. xix, pp. 220–1.

[5] _Apologia_, p. 30.

In the *Grammar of Assent* Newman develops his idea of the Object still further. Our imagination keeps the image of Christ before us. This image both creates faith and rewards it. 'It is the Image of Him who fulfils the one great need of human nature.' But our most intimate knowledge of God comes not from his image but from His voice within us, or what we call conscience. Conscience 'always involves the recognition of a living object, towards which it is directed'. Inanimate things cannot arouse our affections as conscience does. Affections are 'correlative with persons'. If we feel ashamed, frightened at transgressing the dictates of conscience, this implies that there is 'One to whom we are responsible'. When we do wrong we feel that 'tearful, broken-hearted sorrow which overwhelms us on hurting a mother'. When we do right, we feel 'the same sunny serenity of mind, the same soothing, satisfactory delight' which a father's praise gives us. We maintain within us 'the image of some person, to whom our love and veneration look, in whose smile we find our happiness, for whom we yearn, towards whom we direct our pleadings, in whose anger we are troubled and waste away'.[1] Conscience, the Evangelicals maintained, is the voice of God in the mind of man, present from birth. It cannot be created or erased by any form of education, though it can be sharpened or dulled.

This theory of the conscience, a theory fundamental to Newman's thought, runs counter to the more radical psychology of his century. In 1829 James Mill published his great *Analysis of the Phenomena of the Human Mind*, containing his doctrine of the association of ideas. Mill saw mental processes as rigidly mechanical, idea following idea purely on the principle of the contiguity of previous experiences. The conscience or 'moral sense' does not represent an echo of the divine Monitor, but merely a complex of associations of certain acts or principles with sensations of pleasure or pain. As he put it, 'the question, then, is, how can those early sequences be made to take place on which the habits, conducive to intelligence, temperance, and benevolence, are founded; and how can those sequences, on which are founded

---

[1] *Grammar of Assent*, pp. 354, 83.

the vices opposite to those virtues, be prevented?'[1] Thus for James Mill it is education and training which produce the moral sense: a good or utilitarian education creates a 'good' man while from the absence of appropriate sequences of associations emerge the socially unfit.

Among the papers in the Birmingham Oratory Newman has left a brief list of 'Arguments against Mill's doctrine of association'. The date is 5 January 1869, the year in which John Stuart Mill published his extensively edited version of his father's *Analysis*. Newman's notes are rough, but he is clearly seeking ways to counter James Mill's theory. First he suggests that 'conscience is too *early* to account for it by association'. Then 'the principle of association itself is to be accounted for'. Thirdly, 'the Greek ethic is too like the Christian' for the similarity to be explained by means of the doctrine of association. Again, '*Why* has punishment always [to be connected with] the *same* act so as to create an association?' But it is Newman's final question which bears directly upon our discussion: 'Is not association, as Mill uses it, a natural cause?'

The question suggests, I believe, that even if Mill's mechanistic analysis of association is correct, it would have no direct bearing upon the doctrine that conscience is the voice of God in the mind of man. Mill, in Newman's view, would simply have shown the natural means by which God's voice comes to be heard. Obviously this suggestion must be viewed as a change in the frame of reference, something in the nature of a last resort, and it sorts ill with the other notes, especially with the notion that conscience appears too early in a child's development to be the product of association. It shows too that the material Newman himself refrained from publishing should be treated with reservation and restraint. But the idea that conscience as a product of education may be the natural working out of a divine intention brings us to a conflict of attitudes which we must understand if we are to appreciate

---

[1] *James and John Stuart Mill on Education*, ed. F. A. Cavenagh (Cambridge, England, 1931), p. 50. The quotation is from an article probably composed in 1818 and published in the supplement to the fifth edition of the *Encyclopaedia Britannica*.

the real force and integrity of Newman's theory. For it has been correctly pointed out that his idea of conscience underlies all his thought;[1] and of all his psychological theories his theory of conscience is perhaps the most alien, certainly the most readily suspect, to uncommitted twentieth-century readers.

Most of us, orthodox or not, assume that our moral sense is indeed the product of education rather than an inherent, universal, directly implanted divine gift. We have a large amount of evidence for this assumption in our knowledge of the development of the moral sense in childhood and in our awareness of the differing moralities of various cultures. But the conclusions we draw from the assumption are what really ought to be of primary interest. In order to illuminate by contrast Newman's now unfamiliar position it is worthwhile to examine an extreme twentieth-century view, a view as extreme for most of us as Newman's seemed to many of his contemporaries, a view which nevertheless characterizes popular religious scepticism. And this view has been in part established and certainly most boldly stated by Freud.

Newman felt in our responses to the dictates of the moral sense 'a tenderness almost tearful on going wrong, and a grateful cheerfulness when we go right which is just what we feel in pleasing or displeasing a father or revered superior'.[2] As we know, Freud also found in our sensations of guilt and love strong resemblances to the responses of a child to its parents. From these observations Freud deduces—and in *The Future of an Illusion* argues —that these sensations must be the enduring effects of parental and social prohibitions, diffused and disguised, but rooted and powerful. The idea of God results from the survival of these prohibitions, an illusion created by the enduring fears and affections of childhood.' Religion', Freud concludes, 'is comparable to a childhood neurosis, and [the psychologist] is optimistic enough to assume that mankind will overcome this neurotic phase, just as so many children grow out of their similar neuroses.'[3]

[1] J.-H. Walgrave, O.P., *Newman the Theologian*, trans. A. V. Littledale (London, 1960), p. 342.
[2] Quoted in Boekraad and Tristram, *The Argument from Conscience*, p. 118.
[3] *The Future of an Illusion*, trans. W. D. Robson-Scott (London, 1928), p. 92.

Newman, however, finds in the paternal voice of conscience not the evidence for an illusion, but the proof of a divine Father:

so that contemplating or revolving on this feeling the mind will reasonably conclude that it is an unseen father who is the object of the feeling. And this father has necessarily some of those special attributes which belong to the notion of God. He is invisible—He is the searcher of hearts—He is omniscient as far as man is concerned—He is (to our notions) omnipotent.[1]

From the observation of similar psychic phenomena, then, Newman and Freud draw precisely opposite conclusions about the existence and nature of what they call God. The confrontation, I think, is most exciting when we ask why this is so, when we ask what premises lead them to their opposite conclusions. 'Am I', asks Freud, 'to be obliged to believe every absurdity? And if not, why just this one? There is no appeal beyond reason.' But what actually makes Freud suspicious of God's objective existence is not a rational proof of the absurdity of the idea. This he does not and cannot be expected to supply. What makes Freud suspicious is that the existence of God is *what we desire:*

We say to ourselves: it would indeed be very nice if there were a God, who was both Creator of the world and a benevolent providence, if there were a moral world order and a future life, but at the same time it is very odd that this is all just as we should wish it ourselves.[2]

Newman's position is again the antithesis of Freud's. For Newman, guilt and fear, desire and love, are not chiefly sources of illusion but chiefly sources of knowledge. Passions and affections may be felt before we discover their objects, 'and their activity would of course be an antecedent argument of extreme cogency in behalf of the real existence of those legitimate objects, supposing them unknown'.[3] So in Newman's second novel the bishop Caecilius tells Callista that her spiritual longings ' "imply, by their very existence, that such an Object does exist also" '.[4]

[1] Quoted in Boekraad and Tristram, *The Argument from Conscience*, p. 118.
[2] *The Future of an Illusion*, pp. 49, 58. The last-quoted passage continues: 'And it would be still odder if our poor, ignorant, enslaved ancestors had succeeded in solving all these difficult riddles of the universe.'
[3] *Essay on Development*, p. 45.　　　　[4] *Callista*, ch. xix, p. 220.

'Mental acts of whatever kind', Newman writes in the *Grammar*, 'presuppose their objects'. Christianity's 'very divination of our needs is in itself a proof that it is really the supply of them'.[1]

I have used Freud's argument on illusion in religion—it is not one of his best—as a contrast to or inversion of a Christian theory of conscience because I believe that most readers require some sort of intellectual or historical bridge by which to approach that more orthodox idea. Both arguments are in some sense presumptive, but Newman's no more so than Freud's, despite the latter's claim to the methods of reason and science.

FAITH AND THE PRINCIPLE OF DOGMA

Edmund Burke once observed that a man becomes a Christian in the most enlarged sense 'by examining into his *own nature* and finding that there were chasms in his soul which could be filled only with Religion!'[2] Much of Newman's epistemology is based on an assumption that the mind's operations carry with them their own rationale or justification. If experiences of guilt and fear seem general among us, then the probability is strong that they are designed to serve necessary functions in human life, and, most important, religious functions. If most men achieve a sense of spiritual life by impulses of desire and love rather than the workings of the reason, then desire and love are probably the appropriate means to such knowledge. In fact, one of the implications of the preceding discussion is that an investigation of the mind's operations can lead us to knowledge about external reality: 'Mental acts of whatever kind presuppose their objects.' A longing for God implies His existence while a devout love protects the believer against superstition. In the language of the *Grammar of Assent*, 'the human mind is made for truth, and so rests in truth, as it cannot rest in falsehood'.[3]

Newman, characteristically aware of the potential weaknesses in his own theories, early recognized that this justification of

[1] *Grammar of Assent*, pp. 5, 372.
[2] Reply to a message from a sceptic, undated letter (1790s?), Sheffield Central Library.
[3] *Grammar of Assent*, p. 167.

irrational mental activity could not invariably be applied with confidence to the inner life of any particular individual. In any intense examination of one's private spiritual state there is a danger that egocentric preoccupation will obscure the vision of external realities and that exercises of introspection may be substituted for exercises of faith. Thus, though he argues that an intimate knowledge of the mind points to realities beyond the mind itself, Newman also stresses the individual liability to error.

An awareness of personal fallibility, sharpening at times to a sense of weakness, runs through most of Newman's work, though countered in tone by the assurance with which he articulates the dogmas of orthodox Christianity. Even his 'natural religion', those ideas derived independently of revelation from the workings of the conscience and the constant experience of pain, together with a knowledge of past suffering and the secure anticipation of suffering to come, leads him to comment on the limits of human vision: 'How are we to explain it, the existence of God being taken for granted, except by saying that another will, besides His, has had a part in the disposition of his work, that there is a quarrel without remedy, a chronic alienation, between God and man?'[1] The doctrine of original corruption, stated here with an interesting modernity, appears periodically in Newman's Anglican sermons, qualifying his confidence in the integrity of the heart's impulses.

But it is when men begin to act independently, without the corrective guides of tradition and authority, that Newman finds them most in danger of error. 'What is meant by the right of private judgment?' he asks Hurrell Froude in a letter of 1830, 'The *duty* I understand: but no one can *help* another's thinking in private.'[2] As he left aspects of his Evangelicalism behind him, Newman grew increasingly aware of the danger to dogma implied in religious introspection. His sermons more frequently exhort his congregation to lose the consciousness of self in the contemplation of the immense traditional assertions of Christianity. As Horton Davies puts it, 'Newman came increasingly to feel that the defect of Protestant worship was its subjectivity, its

[1] Ibid., p. 303.　　　　[2] Mozley, i. 221.

perpetual scrutiny of the feelings, its emphasis on our faith, not on the Object of faith, while the strength of Roman Catholic worship was its objectivity, its steady contemplation of God as revealed in the Incarnation.'[1]

Both Evangelicalism and Tractarianism preached the depravity of the times, stressed the importance of internal holiness, and encouraged the disciplining of the heart and will. To these emphases, however, Tractarians added a sense of the high value of tradition, of the sacramental principle and liturgical worship, of understanding the catholicity and apostolicity of the English Church, and, primarily in the second generation, of the full exercise of ceremony. The great contribution of the Oxford Movement to English Christianity was to re-establish the objective bases of belief as preserved in dogma, in the history of the primitive church, and in ritual.[2]

As his friendship with Froude grew and his alliance with Keble and Pusey was established, Newman's idea of religious duty became less that of examining one's private inner life and more that of contemplating the objects of devotion. He began to lay the groundwork for those great defences of dogma for which he is both loved and ignored. By 1839, he can write with remarkable vehemence against those in whom 'spiritual-mindedness' has been substituted for a real apprehension and active imitation of Christ.

Poor miserable captives, to whom such doctrine is preached as the Gospel! What! is *this* the liberty wherewith Christ has made us free, and wherein we stand, the home of our own thoughts, the prison of our own sensations, the province of self, a monotonous confession of what we are by nature, not what Christ is in us, and a resting at best not on His love towards us, but in our faith towards Him! This is nothing but a specious idolatry; a man thus minded does not simply think of God when he prays to Him, but is observing whether he feels properly or not; does not believe and obey, but considers it enough to be conscious that he is what he calls warm and spiritual; does not consider

---

[1] Horton Davies, *Worship and Theology in England, Vol. IV: From Newman to Martineau* (Princeton, 1962), pp. 35–6.
[2] Ibid., *Vol. III: From Watts and Wesley to Maurice* (Princeton, 1961), pp. 243–54.

the grace of the Blessed Eucharist, the Body and Blood of his Saviour, Jesus Christ, except—O shameful and fearful error!—except as a quality of his own mind.[1]

'By objective truth', writes Newman in a tract of 1835, 'is meant the religious system as existing in itself, external to this or that particular mind'. 'Subjective' truth includes what each mind receives in particular and considers to be objective. If we wish to apprehend an objective truth, we must 'throw ourselves forward upon that which we have but partially mastered or made subjective'. We must embrace and maintain convictions which transcend our capacity, convictions 'of which we cannot see the bottom'. The objects of these spiritual convictions resemble the temporal 'ideas' discussed earlier in this chapter, ideas so vast that the individual mind cannot comprehend all their details nor words express their harmony and precision. We must, the Tract continues, 'bow before the import of such propositions, as if we were contemplating what is real and independent of human judgment'. To the rationalist, such humility and faith as are implicit in the submission to creeds and dogma seem to be superstitions. He relegates them to the realm of subjective truth, thinking that they meet different needs and carry different significances for different persons. He imagines that we have some chance of analysing our own nature, but none of understanding God's.[2]

Newman admits that Christian doctrine is variously received by different minds. As a 'Manifestation', or subjective truth, it cannot be more than that which each mind comprehends it to be. As a 'Mystery', however, it exists independently of human apprehension. Mystery is doctrine hidden in language, its only possible medium. Each mind receives it according to its own individual capacity for receiving—and the more diligent the mind the more complete the manifestation. But as mystery it remains 'one and the same, independent and real, of depth unfathomable, and illimitable in its extent'.[3]

---

[1] Quoted in *Autobiographical Writings*, p. 142.
[2] 'On the Introduction of Rationalistic Principles into Revealed Religion', *Essays and Sketches*, i. 186, 190.   [3] Ibid. i. 191–2.

Christian mysteries come to us in the writings of Scripture and the doctrines of the Church. Christians accept them as dogma, a body of doctrines formally and authoritatively affirmed, and received on the testimony of their Church. We have seen that for Newman the 'voice' of conscience implies the existence of a transcendent personality. This implication is confirmed when men find in the image of Christ the Object correlative of their religious needs and aspirations. The human mind is so constituted as to desire an idea of God, and this furnishes us with a particular example of its capacity, its need, to be provided with such dogma as those Scriptures describing the nature and life of Jesus. But Newman also writes of the general need of the mind for dogmatic assurance, a need which he considers by no means limited to a love of Christ's image.

Christians accept dogma, the mysteries of Christianity for example, not because they altogether comprehend their meaning, but because they have faith in their source. A Christian may have a certain imperfect apprehension of each of the 'persons' of the Trinity. To understand how they form a unity, however, is quite beyond him. If he believes in the Trinity, his mind affirms what it cannot understand. Faith, in this sense, is 'the absolute acceptance of the divine Word with an internal assent, in opposition to the informations, if such, of sight and reason'.[1]

Such assents are often formal, as in the use of creeds; but for Newman they are not arbitrary. They find a partial justification in the nature of our minds. 'It is as if a law of the human mind, ever to do things in one and the same way.' We speak in the same tones, adopt the same phrases and turns of thought. We love order and arrangement. 'Method approves itself to us.' Even sceptics must adopt principles of action; the illiterate find rude rules for classifying their experiences; children attempt to relate their discoveries to some law or system; even Latitudinarians vigorously defend the principle of latitude:

Thus, what is invidiously called dogmatism and system, in one shape or other, in one degree or another, is, I may say, necessary to the human

[1] *Essay on Development*, p. 303.

mind; we cannot reason, feel, or act, without it; it forms the stamina of thought, which, when it is removed, languishes and droops. Sooner than dispense with principles, the mind will take them at the hand of others, will put up with such as are faulty and uncertain.[1]

Thus, dogma, as a principle, is not for Newman the arbitrary imposition of opinion from without, but the meeting of a fundamental psychic need. Because our minds characteristically pass judgement on whatever comes before them, and will adopt principles of some sort to explain what they perceive, Newman has no hesitation in indoctrinating receptive seekers with dogmas whose claim to divine truth is in logical terms 'probable' at best.

To greet the dogmas of the Church with suspicion and distrust, he argues, is to treat them with less respect than that which we reserve for other alleged facts and truths. When we hear accounts of daily occurrences which come to us with a 'fair presumption' in their favour, we do not greet them with doubt, but with spontaneous confidence. We take them on trust, behaving as if we had proved that they are true.[2] It is natural in us to do so. If assent to the truth of what comes before us, whether through our senses or the teachings of a church, were not congenial to and spontaneous with us, we could learn nothing. We could gather no evidence, because no evidence carries with it a philosophically irrefutable proof of its own validity. We must assent before we can question, and evidences in general are not the bases of faith; they are its rewards. We advance in knowledge by assenting, discovering errors, and assenting again. For this reason wisdom is the last gift of the spirit. Faith is the first.[3] And faith is the 'correlative of dogma'.[4]

The satisfactions which the exercise of religious faith gives the Christian argue strongly in favour of its validity as a means to truth. Physical pain and grief, spiritual anxiety and self-chastisement, Newman claims, do not affect the 'vision of faith'. 'We

[1] 'Wisdom, as Contrasted with Faith and Bigotry' (1841), *University Sermons*, pp. 295–7.
[2] *Essay on Development*, pp. 93–4.
[3] 'Wisdom as Contrasted with Faith and Bigotry' (1841), *University Sermons*, p. 294.
[4] *Essay on Development*, p. 303.

are two or three selves at once, in the wonderful structure of our minds, and can weep while we smile, and labour while we meditate.' Man's highest glory is obedience, and 'It is our shame, not our privilege, that we do not obey as the Angels do'.[1] No irreligious person should be surprised that religious obedience is 'so pleasant in itself'. They cannot know its 'secret pleasure' until they attempt to live a Christian life.[2]

ANTECEDENTS OF THE ILLATIVE SENSE

Creeds and dogmas, then, satisfy the mind's need for forms and principles. They also enable Christians to deal with those highly complex 'ideas' discussed earlier in this chapter. 'Creeds and dogmas live in the one idea they are designed to express.' We need them because our minds cannot apprehend these 'ideas' except in their separate aspects. By means of dogmas we realize ideas in their variously related parts.[3]

These aspects or parts of ideas exist in dogma as distinct facts and actions rather than as abstract arguments. In a sermon called 'The Influence of Natural and Revealed Religion Respectively' (1830), Newman refers to 'The Roman Stoic' who, 'as he committed suicide, complained he had worshipped virtue, and found it but an empty name'. Christian Revelation presents us not with abstractions and generalized laws, not with metaphysical conjectures, but with the life of Christ, his death and resurrection. 'Facts such as this are not simply evidence of the truth of the revelation, but the media of its impressiveness.' They bring vividly before us a realization of truths necessary to our religious being, truths which otherwise would 'wander idle and forlorn over the surface of the moral world'. The 'Revealed system' teaches religious truths historically and dramatically, not by deductions drawn from evidences, not in natural laws, but in spoken commands, 'not in works, but in action'.[4]

Scripture, therefore, offers us what Newman in the *Grammar of Assent* calls 'real apprehension'. Real apprehension is stronger

[1] 'The State of Grace' (1836). *Parochial and Plain Sermons*, iv. 146–7, 142.
[2] 'Religion Pleasant to the Religious' (1840), ibid., vii. 198.
[3] *Essay on Development*, pp. 49–50.   [4] *University Sermons*, pp. 27, 30.

than 'notional' because the perception of objects external to us affects us more strongly than our apprehension of notions: 'intellectual ideas cannot compete in effectiveness with the experience of concrete facts'. Images and experiences strike us individually as the notions abstracted from them do not. Newman values this immediate perception of facts and images far above abstract reasoning, which he calls 'Inference' in the *Grammar*. Inference is most perfect when exercised on propositions apprehended as notions, 'that is, which are creations of the mind'. Assent, on the contrary, is most perfect when exercised on propositions apprehended as experiences or images.[1]

Newman stresses the unreal nature of abstractions throughout his Anglican as well as his Catholic career. Reality, for Newman, is in nature always unique and individual, for as in physics nature abhors a vacuum, so in 'moral subjects' she seems to abhor identity. There exists in nature no identity between objects, no identity of the 'narrow, absolute, formal kind', and a system which requires that everything be shaped into one mould is false to our actual experience. A 'true system', such as Christianity, can afford to be 'free and spontaneous, to vary its aspect, to modify, enlarge, and accommodate itself to times and places without loss of principle'.[2] Similarly, in the *Grammar of Assent*, Newman observes that science reaches truth in the abstract and only achieves probability in the concrete. But 'what we aim at is truth in the concrete'.[3] The dogma of Revealed Christianity, we learn later in the *Grammar*, provides us with truth in the concrete.

In Newman's epistemology, the entire complex of faculties by which we are able to judge truth in the concrete operates collectively as the Illative Sense. The Illative Sense partakes of

[1] *Grammar of Assent*, pp. 8–9, 30–2.

[2] 'Prospects of the Anglican Church', in *Essays and Sketches*, i. 352–3. In an undated note among the Birmingham papers we find this observation: 'Classes are not external facts but ideas derived from the sight *or* experience of resemblance, purely mental, and without corresponding objects. Individuals are the only facts.'

[3] *Grammar of Assent*, p. 212. 'This dependence upon the concrete is interesting for several reasons. It is typical of the whole Romantic Movement in literature, a reaction against the abstract philosophy of the Eighteenth Century' (W. R. Castle, Jr., 'Newman and Coleridge', *The Sewanee Review*, xvii, April 1909, 140).

the functions of other faculties discussed in this chapter but is not bound by their limitations. It shares with reason the ability to form conclusions from evidences but abandons methods of reasoning and logic when they are inappropriate to the subject in question. Like imagination the Illative Sense is closely allied with memory, for it expands and perfects itself with experience, but unlike imagination its subtle sensitivity to moral value prevents it from being seduced by the glamour of worldly temptations. Though its operation appears to be rapid and immediate, though it takes account of such emotions as love and fear, and though the bases of its judgements lie too deep in the mind and are too complex for verbal expression, the Illative Sense possesses a degree of consciousness and deliberation which preserves it from the errors and excesses of intuition. Because the Illative Sense is so complex and comprehensive, Newman cannot provide it with the same sort of psychological and philosophical justification which can be found historically for reason, imagination, intuition, and conscience. This does not mean that the Illative Sense is not real, real to Newman, perhaps, in the same way that the ego was to Freud, as a hypothetical characterization of a large range of psychic activity. But the Illative Sense differs from Freud's constructs in being ideal, the 'power of judging and concluding, when in its perfection'. The Illative Sense is that 'subtle and elastic logic of thought' which provides the only ultimate test of truth or error in any class of concrete reasonings, experimental science, historical research, or theology.[1]

Only the Illative Sense is elastic and delicate enough to take account of the variousness of reality, the uniqueness of each thing experienced. It therefore fills a hiatus in Newman's epistemology which goes back to his first distrust of reason as a means to truth. It satisfies the demand that the Christian take his religion as a practical and immediate concern, not as a subject for speculation, or what Newman calls in a sermon preached in his early thirties, a 'mere matter of philosophical or historical research'.[2] The Illative Sense makes use of that Christian self-

---

[1] *Grammar of Assent*, pp. 268, 272–3.
[2] 'Faith Without Sight' (1834), *Parochial and Plain Sermons*, ii. 21.

consciousness so important to Newman's Evangelical period. But, based as it is upon concrete experience, and judging principally of the truth of things outside the self, it avoids the dangers of self-contemplation to the exclusion of the objects of faith.

The Illative Sense is personal. 'It is seated in the mind of the individual, who is thus his own law, his own teacher, and his own judge in those special cases of duty which are personal to him.' Formed by our experience of reality in all its diversity, the Illative Sense can be developed and perfected. But, because of its personal character, the Illative Sense cannot perform the function of logic which is to supply a 'common measure between mind and mind.'[1] Not to do so is a condition of its flexibility, of its spontaneity. We have seen that language is, in Newman's view, a crabbed and distant representation of reality, that in being common and general it becomes inexact and misleading. In his *Essay on Development*, written more than twenty years before the *Grammar of Assent*, Newman argues in a discussion of reason and faith that

the spontaneous process which goes on within the mind itself is higher and choicer than that which is logical; for the latter, being scientific, is common property, and can be taken and made use of by minds who are personally strangers, in any true sense, both to the ideas in question and to their development.[2]

The need for and existence of some spontaneous and elastic personal faculty for judging truth had occurred to Newman before he wrote the *Grammar of Assent*. As an Anglican, he characteristically advised his congregation to follow their intuition in matters of duty, to attend to the voice of conscience, to be led by a love of Christ. In a letter to Mrs. J. W. Bowden in 1846, Newman urges that lady to overcome her religious difficulties by the means which God has given her: if she is led to Catholicism by Newman's own example, by the Catholic tendencies of her son, by her judgement of the 'present state of things', by

---

[1] *Grammar of Assent*, pp. 269, 273, 275.
[2] *Essay on Development*, pp. 177-8.

her general impression of history, then these are the legitimate ways 'in which you are called upon to use your reason. God will bless you in such a calm spontaneous use of it.' Newman then indicates that in this letter he means by reason not systematic reasoning, but the intimate workings and impulses of the mind, as he goes on to disparage disputes and arguments.[1] There can be no doubt that if we apply the terminology of the *Grammar of Assent*, Newman is encouraging Mrs. Bowden to make use of impressions and experiences so diverse that they can only be assembled and employed by an Illative Sense.

I began this chapter by emphasizing the difficulties which Newman thought accompany the analysis of mind. Among these he placed eccentricity and untrustworthiness of the mind, the ambiguity of the terms employed, and the limitations of the perceptive faculties themselves. Our reason operates in closed systems based on limited experience. Our calculi are 'economies' running parallel with reality for a space, then in some contradiction betraying their insufficiency to comprehend experience beyond their range. Reason fails to explain historical developments in religious doctrine just as it often fails to lead men to religious truth. It cannot help us to break out of our spiritual isolation. Christians reach into the spiritual universe by means of love, a love created in man by God which leads to a perception of Him. As the Object correlative of our spiritual needs, God's Image, kept before the Christian by his imagination and the voice of conscience, preserves him from superstition. Dogma provides the orthodox with assertions at once objective and specific; it alone avoids the dangers of subjectivity and the unreality of abstract speculation. Its language, though containing apparent contradictions, is nevertheless for human perception coincident with the truths received from it. The religious mind throws itself forward by means of love to assent to mysteries as the ultimate objective truths.

In much of Newman's epistemology before 1845 we can discern lines of thought which ultimately lead him to his dis-

[1] *Letters and Diaries*, xi. 187.

covery of the Illative Sense. The Illative Sense grows out of our individual experiences of reality. It is personal and practical, not general or abstract. It provides a private means to truth, and is unfettered by any need to express its judgements in language. The Illative Sense takes account of the uniqueness of each object and each experience. It comprehends love and desire, fear and guilt as relevant to the search for truth and does not dismiss them as potential distorters of our vision.

CHAPTER THREE

Liberalism: Newman's Social Criticism in Relation to his Philosophy of Mind

... she was as low down, in the school, as low could be;
... after eight weeks of induction into the elements of
Political Economy, she had only yesterday been set right
by a prattler three feet high, for returning to the question,
'What is the first principle of this science?' the absurd
answer, 'To do unto others as I would that they should do
unto me.'

(DICKENS, *Hard Times*)

A WORK exclusively devoted to Newman's criticism of
English society is much needed. His life nearly spans the century
and in one way or another his writings are related to currents
of English social thought as different from each other as romanticism and utilitarianism. This chapter is not intended to substitute
for such a book, but to show how Newman based his criticism
of society, including his reaction to the romantics and the utilitarians, upon his philosophy of the mind. In *The Tamworth Reading
Room* and in *The Idea of a University* his views on the scope and
limitations of knowledge led him not only to a complex of
qualifications about the aims and limits of education but to a
direct attack on what he ironically termed his 'civilized age'. It is
my hope that by relating Newman's epistemological and psychological theories to his social criticism I shall be able to suggest
some of the bases for his attitudes towards his society in its relation to Christian principles and to continue to deepen our understanding of his contemplation of mind.

John Stuart Mill pointed out that Bentham and Coleridge
agreed in perceiving 'that the groundwork of all other philosophy
must be laid in the philosophy of the mind'.[1] Newman also

[1] *Bentham and Coleridge*, ed. F. R. Leavis (New York, 1962), p. 102.

tried to lay such a 'groundwork'. In the preceding chapter I have
attempted to outline his philosophy of the mind without relating
it either to his social criticism or to his imaginative and autobiographical achievements. I tried instead to abstract this 'philosophy' primarily from his sermons, letters, and journals, and
from the *Grammar of Assent*, stripping it for the sake of clarity
of all except those religious and theological associations without
which any theory of Newman's can scarcely be said to exist at
all. But this skeletal psychology and epistemology taken by itself
is in an important sense not false or artificial but misleading.
Before he wrote the *Grammar of Assent*, Newman rarely dissociated
his analyses of mind from social, personal, and literary considerations. In the two chapters to come I discuss Newman's theories
of psychic activity as they influence his views on education and as
they function dramatically in his novels and in the *Apologia*. In this
chapter we view them as they operate in his social criticism.

Most of Newman's social criticism takes the form of an attack
on 'liberalism'. The word appears frequently in his writing but
its meaning is somewhat complex, always rich in religious
connotations. Newman associates it with rationalism, or human
reason operating uninformed by Christian dogma, giving rise
to those epistemological 'usurpations' which he had attacked
since his Evangelical youth. When in 1851 a rumour spread
that Newman was to be made a bishop, he wrote to George
Talbot in Rome arguing that his great value lay in his literary
work, not in canon law. He expresses the fear that with the duties
of a bishop 'the work of a *life* would be lost. For twenty years I
have been working on towards a philosophical polemic, suited
to these times.'[1] This philosophical polemic is directed against a
variety of attacks on Catholic Christianity, nearly all of which
Newman associates with liberalism. In the *Apologia* he traces the
development of liberalism during his adult life:

> The Liberalism which gives a colour to society now, is very dif-
> ferent from that character of thought which bore the name thirty or
> forty years ago. Now it is scarcely a party; it is the educated lay
> world. When I was young, I knew the word first as giving name to a

[1] *Letters and Diaries*, xiv. 206.

periodical, set up by Lord Byron and others. Now, as then, I have no sympathy with the philosophy of Byron. Afterwards, Liberalism was the badge of a theological school, of a dry and repulsive character, not very dangerous in itself, though dangerous as opening the door to evils which it did not itself either anticipate or comprehend. At present it is nothing else than that deep, plausible scepticism, of which I spoke above, as being the development of human reason, as practically exercised by the natural man.[1]

We have seen in the preceding chapter how Newman thought reason operates in the natural man. His growing knowledge of its epistemological limitations during his Tractarian career corresponded with a developing awareness of the religious depravity of the times, a depravity he found evident in the Anglican Church and in all of English society.

Newman found one of the earliest indications that a reforming and rational spirit threatened Anglicanism in the enactment of the bill for Catholic Emancipation. 'Its passing', he writes to his sister in 1829, 'is one of the signs of the times, of the encroachment of Philosophism and Indifferentism in the Church'.[2] Two years later Newman tells John William Bowden that he fears that 'society is rotten, to say a strong thing'. Most people one meets cannot be expected to be consistently religious, but they are not even believers in Christianity in any true sense. 'No, they are Liberals, and in saying this I conceive I am saying almost as bad of them as can be said of anyone.'[3] In Rome in 1833, Newman finds the Roman clergy superior in appearance to the Neapolitan priests with their 'trumpery ornaments' and 'absurd inscriptions'. But even in Rome he finds 'timidity, indolence, and that secular spirit which creeps on established religion everywhere'.[4] Eighteen months later, with the Tractarian Movement just a year old, Newman writes to Whately about certain principles which he believes his former mentor holds and which betray the same

[1] *Apologia*, pp. 233–4.
[2] Mozley, i. 199. Newman did not react strongly to the bill itself, but to what he felt to be Peel's insult to the university in expecting it to follow unprotestingly his changes of mind and policy. See Meriol Trevor, *Newman: The Pillar of the Cloud* (London, 1962), pp. 81–2.
[3] Mozley, i. 237.   [4] Ibid., i. 360.

secular spirit: 'principles which bear upon the very fundamentals of all argument and investigation, and affect almost every doctrine and every maxim on which our faith and our conduct depend'. Newman continues this painful letter by admitting that if 'something from within' had not held him back, he might have adopted certain views of Whately's on social and religious questions, views which he sees to be grounded in 'the pride of reason'.[1] In 1835 Newman warns his aunt that 'one must expect a flood of scepticism on the most important subjects to pour over the land, and we are so unprepared, it is quite frightful to think of it'.[2] A year before the publication of *Tract XC*, Newman asks Keble whether he should give up his position at St. Mary's in Oxford. Newman argues that the liberal Protestant spirit is the great evil, the present threat to Anglicanism, and that the important struggle is not with Roman Catholicism but with rationalism: 'Rationalism is the great evil of the day. May not I consider my post at St. Mary's as a place of protest against it?'[3]

The rejection of *Tract XC* by the Anglican bishops meant to Newman that the Anglican Church had denied the only possible Catholic interpretation of the Thirty-nine Articles. In *Loss and Gain*, the hero, Charles, wonders whether there is any authority for a Catholic interpretation of the Articles based on the doctrines of the Fathers. He is told that such an interpretation has never been officially condemned, but has been much opposed. Newman permits himself an obviously autobiographical note in Charles's observation that the Anglican Church once had the chance to sanction a Catholic interpretation but rejected it. The Catholic interpretation of the Articles remains ' "a mere theory struck out by individuals" '.[4]

But if the Anglican Church was not to be Catholic, then it must become either perfectly innocuous or dangerously liberal. Along with his growing awareness of irreligion in England,

---

[1] Ibid., ii. 70.   [2] Ibid., ii. 129.

[3] Newman quotes himself from a letter of 1840 in the *Apologia*, p. 127.

[4] *Loss and Gain, The Story of a Convert* (London, 1919), pt. i, ch. xv, p. 135. *Loss and Gain* first appeared in 1848.

Newman was developing the idea of a fundamental dialectic in the intellectual life of the times, a dialectic in which Catholicism was the thesis and liberalism the antithesis. In 1837 he observes that England has many high virtues, but a 'low Catholicism'. How, he asks, can the English Church avoid Scylla and Charybdis, by which he probably means Rome and liberalism, and go 'straight on to the very image of Christ'?[1] By 1839 Newman had become impatient with whatever held a neutral position, with the 'motley protestantism' of the day. Protestantism, he decides, merely occupies the space between the two great powers, Catholic truth and rationalism:

neither of these owning it, or making account of it, or courting it; on the contrary, both feeling it to be a hindrance in the way of their engaging with each other, and impatiently waiting to be rid of it. Then, indeed, it will be the stern encounter, when two real and living principles, simple, entire, and consistent, one in the Church, the other out of it, at length rush upon each other, contending not for names and words, or half views, but for elementary notions and distinctive moral characters.[2]

One of Newman's few immediate intellectual gratifications in his conversion to Roman Catholicism must have been the sense that he had shed the last of his associations with the attitudes of Protestants and liberals. The *via media* had narrowed and disappeared, leaving him in an insupportably anomalous position. The Anglican bishops in their reaction to *Tract XC* treated him as a sort of acutely embarrassing irrelevance in the English Church. In September of 1843 he preached his last sermon at St. Mary's and retired to Littlemore to reconstruct his religious identity.

Newman points out in the *Apologia* that he particularly feared that many of his followers would not come to Rome but, finding

---

[1] Newman quotes himself in the *Apologia*, pp. 38–9.

[2] 'Prospects of the Anglican Church' (1839), *Essays and Sketches*, i. 363. Newman had already begun to doubt the reality of a *via media* for the English Church. After he becomes a Catholic he writes: 'The *Via Media* is really nothing else than Protestant. Not to submit to the [Roman] Church is to oppose her, and to side with the heretical party; for medium there is none' (*Certain Difficulties Felt by Anglicans in Catholic Teaching*, London, 1901, i. 377). These lectures were delivered in 1850.

a middle position to be as untenable for them as it was for him, would join the liberal camp. Only two alternatives present themselves to a philosophically consistent mind, the *Apologia* tells us, 'the way to Rome, and the way to Atheism: Anglicanism is the halfway house on the one side, and Liberalism is the halfway house on the other'. The famous words have the gravity of prophecy. Less often quoted is the observation which follows them, and which will conclude this introductory sketch of Newman's growing sense of irreligion in England before his conversion: 'It is not at all easy (humanly speaking) to wind up an Englishman to a dogmatic level.'[1] This remark, with its demure parenthesis, must have seemed to the exiled leader of the Tractarian Movement one of the gentlest understatements ever made by an Englishman to Englishmen. For our purposes, it serves to introduce a discussion of what is perhaps at once the most intimate and the most public of civilized practices, private judgement.

PRIVATE JUDGEMENT

Liberalism, for Newman, is a development of human reason as exercised by the natural man which results in a broadly sceptical attitude towards all information appealing to trust or authority. In principle and practice it is anti-dogmatic. As the foregoing quotations indicate, liberals and English rationalists are closely connected in Newman's mind. But when Newman writes of

[1] *Apologia*, p. 185. In a letter of January 1846, Newman defended his dialectic and its effects upon his followers: 'I fully grant that my mode of reasoning, as you object, tends, as was objected to Bishop Butler's great work, to drive people into one extreme or the other. All disquisitions, which contemplate things as they are, more or less destroy middle views as unreal and untenable. Butler was accused of making atheists—but no religious person is in danger of this extreme—his intellectual difficulties, whatever they are, will clearly seem to him, in the eye of reason, nothing but *temptations*. The other extreme is open to him—and if he embrace it, he will have strength given him to resist temptation to infidelity. But it is miserable to stand in the middle, with the temptation and without the grace' (*Letters and Diaries*, xi. 86). J. A. Froude, who rejected Christian orthodoxy before Newman's conversion and despite his influence, supports the validity of his dialectic in the autobiographical novel, *The Nemesis of Faith* (London, 1849): 'It was enough for me to learn, as now I soon did, that all real arguments against Catholicism were, in fact, arguments against Christianity' (p. 148).

reason and logic he works in the realm of epistemological theory and theological controversy. His available antagonists are generally limited to academic clerics and philosophers. When Newman attacks liberalism, however, he seems to take John Bull by the horns, not so much in the political arena, but on the wide, treacherous field of national prejudices and values, assumptions and traditions. Of his hypothetical eighteen propositions of liberalism annexed to the 1865 edition of the *Apologia*, each of which he denounced and abjured, the ninth reads:

There is a right of Private Judgment: that is, there is no existing authority on earth competent to interfere with the liberty of individuals in reasoning and judging for themselves about the Bible and its contents, as they severally please.[1]

In 1865 Newman was well aware that most Englishmen, including perhaps some Roman Catholics, had never questioned the right of private judgement. Earlier in the *Apologia* he compares the growth of liberalism in religion with Phaeton, who 'has got into the chariot of the sun; we, alas! can only look on, and watch him down the steep of heaven. Meanwhile, the lands, which he is passing over, suffer from his driving.'[2] The metaphor is appropriate. The mortal who presumed to attempt the work of the gods symbolizes the usurpation of dogmatic religion by liberalism, of assent by reasoning.[3]

This usurpation Newman characterizes in an important note to the *Apologia*:

Now by Liberalism I mean false liberty of thought, or the exercise of thought upon matters, in which, from the constitution of the human mind, thought cannot be brought to any successful issue, and therefore is out of place. Among such matters are first principles of whatever kind; and of these the most sacred and momentous are especially to be reckoned the truths of Revelation. Liberalism then is the mistake of subjecting to human judgment those revealed doctrines which are in their nature beyond and independent of it, and of claiming to determine on intrinsic grounds the truth and value of propositions which

---

[1] *Apologia*, p. 261.   [2] Ibid., p. 62.
[3] See Robert Colby, 'The Poetical Structure of Newman's *Apologia pro Vita Sua*', *Journal of Religion*, xxxiii (1953), 48.

rest for their reception simply on the external authority of the Divine Word.[1]

No Christian, according to Newman, has the right to challenge the validity of Catholic dogma. As reasoning can destroy the habit of assent in the private mind, so liberalism usurps the position of dogmatic Christianity in society. And this provides us with another indication of the connection between Newman's social thought and his epistemology. His awareness of the liabilities to which the mind is subject and the seductions to which it yields enabled him to appreciate the scope and power of what he termed liberalism. By 1865 liberalism was no longer the title of Byron's publication or a dull party of dry Oxford dons, but the spirit of the age, an increasingly general cultural calamity.

As early as 1829, about the time when he first sensed the tendency of excessive religious introspection to distract the Christian from the objects of worship, Newman began to sense the presence of a pervasive liberal spirit in society. The popular insistence upon the right of private judgement was a manifestation of that spirit. In a letter to his mother he observes that 'we live in a novel era—one in which there is an advance towards universal education'. Previously, Newman continues, men accepted the religious teachings of the clergy. Now they try to judge for themselves. Christianity, of course, is not opposed to free inquiry, but 'still I think it *in fact* at the present time opposed to the particular form which that liberty of thought has now assumed'. A spirit is at work against Christianity, 'a spirit which tends to overthrow doctrine, as if the fruit of bigotry and discipline—as if the instrument of priestcraft. All parties seem to acknowledge that the stream of opinion is setting against the Church.'[2]

In 1832 Newman tells his congregation that when dogma has been rejected as the medium of religious truth, men fall back on themselves and on the world. Religion becomes 'a mere *civilization*', and society carries on much as it would have done 'even supposing Christianity were not the religion of the land'.[3] This

---

[1] *Apologia*, pp. 255–6.   [2] Mozley, i. 204.
[3] 'Knowledge of God's Will without Obedience' (1832), *Parochial and Plain Sermons*, i. 30.

is true because the great majority of people are utterly incapable of using private judgement to arrive at religious truth. In an article called 'Private Judgement', published in the *British Critic* in 1841, Newman argues convincingly that the mass of English people either do not really believe in private judgement or are 'deplorably dark about it'. Even those who profess to employ their own judgement do not really hold the right of private judgement, 'but their own private right, and no one's else'.[1]

In 'Obedience without Love' (1837), Newman speaks of the credit Englishmen give to anyone who acts up to his own standard, *'whatever that is'*.[2] Society admires those who are true to themselves and is not scrupulous about the correspondence of private opinions to Christian doctrine. In *The Tamworth Reading Room*, Newman indignantly quotes Lord Brougham, who had 'laid down at Glasgow the infidel principle, or, as he styles it, "the great truth", which "has gone forth to all the ends of the earth, that man shall no more render account to man for his belief, over which he has himself no control" '.[3] Similarly, the tenth proposition of liberalism states:

> There are rights of conscience, such that every one may lawfully advance a claim to profess and teach what is false and wrong in matters, religious, social, and moral, provided that to his private conscience it seems absolutely true and right.[4]

Liberalism, in Newman's view, not only gives this unauthorized freedom to the individual, but also in fact forces it upon him. Propositions four and five hold that no one should make an act of faith in anything which has not been brought home to him by actual proof and that it is 'immoral in a man to believe more than he can spontaneously receive as being congenial to his moral and mental nature'.[5] G. M. Young's response, 'Indeed why should he? Or indeed, how can he?',[6] illustrates the almost prophetic nature of the propositions of liberalism. The principles which Newman denounced and abjured in 1865, most of us now

---

[1] *Essays and Sketches*, ii. 141. [2] *Parochial and Plain Sermons*, iv. 32–3.
[3] *Essays and Sketches*, ii. 177. [4] *Apologia*, p. 261.
[5] Ibid., p. 260. [6] *Daylight and Champaign*, p. 100.

take as truisms. How, indeed, are we to reject proposition number two? 'No one can believe what he does not understand. There-fore, e.g. there are no mysteries in true religion.'[1]

The solution to Young's dilemma, a dilemma which is perhaps shared by most twentieth-century readers of Newman, may be found in an understanding of his philosophy of mind. In the pre-ceding chapter I discussed in detail Newman's analysis of the pro-cess by which the devout mind, recognizing its own limitations and being drawn to a Divine Object for its fear and love, throws itself forward by an act of longing and will to accept what it cannot understand. That the Mysterious Object satisfies the Christian's desire and that the dogma which conveys the mystery in language meets a fundamental psychic need suggest to New-man that we can and should accept what has not been demon-strated to us and what we do not understand. If we do not find it congenial it is because our own egocentricity and the seduc-tions of the world, for both of which liberalism is in part a rationalization, have corrupted us. It is natural in us not to doubt but to assent: our most 'obstinate and most reasonable certitudes depend on proofs which are informal and personal. ... If we must speak of Law, this recognition of a correlation between certitude and implicit proof seems to me a law of our minds.'[2]

In a letter of 1850, Newman criticizes his old Oxford pupil and friend, Frederick Rogers, for maintaining a deep scepticism, a shrinking from accepting the truth of what others tell him, 'an utter suspiciousness of what does not approve itself to his moral feeling'.[3] Rogers, and perhaps other admirers of Newman whose mental and moral natures have been shaped in such a way as to find dogmatic Christianity uncongenial, have the right to ask how they can persuade themselves to receive it. Charles, the hero of *Loss and Gain*, meets one of the several mysterious priests of nineteenth-century fiction on the way to London where he will become a Catholic, and puts the question to him. Since the authority of revealed doctrine logically rests at best on a convergence of probabilities, how can it be introduced into a

---

[1] *Apologia*, p. 260.   [2] *Grammar of Assent*, p. 229.
[3] *Letters and Diaries*, xiv. 182.

community where reason has been cultivated and argument is the test of truth? A man may wish that he had been educated a Catholic, but he has not been, and the evidence presented to him is not sufficient to subdue his reason. ' "What" ', asks Charles, ' "is to make him believe?" His fellow-traveller had for some time shown signs of uneasiness; when Charles stopped, he said, shortly, but quietly, "What is to make him believe! the *will*, his *will*".'[1]

During the year in which *Loss and Gain* was published Newman wrote to Mrs. William Froude on the subject of faith, considering it for the moment not as a gift of God, but 'as a human process and attained by human means'. Faith is not a conclusion from premises but 'the result of an act of the *will*, following upon a *conviction* that to believe is a *duty*'. As soon as one feels a conviction that he ought to believe, reason has done all it can, 'and what is wanted for faith is, not proof, but will'. Newman finds it necessary to insist upon what would probably have seemed a commonplace to the Bible Society of his youth. '*We can believe what we choose.*'[2] He repeats this advice to Catherine Ward, again emphasizing his point with italics: '*You can believe what you will.*'[3]

There is no denying, however, that a difficulty of some magnitude remains: How, in fact, does the process by which a potential convert achieves his 'conviction that to believe is a *duty*' differ from those exercises of private judgement which Newman condemns? Newman seems not to have given an extended answer to the question in the abstract, but a reading of the experiences of particular converts, such as Charles Reding in *Loss and Gain* and Newman himself in the *Apologia*, suggests that the vital difference lies in the subject-matter upon which individual inquiry is exercised. The liberal feels free to employ his private

---

[1] *Loss and Gain*, pt. iii, ch. vi, pp. 383-4.

[2] *Letters and Diaries*, xii. 228.

[3] Ibid., xii. 289-90. This letter was also written in 1848. Newman, in an unfinished letter to William Froude in 1879, again argues that religious difficulties should be put aside with a strong act of will. As an example of how the will ought to be exercised, Newman, somewhat irrelevantly, employs the plight of Othello as a temporal analogy: 'Wives may be unfaithful, but Othello ought by a strong act of the will to have put aside his suspicions' (Ward, ii. 592).

judgement upon any assertions of dogma and revelation. The potential convert seeks the appropriate authority to which he may submit himself. The liberal makes inquiries into and judgements upon questions which transcend, in Newman's opinion, the range of his individual capabilities. The potential convert employs his judgement on historical evidence for authority, such as the consistency and integrity of doctrinal development, and on the dogma's epistemological correspondence to the nature of the human mind. The liberal rejects the Trinity as logically absurd. The convert submits to the doctrine on the testimony of the church which he has found contains the authority to assert it.

W. G. Ward hailed the appearance of the *Grammar of Assent* as providing Catholics with a defence and an explanation of the fact that their religion made it a duty for them to submit to dogma. The *Grammar* demonstrated that nearly all certitude in nearly all subjects depends logically upon mere probability, and that many of the propositions which most minds hold as truths are received on some sort of trust or authority. That a Catholic's faith does not weaken when a difficulty is presented to him may surprise the rationalist. The Catholic, however, retains his faith in the truth of what he cannot fully understand.[1] Nor was Ward the only one who interpreted the *Grammar* as an attempt to fill this hiatus for modern Catholics. One female reader, however, argued that there were persons who believed in Christianity because they had strictly proved it. No one, answers Newman, really believes for this reason. She has confused a conclusion drawn from evidence with an assent which is reached by an act of the will. 'Everyone believes by an act of will, more or less ruling his intellect (as a matter of duty) to believe absolutely *beyond* the evidence.'[2]

In the second discourse of *The Idea of a University*, Newman traces part of the process by which the act of faith comes to be regarded as subjective and involuntary. The philosophically disposed but irreligious man doubts that anything can be known

---

[1] Ward, ii. 272. W. G. Ward was the biographer's father.
[2] Ibid. ii. 276.

for certain about the origin of the world or the ultimate purposes of its inhabitants. This scepticism creeps into religion until even the religious world holds that feeling and sentiment, rather than knowledge, constitute religion. The old Catholic idea, according to Newman, was 'that Faith was an intellectual act, its object truth, and its result knowledge'. But 'in proportion as the Lutheran leaven spread' it became 'fashionable' to hold that faith is not an act of the intellect but a 'feeling, an emotion, an affection, an appetency'. The view spread that religion is grounded on taste and sentiment, with nothing objective, everything subjective in its doctrine. Even those who were disgusted by the affectation of such pietism came to take it for granted 'that Religion was nothing beyond a *supply* of the wants of human nature, not an external fact and a work of God'.[1]

Newman realized that the assumption that each man's religion arises from his personal needs permits the sceptic to challenge the motives of belief. The tenth proposition of liberalism holds that each man has the right to profess and teach whatever seems true and right to his private conscience, but this 'right' has the effect of making each individual responsible for the truth of his religion. In dogmatic Christianity the church authorizes each doctrine and the responsibility of the individual lies in accepting the testimony of the church. If, however, religion is merely personal, each believer must bear with him a burden of proof justifying his religion—if, that is, he regards it as more than a 'feeling'. Society tends to demand such justification not merely from the unorthodox, to whom the demand may perhaps properly be put, but from the orthodox as well. In an important manuscript dated 12 July 1860, Newman notes that

---

[1] *The Idea of a University*, ed. C. F. Harrold (New York, 1947), pp. 25–6. The third proposition of liberalism holds that 'No theological doctrine is any thing more than an opinion which happens to be held by bodies of men' (*Apologia*, p. 260). In a note among the Birmingham papers, dated 23 July 1868, Newman observes that 'The prevailing school of unbelief just now goes on the principle that what a man's heart tells him is truer than any revelation, and that there can be no truth, no external revelation of truth which in its nature can possibly be received as that which his own self, his reason and heart, tell him is received.' This, says Newman, is a libertine's argument to a married woman.

just now a scepticism is on foot, which throws on the individual believer the *onus probandi* in a way never *contemplated*, or at least recognized before. Hitherto a man was allowed to believe till it was logically brought home to him that he ought not to believe, but now it seems overtly to be considered that he has no liberty to believe till it has been brought home to him in a rational form that he has a right to do so (till he can state (show cause) distinctly or at least till others can do it for him, why he has a right to believe).[1]

This '*onus probandi*' is heavy enough to interfere with the process of assent. In the section on 'Words and Ideas' in the preceding chapter I discussed Newman's apprehension of the limitations of language. Words convey at best a shadow of spiritual reality. Verbal methods of communicating religious convictions, essentially bound by patterns of reasoning and logic, differ from those by which the mind achieves faith. The truths of Scripture are *hidden* in language because language provides the only human medium for their expression. Newman makes it clear that his Illative Sense, by which men judge truth in the concrete, provides no medium of communication from mind to mind. If, therefore, the believer is to justify his religious convictions to liberals, he must surrender as inadequate or merely personal those elastic and emotional impulses which lead him in some degree to realize the Divine Object correlative of his religious being. Almost paradoxically, the believer's attempt to justify his convictions in a common language undermines his apprehension of them as objective truths. He must eliminate from his verbal justification those immediate perceptions which make his religion real to him.[2]

Thus Newman's interest in epistemology is intimately related to his attack on the insinuation of liberal attitudes into English religious and social life. As we have seen, he believed one of the most dangerous of these liberal attitudes to be the notion of a

[1] Quoted by Boekraad and Tristram, *The Argument from Conscience*, p. 173. The parentheses are Newman's.

[2] In his Inaugural address at St. Andrews, J. S. Mill voiced what Newman took to be the rationalist view of the accuracy of language: 'If you want to know whether you are thinking rightly, put your thoughts into words' (*James and John Stuart Mill on Education*, p. 133).

right to private judgement. The right, he knew, was becoming a burden and ultimately a duty. On the occasion of his becoming a cardinal, Newman speaks of his lifelong attack on liberalism, which he represents as the doctrine that all religions are to be tolerated because all are matters of opinion. Liberalism holds, Newman tells the assembled clerics and the pope, that 'Revealed religion is not a truth, but a sentiment and a taste; not an objective fact, not miraculous; and it is the right of each individual to make it say just what strikes his fancy.' Since religion is 'so personal a peculiarity and so private a possession', it ought, according to the liberal view, to be ignored in social intercourse. 'Religion is in no sense the bond of society.'[1]

Newman, then, understood that insistence on the exercise of private judgement in matters of faith led many nineteenth-century Englishmen to treat religion as a subjective matter, the reality of which exists only within the mind of the individual. But this does not mean that Newman found no place for private judgement in the intellectual life of the Christian. In a sermon called 'Dangers to the Penitent' (1842), he characteristically urges submission to the teachings of the church. Nothing healthy can be expected of religion in the community until its members learn that they cannot manage themselves by private judgement. The discipline of the heart is hard to learn. Most men cannot be their own divines or their own casuists, just as they would not attempt to be their own physicians.[2] In another sermon written about the same time, however, Newman argues that once Christians have made a sincere and unqualified submission to orthodox doctrine they may exercise private judgement in questions of personal duty. Such a question may be the choice between a secular and a religious life. Christians should employ private judgement not in questions of doctrine, not in points 'public and ecclesiastical and eternal and independent of

---

[1] Ward, ii. 460. In June of 1885, Wilfrid Ward visited the aged cardinal in Birmingham. Newman amused himself by speaking to his future biographer in a hypothetically sceptical manner. He argued for the common sense of worldliness and the folly of otherworldliness. Does our nature really testify to the truth of Christianity? 'Is it not only a mood which so testifies?' (ibid. ii. 492).

[2] *Sermons Bearing on Subjects of the Day* (London, 1898), p. 50.

ourselves, but personal,—in the choice of life, in matters of duty!'[1]

After Newman had fought his battle for liberal education in Ireland, had tried to reconcile his own attacks on reason with the position taken by Italian scholastics, and had lost ground in Rome by his opposition to English ultramontanism, he came to feel that the intellectual champions of the Roman Church ought to allow priests greater liberty in their private intellectual lives. In a letter of 1863 he complains that whenever he puts anything in print Propaganda answers him at once:

How can I fight with such a chain on my arm? It is like the Persians driven to fight under the lash. There was true private judgment in the primitive and medieval schools,—there are no schools now, no private judgment (in the religious sense of the phrase), no freedom, that is, of opinion. That is, no exercise of the intellect. No, the system goes on by the tradition of the intellect of former times.[2]

Newman goes on to predict correctly that its own needs will force the Roman Church to be more flexible. Similarly, in 1879, he writes that theology is necessarily more restrained than the physical sciences because it involves more 'questions which may be called burning'. But what is true of physics is true of theology, for each makes progress by being ' "alive to its own fundamental uncertainties" '.[3]

In concluding this section, I wish to observe that Newman's advocacy of private judgement in matters of personal duty and theological investigation should not be isolated from his distrust of its suitability for questions of doctrine. The correct use of private judgement in his view presumed an act of submission to dogma which was and is highly uncongenial to what may loosely be called the liberal mind. He saw the English nineteenth-century attitude towards the 'right' of private judgement as part of the liberalism of the age, and he defined liberalism as false liberty of thought, the error of subjecting Christian dogma to human reason. Newman saw the exercise of private judgement

---

[1] 'The Apostolical Christian' (1843), ibid., p. 292.
[2] Ward, i. 588.
[3] Ibid. ii. 591. Newman is quoting William Froude.

in matters of personal duty so exaggerated in English social attitudes as to include the right and assume the ability of each individual to determine for himself what is false and what is true in Christianity. He understood that society had begun to place the burden of proof on the individual believer, that it had begun to assume that the individual was responsible for the accuracy of his own religious convictions, and that it had begun to regard each Christian as being bound to accept only those doctrines which he could prove and communicate. The liberal spirit in society treats religion not as a body of objective truth, but as the means by which individuals define themselves and their place in the universe. Religion thus becomes not the glorification of God but the satisfaction of needs which vary with individuals. Newman countered these assumptions by stressing the ability of the individual to submit himself to dogmatic Christianity by an act of the will, and, as we shall see, by an increasingly intense effort to distinguish religious knowledge from secular in a profound attack upon utilitarian attitudes in education. But before dealing with his distrust of the relation of knowledge to virtue, we need a more precise idea of what Newman has in mind when he speaks so ironically of his 'civilized age', when he characterizes 'the times' with such acute disdain.

THE LIBERAL SPIRIT IN SOCIETY

According to the sixteenth proposition of liberalism,

> It is lawful to rise in arms against legitimate princes. Therefore, e.g. the Puritans in the 17th century, and the French in the 18th, were justifiable in their Rebellion and Revolution respectively.

For Newman the liberal spirit threatens the established social structure. Antichrist, the *Apologia* reminds us, is traditionally described as 'exalting himself above the yoke of religion and law. The spirit of lawlessness came in with the Reformation, and Liberalism is its offspring.'[1] In the three works written in 1849, 1850, and 1851, *Discourses to Mixed Congregations, Difficulties of*

---

[1] *Apologia*, pp. 261, 174.

Anglicans, and *The Present Position of Catholics*, Newman considers the role of the Catholic in English society and the relation of Roman Catholicism to the Established Church. Nowhere in any of these volumes does he advocate a fundamental change in the social structure. On the contrary, he urges Catholics to explain themselves to their contemporaries by leading the sort of personal lives which will at once demonstrate their moral, or at least religious superiority and prove the prejudices against them and their church to be groundless. He admits that Catholics as a class have not enjoyed the privileges of birth or liberal education, that they lack the 'tone of good society':

you have no share of the largeness of mind, the candour, the romantic sense of honour, the correctness of taste, the consideration for others, and the gentleness which the world puts forth as its highest type of excellence.

But the fact that English society has not provided the means by which Catholics might become gentlemen does not, in Newman's view, justify institutional reform. The Catholic's primary duty is to be devout, not elegant. And anyway, Newman observes, social ambitions are vulgar. No position of life is dishonourable; 'no one is ridiculous who acts suitably to his calling and estate; no one, who has good sense and humility, but may, in any station of life, be truly well-bred and refined'.[1]

Newman's toleration of class distinctions primarily derives not from a strong desire to preserve them for their own sake, but from a sense of the irrelevance of social reform to the real business of life, the attainment of salvation. Although he probably accepted the social hierarchy as an appointment of Providence and although he accepted society's conventions of behaviour, it is characteristic of Newman to speak of its amenities with contempt. 'What, indeed, is the very function of society, as it is at present, but a rude attempt to cover the degradation of the fall, and to make men feel respect for themselves, and enjoy it in the eyes of others, without returning to God.'[2] Society he

---

[1] *Discourses Addressed to Mixed Congregations* (London, 1899), pp. 114, 115.
[2] 'Ignorance of Evil' (1836), *Parochial and Plain Sermons*, viii. 266.

sees as a misleading show, full of ostentation, affectation, and ambition.

In a discourse called 'God's Will the End of Life' Newman speaks of St. Paul's comparison of the world to a play. The actors assume the roles of kings and soldiers, but it would be absurd in them to pride themselves on their crowns and swords off-stage. The hierarchy of the stage becomes a metaphor for the social hierarchy. Neither has spiritual importance. While the play lasts, the actors have the duty to act their parts well. Spiritually, however, 'we are one and all equal, we shall be judged as equals as soon as life is over'.[1]

After his conversion, Newman came to see the Anglican Church as the minion of secular society, subject to its political leaders and corrupted by its values. In a letter to his mother in 1829, with most of his great work for Anglicanism before him, Newman identifies those whom he considered the enemies of the church. The list includes the uneducated or partially educated masses, the utilitarians, the schismatics, the Baptists and consistent Calvinists, high circles in London, and political indifferentists.[2] Who, one wonders, are its friends, and from what class will they come? Newman's growing awareness of the secular temper of the age drove him to attempt to shape the Anglican church into a bulwark against it. Late in his Tractarian career he thought he saw Anglicanism sliding into the very liberalism he wished to combat. As a Roman Catholic he argues, especially in *Difficulties of Anglicans*, that the English Church supplies no place for a Catholic. The Tractarian Party has become an anomaly: it cannot remain Anglo-Catholic because the Anglican Church has provided no sanction for that position. 'You will no longer be Anglo-Catholic, but Patristico-Protestants.' The basis of the Tractarian Movement, Newman continues, was the professed abnegation of private judgement. But if the Tractarian party is to continue it must create a religion for itself, a process which entails the improper exercise of private judgement.[3]

---

[1] *Discourses to Mixed Congregations*, p. 112.   [2] Mozley, i. 204–5.
[3] *Certain Difficulties Felt by Anglicans in Catholic Teaching* (London, 1901), i. 153–4.

In a large measure the Oxford Movement was itself a reaction against what its leaders regarded as the corruptions of the eighteenth century. It is perhaps the one issue on which they agreed with the liberals. John Stuart Mill could describe the submission of the late eighteenth-century English Church to secular pressures with ironic humour:

on condition of not making too much noise about religion, or taking it too much in earnest, the Church was supported, even by philosophers—as a 'bulwark against fanaticism', a sedative to the religious spirit, to prevent it from disturbing the harmony of society or the tranquillity of states. The clergy of the establishment thought they had a good bargain on these terms, and kept its conditions very faithfully.[1]

With this appraisal Newman substantially agrees. In what he feels to be the failure of the Oxford Movement he sees the large body of the Anglican clergy as still faithful to this bargain with the state. This point may be illustrated by the following passage in which Newman says essentially what Mill does above; even Newman's irony, though perhaps not quite so good-humoured, is of the same character as Mill's:

For, it is evident enough, a National or Branch Church can be of the highest service to the State, if properly under control. The State wishes to make its subjects peaceful and obedient; and there is nothing more fitted to effect this object than religion. It wishes them to have some teaching about the next world, but not too much: just as much as is important and beneficial to the interests of the present. Decency, order, industry, patience, sobriety, and as much of purity as can be expected from human nature,—this is its list of requisites; not dogma, for it creates the *odium theologicum*; not mystery, for it only serves to exalt the priesthood. . . . The parochial clergy are to be a moral police; as to the Bishops, they are to be officers of a State-religion.[2]

---

[1] *Bentham and Coleridge*, p. 136.

[2] *Difficulties of Anglicans*, i. 187–8. In a letter written three years after this lecture, Newman points out that all churches except the Roman Catholic are national: 'the *nationalism* of all religions but the Catholic is one of the very evidences of Catholicism. St. Augustine says that heresy *lies where it first took up its position*' (*Letters and Diaries*, xv. 388).

As the moral guardian of society, the Anglican Church partakes of the greatest blessings society can confer, 'decency and order, propriety of conduct, justness of thought, beautiful domestic tastes'.[1] What Newman thinks it lacks, of course, is authority. From the beginning of his Tractarian career he was suspicious of the aesthetic appeal of Anglicanism. As we shall see, he harboured a distrust of sensuous beauty whether natural, human, or artistic. Primitive Christianity attracted him in part because it lacked the elegance of late eighteenth-century Anglicanism. In a sermon on 'The Religion of the Day' (1832), Newman preaches, 'I will not shrink from uttering my firm conviction, that it would be a gain to this country, were it vastly more superstitious, more bigoted, more gloomy, more fierce in its religion'. Such tempers of mind, he continues, are not desirable in themselves, but are more promising than 'a heathen obduracy, and a cold, self-sufficient, self-wise tranquillity'.[2] Two years later, speaking of the spirit in which John wrote the Apocalypse, Newman laments the absence of such 'zeal and holy sternness' in England. We need it, he preaches, 'to temper and give character to the languid, unmeaning benevolence which we misname Christian love. I have no hopes of my country till I see it'.[3]

Newman understood that an established national church must become involved in customs and practices which have nothing directly to do with religion, and that it tends to become corrupted by the pervasive hedonism of its society. As a national institution the church partakes of that insularity characteristic of Englishmen who, like Podsnap in *Our Mutual Friend*, treat English customs as divinely appointed. Such a man, Newman tells us, believes that the whole world should rise at half-past eight, breakfast, read the papers, lunch, drive, and dine:

> Here is the great principle of the day—dine; no one is a man who does not dine; yes, dine, and at the right hour; and it must *be* a dinner,

---

[1] *Discourses to Mixed Congregations*, p. 102.

[2] *Parochial and Plain Sermons*, i. 320–1. Newman's view that it is better to be superstitious than sceptical is examined in the preceding chapter. He wishes his congregation to form habits of assenting rather than of questioning, of submission rather than independence.

[3] 'Tolerance of Religious Error' (1834), ibid. ii. 286.

with a certain time after dinner, and then, in due time, to bed. Tea and toast, port wine, roast beef, mince-pies at Christmas, lamb at Easter, goose at Michaelmas, these are their great principles. They suspect anyone who does otherwise. Figs and maccaroni for the day's fare, or Burgundy and grapes for breakfast!—they are aghast at the atrocity of the notion.[1]

In perhaps his most famous representation of the insular mentality, Newman also employs national prejudice, this time as a metaphor for religious bigotry. *The Present Position of Catholics* attempts to explain and describe the difference between Roman Catholic and Anglican sensibilities in order to equip Catholics to deal with the persistent misunderstanding which surrounded them. In the first and most widely known lecture in the work he presents a Russian count who proposes to explain the British Constitution by using Blackstone as a gloss. The true Russian audience learns to its horror that the king can do no wrong, that the king never dies, that Parliament is omnipotent, and that Queen Victoria's age of 18 when she ascended the throne in 1837 multiplied by 37 equals 666, the number of the Beast of the Apocalypse. The Russian indignation is roused because the audience does not perceive the sophistry nor understand the meaning of the legal formulae, just as Protestants fail to understand the forms of Catholic worship. The climax of the lecture occurs when the Count, in a storm of exclamations utterly devoid of significance, drives the mob to anglophobic

---

[1] *Lectures on the Present Position of Catholics in England* (London, 1924), p. 296. Newman's antagonism to the hedonism of much of English society was aroused early in his Anglican career: 'Perhaps you have your pleasure parties; you readily take your share in them time after time; you pass continuous hours in society where you know that it is quite impossible even to mention the name of religion' ('Religion a Weariness to the Natural Man', 1828, *Parochial and Plain Sermons*, vii. 18). 'Pleasure parties' has the true Evangelical ring. Also relevant is the passage quoted in my second chapter, in which Newman presents as Plutarch's notion of superstition his own vision of primitive Christianity (*Essay on Development*, p. 211). In *Callista* as well, the sunny, rational pagans make the glorification of their convenient gods an excuse for reveling and licence. Anglicans, of course, are more moderate: lamb at Easter, goose at Michaelmas. It should be added, however, that Newman was more interested in encouraging Christians to be devout than in terrifying them into asceticism.

riot by railing against the perfidious provisions of *habeas corpus*, 'accursed fee simple and fee tail, villanage, and free soccage, fiefs, heriots, seizins, feuds . . .'.[1]

But we have seen that the true opposition in English religious life became, for Newman, not a struggle between Protestants and Catholics, but between Catholicism and liberalism. As early as 1835, he insists upon the almost unbridgeable gap between what he terms 'the mind of dissent' and 'the mind of Christ and His Holy Church Catholic'. He condemns the 'mind of dissent' and warns his congregation of its seductions.[2] Protestant and dissenting minds develop habits of private judgement, of questioning. Faith, argues Newman in *Discourses to Mixed Congregations*, is 'a particular mode of thinking and acting'. Most Englishmen have lost this 'habit or character of mind'. They do not even have faith in their own religion. The lack of faith 'is a definite defect in their minds'. And, characteristically, Newman goes on to give his familiar analysis of rationalism as the explanation for this defect, the inappropriate application to religious subjects of the methods by which men learn about the visible world.[3]

The sceptical attitude is to regard religion as merely another phenomenon, to be analysed like politics or investigated like physics. In a letter of 1852, Newman observes that Bulwer Lytton's attitude is characteristic of the 'prevailing school, who look down on all religions, and think they can measure them'. Perhaps the prevailing school, by which Newman means the religious liberals, assigns Catholicism a high intellectual position 'as being the greatest idea, faith being the highest exercise of reason, and (I suppose) *imagination* the second, but, as imagination does not deal with truths, neither does faith'.[4] In *The Idea of a University*, Newman acidly characterizes this prevailing attitude,

---

[1] *The Present Position of Catholics*, p. 40.
[2] 'Religious Worship a Remedy for Excitements' (1835), *Parochial and Plain Sermons*, iii. 342.
[3] *Discourses to Mixed Congregations*, pp. 193–5. In the *Grammar of Assent* Newman condemned the 'lawyerlike qualifications' of those 'who resolve to treat the Almighty with dispassionateness, a judicial temper, clearheadedness, and candour' (p. 324).
[4] *Letters and Diaries*, xv. 16.

the 'state of society such as ours', as being contemptuous of authority, tradition, moral instinct, and 'divine influences'. Instead, free discussion and private judgement are 'prized as the birthright of each individual'. He begs permission to exercise towards the religion of the age 'some portion of that scepticism which it exercises itself towards every received but unscrutinized assertion whatever'.[1]

In a letter to Faber in 1849 Newman points out that Christ performed no miracles where there was no faith.[2] Newman had himself come to believe that communication between a liberal and a devout mind on matters of mystery and dogma was impossible. In his *Discourses to Mixed Congregations* he addresses himself only to the devout: 'I speak to those who do not narrow their belief to their experience.'[3] A gulf had opened in English society between the religious and the irreligious. By the time Newman writes the *Grammar of Assent*, he feels that it has widened unbridgeably. The irreligious have blinded themselves to the most important perceptions in the intellectual life of Christians.[4]

I wish to conclude this section with an extended quotation from the *Grammar of Assent*. It is one of the most remarkable passages in that great book, and it brilliantly summarizes what Newman had come to regard as the opinions characteristic of the liberal spirit in society:

I have no scruple in beginning the review I shall take of Christianity by professing to consult for those only whose minds are properly prepared for it; and by being prepared, I mean to denote those who are imbued with the religious opinions and sentiments which I have identified with Natural Religion. I do not address myself to those, who in moral evil and physical see nothing more than imperfections of a parallel nature; who consider that the difference in gravity between the two is one of degree only, not of kind; that moral evil is merely the offspring of physical, and that as we remove the latter so we inevitably remove the former; that there is a progress of the human race which tends to the annihilation of moral evil; that knowledge is virtue, and vice is ignorance; that sin is a bugbear, not a reality; that the Creator

---

[1] *The Idea of a University*, p. 33.   [2] *Letters and Diaries*, xiii. 25.
[3] *Discourses to Mixed Congregations*, p. 60.
[4] See C. F. Harrold's introduction to the *Grammar of Assent*, pp. xv–xvii.

does not punish except in the sense of correcting; that vengeance in Him would of necessity be vindictiveness; that all that we know of Him, be it much or little, is through the laws of nature; that miracles are impossible; that prayer to Him is a superstition; that the fear of Him is unmanly; that sorrow for sin is slavish and abject; that the only intelligible worship of Him is to act well our part in the world, and the only sensible repentance to do better in future; that if we do our duties in this life, we may take our chance for the next; and that it is of no use perplexing our minds about the future state, for it is all a matter of guess. These opinions characterize a civilized age; and if I say that I will not argue about Christianity with men who hold them, I do so, not as claiming any right to be impatient or peremptory with any one, but because it is plainly absurd to attempt to prove a second proposition to those who do not admit the first.[1]

THE RELIGIOUS SPIRIT IN SOCIETY

In the preceding section I have tried to give a general account of Newman's awareness of the liberal spirit in English society and his sense of the role of the Established Church in promoting it. I shall use this account as the basis for a forthcoming analysis of his reaction to utilitarianism, which raised questions in his mind of social justice and reform, particularly in the field of education. First, however, some qualification of the material already presented is in order. It is true that when Newman writes of 'society' and 'the times' it is usually to attack them. By far

---

[1] *Grammar of Assent*, p. 316. Twenty-five years before, in his *Essay on Development*, Newman characterized the anti-dogmatic, i.e. liberal, principle as follows: 'That truth and falsehood in religion are but matter of opinion; that one doctrine is as good as another; that the Governor of the world does not intend that we should gain the truth; that there is no truth; that we are not more acceptable to God by believing this than by believing that; that no one is answerable for his opinions; that they are a matter of necessity or accident; that it is enough if we sincerely hold what we profess; that our merit lies in seeking, not in possessing; that it is a duty to follow what seems to us true, without a fear lest it should not be true; that it may be a gain to succeed, and can be no harm to fail; that we may take up and lay down opinions at pleasure; that belief belongs to the mere intellect, not to the heart also; that we may safely trust to ourselves in matters of Faith, and need no other guide,—this is the principle of philosophies and heresies, which is very weakness' (p. 334). These may be termed the epistemological assumptions of liberalism, while those in the quotation from the *Grammar* are social and teleological.

the greater portion of his analysis of society consists of an attack on its irreligion and complacency. The leaders of the Oxford Movement considered themselves not as leading Anglicanism to a new type of Christianity but as attempting to restore the church to its ancient holiness. That is, they were reacting to the evils of the day, and the intensity of their reaction led Thomas Arnold, in the course of a woolly attempt to refute the theory of apostolical succession, to remark that 'Mr. Newman and his friends appear to hate the nineteenth century for its own sake, and to proscribe all belonging to it'.[1]

The Tractarians were in fact attempting to assert the spiritual independence of the Church from the state, to combat the rationalism and liberalism encouraged by the Oriel Noetics, to clarify the Catholic tradition upon which they believed the apostolicity of the English Church depended, and to revive the piety, holiness, and authority maintained by the fathers of the early Church.[2] Especially in reviving a new spirit of holiness and piety the movement met a felt need of the times, and it is Newman's analysis of the social indications of this need which interests students of his philosophy of mind. Behind his assertions that liberalism and utilitarianism do not meet the religious and moral needs of man lies not only a body of theories on psychology and epistemology but the perception of a widely felt dissatisfaction in English society with the tendency to limit meaningful intellectual activity to processes of logic and reasoning.

In a sermon of 1842 called 'Indulgence of Religious Privileges', Newman speaks of a 'more primitive, Catholic, devout, ardent spirit' which he hopes is replacing the colder, more remote attitudes of the preceding age. The 'piercing, and thrilling, and

[1] Introduction dated 14 April 1841, to volume iv of Arnold's *Sermons* (London, 1878), p. xix.
[2] See *English Prose of the Victorian Era*, C. F. Harrold and W. D. Templeman (eds.) (New York, 1959), p. 1617. Of course a history of Tractarianism would be out of place here. Adequate accounts have been written. Newman gives his own analysis after his conversion in *Difficulties of Anglicans*. Church's is still the classic study. Faber's *Oxford Apostles* is less sensational than its reputation suggests. Owen Chadwick's recent anthology, *The Mind of the Oxford Movement*, contains a lucid, balanced introduction, and the third chapter of his history, *The Victorian Church*, provides an excellent general discussion.

kindling, and enrapturing glories' of religion are being felt. Men have begun to understand why the soldier gave up his sword, the philosopher his school. The Gospel has become not an intellectual scheme 'but a reality and a life'. The time for Christian action has arrived, and religion is now a matter of 'public profession' and 'outward manifestation'. The interest in church architecture and religious ceremony indicates this. Books of 'an imaginative cast', painting, music, and poetry of a religious type begin to appear. People attend churches on weekdays. 'External religion' is now seen as the triumph of 'the inward principle' indicating the devotion which the awakened 'religious mind desires to pay to its God and Saviour'.[1]

In this sermon Newman preaches on specifically religious subjects to what is presumably an orthodox audience. The broader cultural indications of the new sensibility he had analysed three years earlier in 'Prospects of the Anglican Church'. The growing religious awareness, he writes there, is 'quite independent of things visible and historical'. It is not a movement, but a 'spirit':

a spirit afloat, neither 'in the secret chambers' nor 'in the desert', but everywhere. It is within us, rising up in the heart where it was least expected, and working its way, though not in secret, yet so subtly and impalpably, as hardly to admit of precaution and encounter, on any ordinary human rules of opposition. It is an adversary in the air, a something one and entire, a whole wherever it is, unapproachable and incapable of being grasped, as being the result of causes far deeper than political or other visible agencies,—the spiritual awakening of spiritual wants.[2]

Among the pre-Tractarian indications which Newman finds for this devout spirit by far the most important and the most frequently mentioned is the literature of the Romantic Movement. In the section on the 'Imagination' in Chapter Two, I

[1] Sermons on Subjects of the Day, pp. 115–16.
[2] Essays and Sketches, i. 341. 'Spirit', obviously, is a favourite word of Newman's. There is, perhaps, a certain irony in the fact that Newman's fine description of the growth of a sensibility may be applied to the triumph of the liberal habit of mind, which he came to see turned out to be more elusive, more difficult to oppose, ultimately more pervasive.

discussed briefly Newman's affinity with Wordsworth and Coleridge in their interest in epistemology. His professed preferences, however, were for Southey and Scott. Their work provided the combination of romance and righteousness which satisfied Newman's predilection for passion directed towards a religious or moral end.[1] Newman considered *Thalaba* the most morally sublime of English poems, for it ended not with marriage but with death and future glory and the versification was 'most melodious'.[2] In 'Prospects of the Anglican Church', he couples Southey with Wordsworth as a poet who, 'in the department of fantastic fiction', carried his readers in the direction of those 'high principles and feelings' congenial to the Tractarian Movement.[3]

In a similar way Newman credits Scott with preparing men 'for some close and more practical approximation to Catholic truth' a quarter of a century before they knew what they should believe or had perceived the truth intellectually. Scott provided his readers with visions which aroused noble ideas; these ideas could in turn be appealed to later as 'first principles'. No doubt, Newman observes, there may be much in his works 'of which a current judgment is forced to disapprove'. But when they are compared with eighteenth-century writers, like Pope, 'they stand almost as oracles of Truth confronting the ministers of error and sin'.[4]

Newman's attitude towards Coleridge is more equivocal. He did not read him until the spring of 1835 and then was 'surprised how much I thought mine, is to be found there'.[5] Later Newman speaks of Coleridge as providing a 'philosophical basis' for the feelings and opinions of the Oxford Movement, though at the

---

[1] John Beer, 'Newman and the Romantic Sensibility', *The English Mind: Studies in the English Moralists Presented to Basil Willey*, Hugh Sykes Davies and George Watson (eds.) (Cambridge, England, 1964), pp. 196-7.
[2] See the letter to J. M. Capes, 22 March 1850, *Letters and Diaries*, xiii. 449.
[3] *Essays and Sketches*, i. 338.
[4] Ibid. i. 337-8. According to Walgrave, by 'first principles' Newman meant 'not only the presuppositions which arise from our personal nature, but a whole crowd of subtle convictions due to the spirit of the time, environment, religion, social habits, the experiences and history of the individual' (*Newman the Theologian*, p. 118).
[5] Mozley, ii. 39, n. 1.

same time indulging in 'a liberty of speculation which no Christian can tolerate' and often arriving at conclusions more heathen than Christian. Newman considers Coleridge's capacity for interesting his age in the principles congenial to Catholicism perhaps more an indication than a cause of the new religious sensibility.[1]

In Wordsworth, Newman (whether he fully realized it or not) found the mind most occupied with the subjects familiar to his own.[2] If Southey carried his readers in the direction of Catholic truth by means of fantastic fiction, Wordsworth did the same in his 'philosophical meditation'.[3] In *The Present Position of Catholics*, speaking of what he sees as the tyranny of the Protestant tradition over English writers, Newman argues that Wordsworth has been 'obliged to do penance for Catholic sonnets by anti-Catholic complements to them'. In 'extenuation of his prevarication' Wordsworth must 'plead pantheism' because English society prefers to see its poets liberals, sceptics, and infidels rather than admit their sympathies to Catholicism.[4]

But Newman's connection with Wordsworth lies deeper than this questionable perception of a latent Catholic sensibility. Both of these great autobiographers retained a profound interest in the nature and development of the mind, and they drew from their explorations some remarkably similar epistemological conclusions. The intellectual affinities of Wordsworth and Newman deserve our extended attention because they illustrate most clearly the degree to which Newman assimilated for Christian orthodoxy a vision of the mind's powers characteristic of Romanticism.

---

[1] *Essays and Sketches*, i. 338–9. In *The Romantic Comedy* (London, 1963), D. G. James has perhaps made as much of the relation of Newman to Coleridge as is reasonably possible. James wisely presents their affinities as a matter of cultural history, rather than of direct influence.

[2] James agrees: 'No doubt Coleridge did more than Wordsworth to renew Christianity in the nineteenth century; but if we think of Wordsworth in his strength, in his love of solitude and silence; and if we think of the great Wordsworth symbols, the wanderers and mourners in his poems who have no abiding city, we see, I think, that Wordsworth, more than Coleridge, leads on to Newman' (*The Romantic Comedy*, p. 270).   [3] *Essays and Sketches*, i. 338.

[4] *The Present Position of Catholics*, pp. 71–2. In the same passage Newman speaks of the Catholic tendencies of Scott, who, he says, is obliged to plead antiquarianism.

The earliest affinity has already been suggested in the opening pages of my first chapter. It lies in an intense experience in childhood of isolation from the external material world. Wordsworth felt that everything he perceived was in fact part of his own material nature; Newman was at times conscious of the real existence only of himself and God. The excitement of the comparison lies not in the uniqueness of the experience—perhaps most children share it in varying degrees of consciousness—but in the intensity of the recollections preserved by the Romantic poet and Victorian priest and the significance which they attach to it in their maturity.

The experience inspired Wordsworth in his greatest ode, and he describes it in the lines which tell us that his 'song of thanks and praise' is not so much for the simple delight and liberty of childhood,

> But for those obstinate questionings
> Of sense and outward things,
> Fallings from us, vanishings;
> Blank misgivings of a Creature
> Moving about in worlds not realized,
> High instincts before which our mortal Nature
> Did tremble like a guilty Thing surprised.

Ignatius Dudley Ryder remembers Newman reading the poem to him during a boyhood illness: 'There was a passion and a pathos in his voice that made me feel that it was altogether the most beautiful thing I had ever heard'.[1] And in a sermon preached in 1833, 'The Mind of Little Children', Newman in fact paraphrases some of the language of Wordsworth's 'Intimations of Immortality from Recollections of Early Childhood', and adopts its meaning to more specifically Christian ideas. The physical beauty of small children, he observes, offers a suggestion of our divine origins. When the child sleeps his mind seems like 'tranquil water, reflecting heaven'. But we should not regret the passing of childhood,

or sigh over the remembrances of pure pleasures and contemplations which we cannot recall; rather, what we were when children, is a blessed

[1] Ward, ii. 354.

intimation, given for our comfort, of what God will make us, if we surrender our hearts to the guidance of His Holy Spirit,—a prophecy of good to come—a foretaste of what will be fulfilled in heaven. And thus it is that a child is a pledge of immortality; for he bears upon him in figure those high and eternal excellences in which the joy of heaven consists, and which would not be thus shadowed forth by the All-gracious Creator, were they not one day to be realized.[1]

Newman's use of the poem here and his references to it in his unpublished papers suggest that he found in it a particular relevance to himself and to the problems with which he worked. The important point, however, is that for Wordsworth and Newman a childhood experience in some way holy or religious or mystical, a sense of isolation from the visible world, was remembered and developed in their later writings, in the 'Immortality Ode' and the *Apologia*. The experience marks for each the beginning of a life's preoccupation with questions concerning the nature of the mind, of the relation of perceiver and object— for Wordsworth primarily in the creation of poetry, for Newman in his investigation into the apprehension of Christian doctrine.

Both Wordsworth and Newman came to believe that reason in its narrow or logical sense could not lead to the perception of truth or fact. Natural objects are perceived directly, the 'life of things', the spirit which informs material reality, comes to us not by any process of inference or reasoning, but as part of what Newman calls 'real apprehension', the immediate act of perceiving. Wordsworth's best poetry implies and insists that material objects are informed by an invisible reality, a natural essence which he often calls 'divine'. The visible object manifests the invisible truth and, for Wordsworth, the imaginative power can be defined as the ability to evoke such meaning from the material world. Poetic creation is the process by which such incarnation of spiritual truth may be realized.[2]

One way of illustrating the influence of Romanticism upon Newman is to point out that although he distrusts the argument

---

[1] *Parochial and Plain Sermons*, ii. 67.
[2] See James A. W. Heffernan, 'Wordsworth on Imagination: The Emblemizing Power', *PMLA*, lxxxi (1966), 389–90.

from design, the rational inference of the existence of God from the order and beneficence of nature, he shares with Wordsworth a belief in a sentient universe: 'Nature is not inanimate; its daily toil is intelligent; its works are *duties*'. He supposes someone examining a flower or a ray of light, an object which the observer treats as beneath him in the scale of being. He might suddenly see, were such power granted him, some wonderful presence, 'whose robe and ornaments those wonderous objects were, which he was so eager to analyse'.[1]

But if for these two writers the visible universe vibrates with spiritual life, there exists an area in which their divergence is fundamental. Newman's primary concern is with the realization in the mind of dogmatic truth, whereas Wordsworth, in his early poems at least, seems directly concerned with the action of a more ambiguous spirit in nature, a force which is not dogmatically defined. Wordsworth's preoccupation with the actual, visible world leads him at times into radical departures from orthodox Christian doctrine. The following lines from the eleventh book of *The Prelude* survived the somewhat pious revision of the poem and appear, surprisingly, in the 1850 version. Wordsworth is speaking of those who were roused to action by the French Revolution, impelled to act

> Not in Utopia, subterraneous fields,
> Or some secreted Island, Heaven knows where,
> But in the very world which is the world
> Of all of us, the place in which, in the end,
> We find our happiness, or not at all.

These superb lines do not contain a Christian message, and Newman could not have read them with approval, concerned as he was with asserting the primacy and transcendence of the invisible world and looking forward to the death of nature.

But Newman did not see this side of Wordsworth. We know that he saw instead in the great poet a Catholic mind forced into the evasions of pantheism by the tyranny of established English Protestantism. In the dialectic Newman had worked

[1] 'The Powers of Nature' (1831), *Parochial and Plain Sermons*, ii, 361, 364.

out by 1839, when he wrote his essay on the prospects of the Anglican Church, Wordsworth and some of his Romantic contemporaries were seen in the drift of their sentiments and opinions, in their sensibility, as opposing liberalism and as favouring Catholicism, at least the Catholic spirit in the English Church. Newman was six years away from his final step towards Rome and he had yet to realize the momentous personal implications which his dialectic held in store for him. In 1839, however, he wants to discover a Catholic spirit within the Established Church and in the religious and aesthetic sensibilities of her congregation.

Perhaps, Newman speculates, poetry in this practical age has taken the place of contemplation characteristic of the early Christian Church. Primitive Christianity was mystical, symbolic. In an age of a more literal or formal religion, and in an age which celebrates the free exercise of reason, poetry may satisfy those psychic needs once met by the metaphorical language of religious mystery. Poetry is more cultivated by nineteenth-century Englishmen than it was by the Christians of the first centuries. And those who have cultivated poetry in the comparatively recent past seem to Newman more Catholic—or at least less Protestant—in spirit than those who scorn or ignore it. Poetry has lately been cultivated by Cavaliers and Tories but coldly looked upon by Puritans and their 'modern representatives':

> Poetry then is our mysticism; and so far as any two characters of mind tend to penetrate below the surface of things, and to draw men away from the material to the invisible world, so far they may certainly be said to answer the same end; and that too a religious one.[1]

In this passage the link with Wordsworth is again evident, for a strikingly similar analysis of the function of poetry appears in the 'Essay Supplementary to the Preface' of 1815. Faith, Wordsworth points out, leads man from 'the treasures of time' to those of eternity, and the elevation of man's nature produced by faith is a 'presumptive evidence of a future state of existence'. The truths of religion cannot be apprehended except by em-

---

[1] *Essays and Sketches,* i. 358.

bodying them in 'words and symbols', and this epistemological limitation of the mind in dealing with spiritual realities suggests to Wordsworth an analogy to poetic creation:

The commerce between Man and his Maker cannot be carried out but by a process where much is represented in little, and the Infinite Being accommodates himself to a finite capacity. In all this may be perceived the affinity between religion and poetry; between religion—making up the deficiencies of reason by faith; and poetry—passionate for the instruction of reason; between religion—whose element is infinitude, and whose ultimate trust is the supreme of things, submitting herself to circumspection, and reconciled to substitutions; and poetry—ethereal and transcendent, yet incapable to sustain her existence without sensuous incarnation.[1]

Here Wordsworth anticipates Newman's idea of poetry and religion as meeting a common psychic need, the need to represent and perceive spiritual realities in material forms. Both men associate the process with passion and excitement, and a passion and excitement which does not distort the perception but on the contrary enables men to perceive realities which lie hidden from rational analysis. In the moment of passion, the moment of fear or love, and in the recollection of it, the ethereal and transcendent poetic essence embodies itself in language, suffering, to use Wordsworth's own passionate phrase, a 'sensuous incarnation', suggesting an analogy—perhaps more than an analogy—with the central mystery of Christianity. In the apprehension of this affinity, Wordsworth raises his art to the level of mystery and suggests that, as Newman was to put it, 'Poetry then is our mysticism'.

But although Wordsworth and Newman find analogies between poetry and doctrine, they are careful to distinguish between the goals of art and the ends of religion. The essential contention of Newman's letters on the Tamworth Reading Room is that literature and science offer no substitute for religious instruction. Literature is the history of the natural man in all his glory and corruption. It neither 'provides a source of moral

strength nor leads man to spiritual salvation. 'Poetry', writes
Wordsworth in the preface to the second edition of his poems,
'sheds no tears "such as Angels weep", but natural and human
tears'.[1]

And yet we know that Wordsworth read nature as a kind
of Scripture, that, in Carlos Baker's words, 'Under "nature's
holy plan," by observing the myriad ways in which the mind is
"fitted" to the external world, as well as the world to the mind,
one could discover a sufficient justification of God's ways to men'.[2]
In *The Recluse* Wordsworth celebrates the marriage of the mind
with the reality it perceives in nature, calling it 'this great consummation':

> How exquisitely the individual Mind
> (And the progressive powers perhaps no less
> Of the whole species) to the external World
> Is fitted:—and how exquisitely, too—
> Theme this but little heard of among men—
> The external World is fitted to the Mind;
> And the creation (by no lower name
> Can it be called) which they with blended might
> Accomplish:—this is our high argument.[3]

The consummation of the union of mind and world proclaimed
in these lines is the product of 'love and holy passion', leading
directly to the apprehension of a divine unity, the unity of
'creation'. Wordsworth is dealing with the apprehension of
unity between mind and nature, and the suggestion seems to me
implicit that the 'fitting' or 'union' between them reveals a
transcendent unity as the source and comprehensor of perceiver
and object. But if this seems an unjustified extension of Wordsworth's idea we can perhaps rest content with the observation
that the apprehension of unity is as important to Wordsworth's
poet as to Newman's Christian and that both achieve it in part
by the exercise of those powers of perception which preclude
and transcend rational analysis.

---

[1] *Poetical Works*, ii. 392.
[2] Introduction to *William Wordsworth's The Prelude* (New York, 1961), p. x.
[3] *Poetical Works*, v. 5.

For either despite or, as I believe, stimulated by their youthful experiences of isolation from the material world (for Wordsworth an experience of unity of ideas and self, for Newman of self with God), both men insist vigorously on the necessity, the duty, of perceiving external objects accurately. Wordsworth's repeated insistence upon an 'accurate taste' in poetry reveals his impatience with those who take forms of expression, patterns of thought, for the objects of nature. In criticizing Macpherson's work he attacks the mentality which proposes to take words for things. To a mind like Macpherson's, every object is 'defined, insulated, dislocated, deadened,—yet nothing distinct'.[1] Macpherson is not a poet because he has not *seen* what he attempts to describe.

Wordsworth insists upon an accurate perception of nature, an accurate perception of external objects, in part because unless nature is perceived accurately, perceived as it *is*, we cannot know what it means. Nature must be apprehended free from rational or linguistic convention if the perceiver or poet is to realize the spirit which informs it. And the very passion which accurate perception arouses becomes, in Wordsworth's critical theory, a verification and a realization of the spiritual force incarnate in nature.

Readers of Newman are familiar with his insistence upon the ultimate validity of what in the *Grammar of Assent* he calls 'Real Apprehension', the direct confrontation of the mind with external objects. And this real apprehension is inseparable from passion, the love and fear which Newman believes to be more certain and more universal sources of spiritual truth than the exercise of reason. 'The heart', he writes in his sixth Tamworth letter, 'is commonly reached, not through the reason, but through the imagination, by means of direct impressions, by the testimony of facts and events, by history, by description. . . . No one, I say, will die for his own calculations; he dies for realities.' It is for this reason that Scripture is not a collection of abstractions, a system of syllogisms, but a history, scenic and descriptive: 'it tells us what its Author is, by telling us what he has done'.[2] Thus

---

[1] Ibid., ii. 423.   [2] *Essays and Sketches*, ii. 204–7.

Newman's view of Scripture resembles Wordsworth's view of good poetry as revealing the fact undistorted by logic, poetic convention, or any other closed or arbitrarily structured intellectual pattern. And in faithfully revealing the fact, the thing, or event, poetry and Scripture, for Wordsworth and for Newman, inform us of that greater presence which exists for them incarnate in the object and the act.

But despite the intensity with which Newman adopted Romantic conceptions of mind and nature, his remarks on the religious spirit in his society occupy a comparatively small proportion of his social comment. And after his conversion Newman seldom discusses Catholic influences as independent of the Roman Catholic Church. Perhaps he had come to view the other Catholic elements in English society as lost causes and loose ends. At any rate, he turns his attentions, as we shall ours, to confront such allies of the liberal spirit as utilitarianism.

UTILITARIANISM

In dealing with Newman's appraisal of the growth of the liberal spirit in society, and especially its insinuation into the Anglican Church, it was my intention to make use of his more general statements and attitudes, reserving specific questions, questions of Providential dispensation and social justice, questions on the aims of education, for this section and the ones to follow.

Newman did not write at length on the political aspects of utilitarianism nor did he minutely examine Benthamite liberalism.[1] Most of his extended attacks on what he calls Benthamism are made in relation to education. As we shall see in the next chapter, Newman distrusted utilitarian education because he thought it was based on faulty assumptions about man's intellectual and moral nature. He believed that utilitarian theories of education depended on a false psychology. But Newman levelled similar charges in his attacks on utilitarian principles as they operate outside the universities and reading rooms. Before turning

[1] Terence Kenny, *The Political Thought of John Henry Newman* (London, 1957), p. 137.

to his theories of education, it will be worthwhile to examine these almost random shots, for they provide insights into Newman's antipathy to most forms of social expediency, an antipathy so spontaneous that it seems as much a matter of temperament as of conviction.

Newman supported the social hierarchy from a belief that it provided the sort of stability necessary for the effective teaching of Christian doctrine and because the primary duty of the Christian is not to attempt to reform the world but to prepare himself for judgement. Nevertheless, the burning nineteenth-century questions concerning social and divine justice confronted him from time to time. As is to be expected, problems of social justice are almost instinctively related by Newman to problems of divine justice, not because he wishes to settle them easily, but because his mind is so constituted as to be unable to return a strictly secular answer to questions so involved with one's attitude towards the dispensations of Providence.

Newman cannot, for example, be charged with evading the problem of the existence of pain. Nor does he adopt the *all's well* approach to it. Take the following vision of a universe of physical agony, which Newman claims is the 'most mysterious' of all suffering:

Sorrow, anxiety, and disappointment are more or less connected with sin and sinners; but bodily pain is involuntary for the most part, stretching over the world by some external irresistible law, reaching to children who have never actually sinned, and to the brute animals, who are strangers to Adam's nature, while in its manifestations it is far more piteous and distressing than any other suffering. It is the lot of all of us, sooner or later; and that, perhaps in a measure which it would be appalling and wrong to anticipate, whether from disease, or from the casualties of life. And all of us at length must die; and death is generally ushered in by disease, and ends in that separation of soul and body, which itself may, in some cases, involve peculiar pain.

And, Newman continues in this brilliant sermon, we cannot console ourselves with the thought that suffering will improve our moral natures. Pain has 'no sanctifying influence in itself. Bad men are made worse by it.' Then Newman turns the cold light of his psychological genius onto his congregation. Not bad men only, but we ourselves are made worse by pain because pain makes us selfish: 'The natural effect, then, of pain and fear, is to individualize us in our own minds, to fix our thoughts on ourselves, to make us selfish.'[1]

This being the case, Christianity's explanation for the existence of pain is, to borrow a favourite phrase of Newman's, 'humanly speaking' most unsatisfactory. And this he is quite ready to grant. In a letter of 1849 to J. M. Capes, he sets forth the atheistic argument that God is wanting in either love or power, which amounts to maintaining that God in the Catholic sense does not exist. Christianity, writes Newman, 'does not *touch* this argument. It leaves it where it was, or adds weight to it.' Christianity offers no adequate rational solution to the problem but 'meets' it indirectly, so that 'The point then is what *degree* of skillful meeting, in a religion, is sufficient to prove it divine.'[2] Or, as he puts it two years later, 'Unanswerable objections *need* not interfere with a moral proof. I believe that God is all good, yet I *cannot* reconcile this belief with the existence of misery in the world.'[3]

In the *Grammar of Assent*, Newman attributes man's pain to his alienation from God, a 'quarrel without remedy, a chronic alienation, between God and man'.[4] He suspects that there are aspects of God's dispensation which will be repugnant to the liberal sense of justice and, as if to beg the question, he makes a special point of vicarious punishment. The final burden of responsibility for our salvation is our own; and yet the exertions of others may help to prepare us for judgement. 'On this vicarious principle, by which we appropriate to ourselves what others do for us, the whole structure of society is raised.' Parents suffer for their children, a wife may suffer a punishment earned by her

---

[1] 'Bodily Suffering' (1835), *Parochial and Plain Sermons*, iii. 142–7.
[2] *Letters and Diaries*, xiii. 320.   [3] Ibid. xiv. 348.
[4] *Grammar of Assent*, pp. 302–3. The complete passage provides a fine example of the vivid way Newman can project the fact of pain: 'Let us say there are a thousand millions of men on the earth at this time; who can weigh and measure the aggregate of pain which this one generation has endured and will endure from birth to death? Then add to this all the pain which has fallen and will fall upon our race through centuries past and to come.'

husband. The innocent suffer for the sake of the guilty. These are the facts of the human condition. Newman quotes Butler as pointing out that those who criticize the practices of sacrifice and atonement for the sins of others ' "forget that vicarious punishment is a providential appointment of everyday's experience" '. Thus, Newman insists, he who undergoes punishment for another 'may be said in a certain sense to satisfy the claims of justice towards that other in his own person'.[1]

That Newman speaks of the whole structure of society being based on a 'vicarious principle' does not necessarily place him in opposition to utilitarian notions of social justice. The distribution of labour is, of course, fundamental to classical economics. But Newman's idea of vicarious punishment has something decidedly anti-utilitarian about it: the voluntary sacrifice of self as an appeasement of divine anger. He is implicitly reacting to those who wish to attribute to the Deity the sort of justice which they think is ideal in society. Newman wishes to be tough-minded as well as orthodox. If vicarious punishment is part of the divine disposition, then we must accept it. That one believes vicarious punishment to be unjust does not give him the right to criticize God's administration of it, or to infer that He is imperfect in one of His attributes. As always, Newman objects to the application of social theories to the spiritual universe, though he himself does not hesitate to confront us with eschatological answers to social questions.

The doctrine of eternal punishment, one would think, should provide another example of how alien the aims and values of liberalism are to Newman's sensibility. Of course he preaches the reality of damnation, but his attitude towards it is a curious one. In the *Grammar* he agrees that we cannot tell what the fact of eternity may add to punishment, for the consciousness of the continuity of suffering is what most gives us pain. Perhaps, he suggests, the damned have no consciousness, or only a partial consciousness of duration and succession. 'For what we know,

---

[1] *Grammar of Assent*, pp. 308–9. In *The Tamworth Reading Room* Newman demands, 'Was there ever a Religion which was without the idea of an expiation?' (*Essays and Sketches*, ii. 212).

the suffering of one moment may have no bearing, or but a partial bearing, on the suffering of the next.'[1] As was to be expected, certain Catholics attacked Newman as explaining away the doctrine of eternal punishment. His opponents argued that unless punishment is conscious it is not punishment. In a note of 1882 to a later edition of the *Grammar*, Newman answers them. He agrees that punishment must be conscious, and that the damned must be aware of the irreversibility of their condition. But he points out that the lost soul need not be conscious of the long course of its suffering, 'in memory and in prospect, through periods and aeons'. Then Newman adds a passage metaphorically explaining this difficult psychological point, a passage which, composed by an orthodox priest, must be considered a vision of transcendent mercy:

The song of the bird, which the monk heard without taking note of the passage of time, might have been, 'And they shall reign for ever and ever;' though of the many thousand times of the bird's repeating the words, there sounded in the monk's ear but one song once sung. And if this may be in the case of holy souls, why not, if it should so please God, in the instance of the unholy?[2]

In all of this I have been attempting to suggest the complicated interaction in Newman's mind between questions of social and divine justice. It would be wrong to imagine that his attack on utilitarianism was ever divorced from religious and even theological considerations. Although he attacks the reformers for applying social theories to religious matters, and for substituting efforts towards social reform for a religious contemplation of man's degenerate nature, he characteristically counters their proposals in favour of reading rooms and libraries with an exposition of man's incorrigibility in the eyes of God.

Despite the severity of such doctrines as that of eternal punishment, however, Christianity, in Newman's view, does make life in the world more bearable. If poverty does not make salvation any easier, at least Christianity maintains that the poor have as much chance of divine mercy as the rich. In a famous passage in

[1] *Grammar of Assent*, p. 321.   [2] Ibid., pp. 386–7.

in Relation to his Philosophy of Mind 113

Difficulties of Anglicans, he preaches the spiritual superiority of a beggarwoman, 'lazy, ragged, and filthy, and not over-scrupulous of truth' but conscientious in her religious devotion, over 'the State's pattern-man, the just, the upright, the generous, the honourable, the conscientious' who possesses merely 'natural virtue'.[1] On the same subject, Wilfred Ward points out that the *Grammar of Assent* answers the question of how the uneducated can have real faith. In arguing that the bases of faith are personal, instinctive, or intuitive, and quite independent of complex reasonings, proofs, and explanations, Newman provided a defence of the validity of religious conviction in the ignorant, the busy, the poor, and the oppressed.[2]

Newman rejected the claim that orthodox Christianity imposes a painful yoke of obedience and submission upon its adherents. He argues in *Discourses to Mixed Congregations* that if we consider man to be the crowning achievement of creation and at the same time recognize his cruelties, enmities, frauds, and oppressions, we are left with the conclusion that God has created nothing perfect, that we are the rebellious occupants of 'a world of order which is dead and corruptible'. In comparison with the dreariness of this conclusion, 'can you venture to say that the Church's yoke is heavy?'[3] On this theme Ward quotes a rough note, dated 1857, in which Newman mentions the pain inherent in scepticism: 'It is as difficult to acquiesce in that we are made for nothing, or that there is no end of our being, as to believe the dogmas of a revelation.'[4] We have seen that dogma and faith are for Newman the fulfilment and the acceptance of truths which meet an innate psychic need, and that the peace they bring with them itself partially indicates their validity. To deprive a man of faith is to cause him pain in this life as well as to endanger his happiness in the next, and it may be inferred that any hedonistic calculus which omits this consideration is incomplete.

In the *Grammar*, Newman gives a brief list of the social achievements of Christianity. It has raised the tone of morality, abolished great social anomalies and miseries, improved the condition of

[1] *Difficulties of Anglicans*, i. 249–50.   [2] Ward, ii. 244.
[3] *Discourses to Mixed Congregations*, p. 274.   [4] Ward, i. 424.

women, protected the poor, destroyed slavery, encouraged literature and philosophy and generally advanced the causes of civilization.[1] But Newman refuses to consider Christianity as a function of civilization. The concerns of the church transcend those of society. For this reason, he insists in *Difficulties of Anglicans*, the argument that Catholic countries have lower social and political conditions does not tell against Catholicism, unless it can be proved as well that 'the standard of civil prosperity and political aggrandisement is the truest test of grace and the largest measure of salvation'.[2]

The social benefits of Christianity, then, are for Newman incidental to its teleology. As Dwight Culler points out, the real issue between Newman and the utilitarians concerns the chief good, the final end of man.[3] There can be no doubt that much of the force and clarity of Newman's attack on utilitarian principles may be attributed to his refusal to treat in detail, at least in his literary work (as distinct from his pastoral), the sort of problems with which the utilitarians, and particularly Bentham, wrestled. Newman did not have to face the terrible question of how the interests of the individual can be made to coincide with those of society. But it is at least equally true that Bentham refused to answer questions which he believed fell outside the province of his hedonistic calculus and that he dismissed as irrelevant facts of man's mental and moral nature so basic as to call into question the value of a calculus which ignores them.

On the subject of Bentham's limitations, Newman and Mill are once again in substantial agreement. Mill points out in his brilliant essay 'Bentham' that the great utilitarian was antagonistic to any philosophy which did not operate by his method of detailed rational analysis or which was not morally based on utility:

He had a phrase, expressive of the view he took of all moral speculations to which his method had not been applied, or (which he considered as the same thing) not founded on a recognition of utility as the moral standard; this phrase was 'vague generalities'. Whatever

---

[1] *Grammar of Assent*, pp. 338–9.   [2] *Difficulties of Anglicans*, i. 259–60.
[3] *The Imperial Intellect* (New Haven, 1955), p. 223.

presented itself to him in such a shape, he dismissed as unworthy of notice, or dwelt upon only to denounce as absurd. He did not heed, or rather the nature of his mind prevented it from occurring to him, that these generalities contained the whole unanalysed experience of the human race.[1]

Bentham, Mill continues, not only rejected as 'vague generalities' all epistemology, all methods of knowing, which did not conform to his criteria of analysis, but was also hampered by a dangerously faulty notion of human psychology:

... all the more subtle workings both of the mind upon itself, and of external things upon the mind, escaped him; and no one, probably, who, in a highly instructed age, ever attempted to give a rule to all human conduct, set out with a more limited conception either of the agencies by which human conduct *is*, or of those by which it *should* be, influenced.[2]

The basis of Newman's attack in *The Tamworth Reading Room* is precisely his apprehension that of the agencies which influence most human conduct, reason is among the weakest. He emphasizes the confusion rather than the order of the mind, its passion rather than its logic, its predisposition to respond to an appeal to faith rather than an appeal to reason:

The heart is commonly reached, not through the reason, but through the imagination, by means of direct impressions, by the testimony of facts and events, by history, by description. Persons influence us, voices melt us, looks subdue us, deeds inflame us. Many a man will live and die upon a dogma; no man will be a martyr for a conclusion.[3]

Because it does not reach the heart, Newman argues, philosophy can never accomplish what was once done by religion. Perhaps Christianity cannot regain the 'organic power in human society' which once it possessed. Philosophy will not elicit from men the passionate and harmonious commitment formerly accorded to Christianity, though a species of philosophy may in fact dominate the state. 'Let Benthamism reign', Newman

---

[1] *Bentham and Coleridge*, p. 59. [2] Ibid., p. 63.
[3] 'The Tamworth Reading Room', *Essays and Sketches*, ii. 204.

writes, 'if men have no aspirations; but do not tell them to be romantic and then solace them with glory.'[1]

Newman proposes no measures to bring Christianity back to its position as the organic centre of society. He attacks a fallacy, resists a pretence. This pretence, he explains in his *Essay on Development*, is the attempt of Benthamism to usurp in men's hearts the place properly held by the values of Christianity:

> Mr. Bentham's system was an attempt to make the circle of legal and moral truths developments of certain principles of his own;—those principles of his may, if it so happen, prove unequal to the weight of truths which are eternal, and the system founded on them may break into pieces; or again, a State may absorb certain of them, for which it has affinity, that is, it may develop in Benthamism, yet remain in substance what it was before.[2]

The passage suggests that Newman hopes for the decline of Benthamism from the fact that it has superimposed itself upon those moral bases of society which are really Christian. As utilitarianism has no real connection with these first principles of conduct it may remain a sort of intellectual and political super-structure, perhaps analogous to the function of art in a Marxist state, exercising no original or fundamental influence upon the moral life of society.

But the violence and complexity of Newman's attack on utilitarian principles elsewhere in his writing leads me to believe that the passage in the *Essay on Development* represents more of a hopeful speculation than a reasoned prediction. Newman considers Benthamism, like liberalism, as being based upon reason and rational analysis. It comes in for a share of Newman's antagonism to rationalism because it attacks the dogmatic principle in religion wherever it finds the dogma inexpedient. In the

---

[1] *Essays and Sketches*, ii. 203.

[2] *Essay on Development*, pp. 174–5. An example of a utilitarian principle which Newman believed liberalism aimed at establishing may be found in the thirteenth proposition of liberalism:

'Utility and expedience are the measure of political duty.

Therefore, e.g., no punishment may be enacted, on the ground that God commands it: e.g. on the text, "Whoso sheddeth man's blood, by man shall his blood be shed".' (*Apologia*, p. 261).

sections on reason and on dogma in my second chapter, I discussed Newman's apprehension of the tendency of reason to usurp the function of dogma, to replace habits of assenting with habits of questioning. However false to man's real needs, however foreign to the true springs of his conduct, if Benthamism weakens dogmatic religion it will be able to insinuate its own principles. The mind, according to Newman, requires principles of some sort in order to act: man cannot act without points of reference or first principles. 'Not that he is very particular whether he finds a good reason or a bad, when he is very much straitened for a reason; but a reason of some sort he must have.'[1] And, as Newman explains in *The Present Position of Catholics*, the more familiar the mind becomes with the principles it has adopted, the more satisfied it is with their validity. The objective truth of any reason or argument does not increase with repetition 'but the effect on any mind, which is passive under the infliction, *is* stronger and stronger everytime it is repeated. In this way almost any idea whatever may be impressed on the mind.'[2] The scientific habit of inquiry into all unproven assertions does provide a 'view' or principle on which the mind can fasten. As Newman observes in a letter of 1850, 'Nothing is clearer than that a *habit* of critical inquiry is wrong. I suspect it leads to infidelity, not to Catholicism.'[3]

Man's natural love of order and need for unity provides Newman with yet another psychological basis for fearing the rational and utilitarian habits of mind. He makes much of the natural tendency of the mind to relate whatever comes before it to whatever it has already apprehended. At the end of a superb passage in *The Idea of a University*, in which he describes the mind's drive towards wholeness and unity, he writes:

[1] *Discourses to Mixed Congregations*, p. 22. On the same theme; 'Not from self-will only, nor from malevolence, but from the irritation which suspense occasions, is the mind forced on to pronounce, without sufficient data for pronouncing. . . . We cannot do without a view, and we put up with an illusion, when we cannot get a truth' (*The Idea of a University*, p. 67).

[2] *The Present Position of Catholics*, p. 230.

[3] *Letters and Diaries*, xiv. 45. Among the Birmingham papers Newman has a note (dated 1857) on this subject in reference to J. S. Mill's *Logic*: 'Right investigation, he says, depends on a *habit of mind*—one man does what another can not. Well, this is just what I say of the investigation which leads to faith.'

It assigns phenomena to a general law, qualities to a subject, acts to a principle, and effects to a cause. In a word, it philosophizes; for I suppose Science and Philosophy, in their elementary idea, are nothing else but this habit of *viewing*, as it may be called, the objects which sense conveys to the mind, of throwing them into system, and uniting and stamping them with one form.[1]

Newman's reference to science in this context is significant. It was from the scientist, or what he terms the 'scientific philosopher', that he anticipated the greatest danger of utilitarianism to Christianity. Scientific philosophers, Newman tells members of the university he has founded, look forward to the time when they shall have triumphed over religion, 'not by shutting its schools, but by emptying them; not by disputing its tenets, but by the superior worth and persuasiveness of their own'.[2] So pervasive have scientific terminology and methods of thought become, that even religious writing of a scientific colour tends to take mere hypothesis for established fact. In 1850 Newman writes to J. M. Capes, editor of the *Rambler*, to caution him against publishing certain Catholic scientific articles: 'We ought not to theorize the teaching of Moses, till philosophers have demonstrated their theories of physics. If "the Spirit of God" is gas in 1850, it may be electro-magnetism in 1860.'[3] In graver tones Newman traces the 'indirect bearing' of scientific discoveries upon religion in the *Apologia*. When the flood of new scientific facts pours in upon us we immediately attempt to relate them to other propositions which we hold as verities, for 'to reconcile theory and fact is almost an instinct of the mind'. Sometimes it turns out to be religion which suffers, and Christians, 'in consequence of the confident tone of the schools of secular knowledge, are in danger of being led away into a bottomless liberalism of thought'.[4]

With this undermining of religion by popular science Newman again associates Bentham. In *The Idea of a University* he attacks the

---

[1] *The Idea of a University*, p. 66.   [2] Ibid., p. 306.

[3] *Letters and Diaries*, xiv. 127. Newman had earlier warned Capes against confidence in his theory, presumably of a scientific tone, about the deluge: 'The "Spiritus Dei" may mean electro-magnetism ten years hence, then the vital principle, and at the end of 50 years "the Spirit of God" as of old' (ibid., p. 68).

[4] *Apologia*, p. 233.

trespass of the rational sciences into the study of morality and religious truth:

Law would seem to have enough to do with its own clients, and their affairs; and yet Mr. Bentham made a treatise on Judicial Proofs a covert attack upon the miracles of Revelation. And in like manner Physiology may deny moral evil and human responsibility; Geology may deny Moses; and Logic may deny the Holy Trinity; and other sciences, now rising into notice, are or will be victims of a similar abuse.[1]

We may observe in passing that although the sciences attack and deny, it is they who, in Newman's prose, turn out to be the 'victims' of an abuse—implying the essential indestructibility of Revelation and the Trinity. At any rate, we cannot doubt that utilitarian economics holds a place among the transgressing sciences. Newman's sixth proposition of liberalism states:

No revealed doctrines or precepts may reasonably stand in the way of scientific conclusions.
    Therefore, e.g. Political Economy may reverse our Lord's declarations about poverty and riches, or a system of Ethics may teach that the highest condition of body is ordinarily essential to the highest state of mind.[2]

Thus when the rational sciences (exclusive of rational theology) are treated as utilitarian, as bases of social conduct, as principles of social action, they threaten religion. We shall see later that Newman's definition of education in the arts and sciences as 'liberal'—capable of being its own end—constitutes part of his attempt to prevent their trespass into the proper sphere of religion and morality.

But before turning our attention to Newman's idea of the connection, or lack of it, between knowledge and virtue, one

---

[1] *The Idea of a University*, p. 84.
[2] *Apologia*, p. 260. One recalls Dickens's creation of Bitzer as the ultimate 'economic man' of classical economics, and also the image of Thomas Gradgrind 'writing in the room with the deadly statistical clock, proving something no doubt—probably, in the main, that the Good Samaritan was a bad economist' (*Hard Times*, Book II, ch. xii).

other possible source of his antipathy to utilitarianism ought to be mentioned. C. F. Harrold points out that the lost sense of a spiritually organic unity in society which Carlyle attempted to recapture through transcendentalism, the Tractarians sought to revive by 'sacramentalizing' the world and restoring man to his 'dual citizenship in the two orders of nature and spirit'. If Newman is a Tory, Harrold continues, his Toryism appears to be of a singularly revolutionary kind, emphasizing the supernatural value of every man. Like the other Tractarians, he recognized condition: in man's dilemma, conditions of an inherited burden of evil which no political or economic reform could ease, 'but which required, for its eradication, a turning to a frame of reference transcending the flux of history'.[1] Social amelioration, in other words, derives from the moral improvement of each citizen, not from sweeping institutional changes. This, certainly, is a commonplace of political conservatism, and it was a commonplace in the middle of Newman's century. But in the following passage from *Difficulties of Anglicans*, even considering the apparently anachronistic reference to the devil, it has not the sound of a platitude, perhaps because of the passion and precision of its articulation, perhaps from its religious fire besides which the projects for institutional reform momentarily pale into irrelevance. The Catholic Church, writes Newman,

contemplates, not the whole, but the parts; not a nation, but the men who form it; not society in the first place, but in the second place, and in the first place individuals; it looks beyond the outward act, on and into the thought, the motive, the intention, and the will; it looks beyond the world, and detects and moves against the devil, who is sitting in ambush behind it. It has, then, a foe in view; nay, it has a

[1] C. F. Harrold, 'The Oxford Movement, a Reconsideration', *The Reinterpretation of Victorian Literature*, ed. J. Baker (Princeton, 1950), pp. 45–8. Harrold urges the twentieth-century relevance of this politically conservative point with remarkable force: 'if we believe, with the secularists, that the Kingdom of Heaven can be established by political and economic programs, then we have no right to object to the claims of the state to embrace the whole of life in order to produce and distribute its secular goods, even though it demands—as it logically will in time—the absolute submission of the individual will and conscience. The realization of this fact drove the religious conscience of the Victorian age to disapprove of unrestricted liberal doctrine' (ibid., p. 50).

battle-field, to which the world is blind; its proper battle-field is the heart of the individual, and its true foe is Satan.[1]

We have seen, then, that although Newman did not ignore the problem of human suffering and although he admitted Christianity's refusal to account for it logically, he nevertheless maintained that to consider religion a means to the alleviation of pain in the world is to make it the servant of society. He insisted that Christianity must not be expected to perform a utilitarian function in the social world. The very approach of religion differs from that of utilitarianism, for it is concerned with the sanctity of the individual rather than the reform of social institutions. The danger of utilitarian sciences lies precisely in their tendency to undermine faith in individuals by their insistence upon analysis rather than assent, an insistence antithetic to the principle of dogma. When utilitarian studies trespass into the field of morality they fail because they make certain false psychological and epistemological assumptions. Men do not receive first principles through their reason, nor are most men moved to action by means of scientific demonstrations: 'The ascendency of Faith may be impracticable', writes Newman in *The Tamworth Reading Room*, 'but the reign of Knowledge is incomprehensible. The problem for statesmen of this age is how to educate the masses, and literature and science cannot give the solution.'[2]

In this discussion of Newman's writings on liberalism, I have treated a wide variety of subjects and ideas. Readers of Newman will perhaps excuse me on the grounds that this variety reflects in some degree Newman's own tendency to insist upon the correspondence and relation of ideas commonly unconnected in formal discussion. I hope, however, that the general purpose, to demonstrate the importance of Newman's philosophy of mind as outlined in my second chapter to the study of his social criticism, has been apparent throughout. I began by sketching Newman's growing sense of irreligion in English society, the triumph of liberal forces within and without the Anglican Church, and his apprehension that the value of the dogmatic principle would be

---

[1] *Difficulties of Anglicans*, i. 236.
[2] *Essays and Sketches*, ii. 203.

lost to Englishmen. We saw that while he remained an Anglican Newman found in romantic literature a Catholic sensibility opposed to rationalism, but that after his conversion he countered the anti-dogmatic forces of his age with a defence of Roman Catholic dogma and its epistemological appropriateness to the transmission and perception of religious truth.

Liberalism, for Newman, is the anti-dogmatic principle, an extension of reason as exercised by the natural man. It cultivates and supports the modern notion that private judgement in all subjects is a matter of duty. Private judgement places the burden of proof on the individual believer, and treats authoritative religion as irrelevant to modern intellectual life. Religion thus becomes not an objective truth discovered by means of faith, but a matter of personal taste adjusted freely to suit needs which vary with individuals.

For Newman, the liberal habit of mind becomes most dangerous when it becomes utilitarian, when men begin to act on its assumptions. Utilitarianism he saw as the extension of rational principles of social reform into the moral life of society. Because Christianity provides no logical solution to the problem of pain, utilitarianism excludes religion from its programme. Benthamism limits the means of knowing to rational analysis, and the unanalysed experience of the human race, including for Newman the means by which most men achieve faith, is derogated in the utilitarian vision of the mind. Political economy, therefore, like physical science, transgresses into areas properly dominated by religion. And then, because the experiences of religion are not comprehended by it, utilitarianism excludes them from its contemplation of society.

CHAPTER FOUR

The Alternative to Liberalism: Newman's Theories of Education as related to his Philosophy of Mind

> Is not the delight of the quavering upon a stop in music the same with the playing of light upon the water?
> *Splendet tremulo sub lumine pontus.*
> Are not the organs of the senses of one kind with the organs of reflection, the eye with a glass, the ear with a cave or strait, determined and bounded? Neither are these only similitudes, as men of narrow observation may conceive them to be, but the same footsteps of nature, treading or printing upon several subjects or matters.
>
> And as concerning divine philosophy or natural theology, it is that knowledge or rudiment of knowledge concerning God, which may be obtained by the contemplation of his creatures; which knowledge may be truly termed divine in respect of the object, and natural in respect of the light.
>
> (BACON, *The Advancement of Learning*)

ON 10 May 1852, Newman delivered in Dublin the first of those discourses which were to form the most important pages of *The Idea of a University*. 'Though it has been my lot for many years to take a prominent, sometimes a presumptuous, part in theological discussions, yet the natural turn of my mind carries me off to trains of thought like those which I am now about to open.'[1] What Newman means by 'the natural turn of my mind' gradually becomes evident in the discussions which follow: that many of his ideas on education grow out of his 'philosophical polemic' on the nature of religious belief, the psychological and epistemological insights of his Anglican career. Indeed, his first extended

[1] *The Idea of a University*, pp. 4–5.

discussion of education appeared in his letters on the Tamworth Reading Room four years before his conversion. These form a brilliant and cruelly unqualified attack on liberal hopes for the moral and social effects of education, and Newman bases his arguments on his view of the mind's limitations and weaknesses. In the Dublin discourses, too, his philosophy of mind forms the foundation of his argument, this time in what finally becomes a celebration of the intellect, a celebration in which he presents a secular and, as I hope to demonstrate, a religious alternative to what he considered the rampant liberalism of his age.

KNOWLEDGE AND VIRTUE

Three years before the beginning of the Tractarian Movement we see Newman making a characteristic attack on the ability of unaided reason to reach moral and religious values: 'Clear-sighted as reason is on other subjects, and trustworthy as a guide, still in questions connected with our duty to God and man it is very unskilful and equivocating'. Here, however, he goes on to challenge those 'men of superior understanding' who hope for moral improvement from enlargement of the intellect, those who 'labour to convince themselves, that as men grow in knowledge they will grow in virtue'.[1] Two years later he makes this point still more specifically by asking how a knowledge of physical science can lead us to a knowledge of virtue or a love of God. Religion, he urges, is 'something *relative to us*,' a system of divine commands and promises:

But how are we concerned with the sun, moon, and stars? or with the laws of the universe? how will they teach us our *duty*? how will they speak to *sinners*? They do not speak to sinners at all. They were created *before* Adam fell. They 'declare the *glory* of God,' but not His *will*.[2]

Closely connected with his view of the moral indifference of the sciences is Newman's profound distrust of the argument from design—that is, the inference of the existence of God from

[1] 'The self-wise Inquirer' (1830), *Parochial and Plain Sermons*, i. 218–19, 223–4.
[2] 'The Religion of the Day' (1832), ibid., i. 317.

the order and beneficence of the natural world. Science, writes Newman in *The Tamworth Reading Room*, can describe nature to us, but it cannot infer religious truths from that description. 'Science gives us the grounds or premisses from which religious truths are to be inferred; but it does not set about inferring them, much less does it reach the inference;—that is not its province.'[1] Newman maintained this conviction throughout his life. In an interesting letter of 1870 he explains that he did not insist upon the argument from design in the *Grammar of Assent* 'because I am writing for the 19th Century, by which, as represented by its philosophers, design is not admitted as proved'. Then he goes on to say that he has been unable to see the logical force of the argument since he was thirty. He accepts the idea of a design because he believes in God, not the idea of God because he believes in design. He knows God primarily through his conscience. 'You will say that the 19th Century does not believe in conscience either—true—but then it does not believe in a God at all.' We must assume something, Newman continues, and in assuming the divine origin of conscience he believes he is being as little presumptive as possible. On the other hand, the mass of men live in ignorance of the argument from design and once they have been taught it they can infer from it very few of the moral attributes of God. 'Design teaches me power, skill, and goodness, not sanctity, not mercy, not a future judgement, which three are of the essence of religion.'[2]

---

[1] *Essays and Sketches*, ii. 204. Of course Newman believed there could in reality be no contradiction between scientific and religious truth, but that apparent contradictions develop as rational science advances. See *The Idea of a University*, p. 314. After his experiences with the College of Propaganda in Rome he came to think it a mistake for Catholic controversialists to argue as if reason and faith are actually and ultimately at odds: 'can a more fatal suicidal act be committed', he asks in a letter of 1853, 'on the part of our controversialists, than to imply an opposition between reason and faith, or at least to encourage the notion that the intellect of the world is naturally and properly on the side of infidelity'. Newman, however, goes on to admit that 'This seems the practical conclusion to which the views would lead, to which I am inclined, when left to myself' (*Letters and Diaries*, xv. 457). But before and after he had converted to Roman Catholicism, Newman spoke of reason and faith as antagonistic *habits of mind*. See the section on Reason in Chapter Two.

[2] Ward, ii. 269.

Thus, in Newman's view, the study of physical nature does not lead to any first principle of morality or religion. And, of course, the study of science and literature takes time which might be spent in the study of religion. 'We must make up our minds to be ignorant of much, if we would know anything. And we must make our choice between risking Science, and risking Religion.'[1] Scientific pursuits benefit the community, Newman writes, and they are worthy of a place in a liberal education. But they begin and end in the material universe, and the material universe by itself provides no system of morality, no ethics, no religion. There is no logical extension available to science by which it can reach religious values.

On the other hand, it is evident that literature, replete with moral and religious significance, does not suffer from this epistemological limitation of physical science. Indeed, we have seen that Newman credits Scott and Southey, Wordsworth and Coleridge, with helping to stimulate the Catholic sensibility which welcomed the Tractarian Movement. Literature appeals vividly to the imagination, and involves moral and religious sympathies as science cannot. In the *Grammar of Assent* Newman quotes a passage from Mrs. Gaskell's *North and South* in which a factory girl, dying from a disease of the lungs, vividly recalls the unremitting misery of her existence and declares that if she believed that there were no future life to compensate for the pain of the one she is leaving, she would go mad. 'Here', comments Newman, 'is an argument for the immortality of the soul.'[2] Why then, one may ask, may we not find our virtue in the reading rooms, in literature which is at once stirring and moral?

Newman gives two closely related answers to this question. First, literature is personal expression. Whereas science proposes to treat of what is 'universal and eternal' (and herein lies the danger of its usurpations), literature is the 'personal use or exercise of language'.[3] Secondly, perhaps because it is personal expression, the moral values or first principles inherent in works of literature are usually neither consistent nor decisive in their relation to

---

[1] *Essays and Sketches*, ii. 194.   [2] *Grammar of Assent*, p. 237.
[3] *The Idea of a University*, pp. 252, 240.

Christianity. Christian values and actions are confused with other values and actions, such as, perhaps, honour and revenge. Literature, therefore, 'is the Life and Remains of the *natural* man, innocent or guilty'. As science reflects physical nature, so literature reflects nature moral and social. And this remains true no matter what locality, period, or language produces it: 'all literatures are one; they are the voices of the natural man'.[1] Thus it becomes as difficult to elicit a consistent morality from literature as to infer one from the physical universe.

And it is with his vision of the natural man that Newman counters the hopes expressed by Sir Robert Peel in an address on the opening of a public reading room at Tamworth:

A distinguished Conservative statesman tells us from the town-hall of Tamworth that 'in becoming wiser a man will become better;' meaning by wiser more conversant with the facts and theories of physical science; and that such a man will 'rise *at once* in the scale of intellectual and *moral* existence'. 'That', he adds, 'is my belief.' He avows, also, that the fortunate individual whom he is describing, by being 'accustomed to such contemplations, will feel the *moral dignity of his nature exalted*'.

Newman responds to these vague encomiums with disproportionate, or at least unexpected, seriousness and precision, stressing from the beginning of his argument a view of the mind as unformed and disordered, 'passions and conscience, likings and reason, conflicting,—might rising against right, with the prospect of things getting worse'. Against the passions of man, Newman points out, even Sir Robert Peel does not pretend to act. Instead Peel offers the passions a bribe, a temporary distraction. At best a reading room will provide this; more commonly it will go unattended: 'Strong liquors, indeed, do for a time succeed in their object; but who was ever consoled in real trouble by the small beer of literature or science?'[2]

[1] Ibid., pp. 201–2.
[2] *Essays and Sketches*, ii. 179, 181, 184. Newman makes the same point in more elegant language in a famous passage from *The Idea of a University*: 'Quarry the granite rock with razors, or moor the vessel with a thread of silk; then may you hope with such keen and delicate instruments as human knowledge and human reason to contend against those giants, the passion and the pride of man' (p. 107).

Why knowledge and reason do not console men in real trouble
or conquer their passion and pride is a question which Newman
refuses to answer in the Tamworth letters. He describes rather
than analyses, maintaining that most men, when they are moved,
are moved by dogmas, not deductions: 'we must resign ourselves
to it as best we may, unless we take refuge in the intolerable
paradox, that the mass of men are created for nothing, and are
meant to leave life as they entered it'. Virtue must be sought in
'graver and holier places than in Libraries and Reading Rooms'.
The mass of men will not find their morality in literature. Vice
cannot be eliminated 'by human expedients'. For the renovation
of the heart and will a higher source must be sought. 'You do but
play a sort of "hunt the slipper" with the fault of our nature, till
you go to Christianity.'[1]

Like literature, Christianity appeals to the imagination. It is
vivid and specific; the apprehension of it is what Newman was
later to call 'real'. Moses did not reason from creation, he performed miracles. 'Christianity is a history supernatural, and
almost scenic: it tells us what its Author is, by telling us what He
has done.' Unlike literature, however, Christianity involves man
in the action; he becomes a character in the drama; he has a stake
in the game. It is for this reason that 'apprehension of the unseen
is the only known principle capable of subduing moral evil,
educating the multitude, and organizing society; and that, whereas man is born for action, action flows not from inferences, but
from impressions,—not from reasonings, but from Faith'.[2]

Literature provides the impressions but omits the motives for
action. In a sermon on 'The Danger of Accomplishments' (1831),
which is one of his best, Newman argues that a 'polite education'
tends to separate feeling and acting. What we read arouses anger,
pity, and affection but provides nothing for us to do with these
emotions. God has given us the power to feel so that we may act,
Newman argues, and if we constantly allow our feelings to be
aroused without acting on them, 'we do mischief to the moral
system within us'. Thus 'a grave question arises, how, after

---

[1] *Essays and Sketches*, ii. 206–7, 185, 189.
[2] Ibid., pp. 207, 213.

destroying the connexion between feeling and acting, how shall
we get ourselves to act when circumstances make it our duty to
do so?'[1] Clearly, literature can weaken the springs of our moral
nature. Not only is literature, as the history of the natural man,
necessarily corrupt, but it has a dangerous tendency to substitute
feelings for actions, feelings which are regarded by its students as
being valuable for their own sake and not as they stir men to the
practice of virtue. 'Literature is almost in its essence unreal; for it
is the exhibition of thought disjoined from practice.'[2]

A GENTLEMAN'S KNOWLEDGE: THE SECULAR IDEAL

Newman did not change his mind about the weak relationship of
secular knowledge to moral action. What he asserts in the Tamworth letters in 1841 he holds in his university discourses eleven
years later. But the circumstances under which the works were
composed differ significantly in two respects. In *The Tamworth
Reading Room* Newman's primary concern is with the education
of the masses and the morality of those who could not afford to
buy books. In *The Idea of a University* he describes the education
of gentlemen. Secondly, in 1841 Newman is on the attack and
does not feel obliged to offer an alternative programme to the
reading rooms. In 1852 he is struggling to found a university, and
his lectures represent an attempt to provide a constructive philosophy of secular education free from the illusions which he
believes characterized Peel's speech on the Tamworth plan.

In his Dublin discourses Newman takes care to dissociate the
kind of knowledge imparted at a university from the sort of
information acquired for any practical or external purpose. He
distinguishes between liberal knowledge and that religious
teaching which leads to the practice of virtue, a distinction we
will return to in the next section in a discussion of what came to
be called with some rancour in orthodox circles the 'philosophy
of severance'.[3] And, more relevant to the present subject, Newman excludes from his ideal university the teaching of practical

---

[1] *Parochial and Plain Sermons*, ii. 371–2.
[2] 'Unreal Words' (1839), ibid. v. 42.
[3] C. F. Harrold, Preface to *The Idea of a University*, p. viii.

secular knowledge, useful or 'utilitarian' training of any sort, at a time in Ireland when professional men were badly needed.

Perhaps the most acute attack on this dissociation of university education from the pressure of social needs appears in T. Cocoran's introduction to a collection of Newman's writings on education. After admiring Newman as a psychologist, 'finely sensitive to types of mental habit', Cocoran launches a telling criticism of early nineteenth-century Oxford, which Newman, he argues, took for his model. At the Oxford of Newman's youth knowledge was indeed pursued for its own sake. The university had degenerated, according to Cocoran, from a medieval community of poor Latinists to a gentleman's club reading a minimum of classics and a smattering of mathematics, bereft of contact with other universities, and fortunately quite unique in its theory of mental cultivation.[1] Cocoran quotes Newman's letters to the effect that because of the emigration and the decline of important Catholic families from centuries of oppression and poverty Ireland seems to be without a ' "*class* to afford members for a university" '. Newman, Cocoran charges, demonstrates a 'defectiveness of moral and intellectual vision as regards grave issues of social justice concerning educational rights and opportunities'. Not only did Newman want an education exclusively to produce gentlemen, but, Cocoran points out, money was collected from the peasants in order to pay for it. And how were they to be repaid when in Newman's philosophy of education 'all specialized training, all pursuit, even of achievement by a student in one branch of learning or science, are clearly excluded from the true activities of a university'?[2]

These charges are difficult indeed to meet. Newman does show, especially in his letters, a certain lack of sympathy for, or

---

[1] *John Henry Newman, Selected Discourses in Liberal Knowledge*, ed. T. Cocoran (Dublin, 1929), pp. xii–xxv. For Newman, of course, Oxford was never a 'club' but a considerable assemblage of effort and brilliance. As is well known, he studied between nine and twelve hours a day for months before his examinations, and later, as Fellow of Oriel, found himself and the best of his fellow tutors attacked for their high academic standards and rigorous moral surveillance. See Culler, *The Imperial Intellect*, pp. 1–123; and Trevor, *The Pillar of the Cloud*, pp. 23–190.

[2] Cocoran, pp. cii, lxi–lxii, xlii–xliii.

understanding of, the social conditions of Ireland in the 1850s. In practice his university made concessions, as in the establishment of a school of medicine. But the important point, I think, is that Newman had been asked to help found a university, not to establish a technical college which could train Irishmen to save their country from depression and poverty. And the function of a university, as John Stuart Mill was to agree, is not to produce professional men but 'capable and cultivated human beings'.[1] 'A university,' writes Newman, 'is, according to the usual designation, an Alma Mater, knowing her children one by one, not a foundry, or a mint, or a treadmill.' She imparts knowledge which her students value for its own sake, liberal knowledge, free from purposes beyond its own possession, knowledge which becomes part of the mind possessing it, a 'special Philosophy, which I have made to consist in a comprehensive view of truth in all its branches, of the relations of science to science, of their mutual bearings, and their respective values'. The possession of such knowledge transforms the student into the 'gentleman', and 'it is well to be a gentleman, it is well to have a cultivated intellect, a delicate taste, a candid, equitable, dispassionate mind, a noble and courteous bearing in the conduct of life;—these are the connatural qualities of a large knowledge; they are the objects of a University'.[2]

The education of such men is not without its effect upon society. Having established that liberal knowledge can be pursued only for its own sake, by which he means its effect upon the mind of the individual, Newman goes on in the seventh discourse to describe the social benefits which a university incidently affords:

a University training is the great but ordinary means to a great but ordinary end; it aims at raising the intellectual tone of society, at cultivating the public mind, at purifying the national taste, at supplying true principles to popular enthusiasm and fixed aims to popular aspiration, at giving enlargement and sobriety to the ideas of the age, at facilitating the exercise of political power, and refining the intercourse of private life.'[3]

---

[1] From Mill's inaugural address at St. Andrews (1867), *James and John Stuart Mill on Education*, p. 133.
[2] *The Idea of a University*, pp. 128, 91, 107. [3] Ibid., p. 157.

These, Newman believes, constitute the social value, the practical conditions of a well-educated citizenry. His phrasing, however, has caused a good deal of confusion. How, after insisting that a university must not impart knowledge with any practical or utilitarian end in view, can Newman call university education a 'means' to an 'end', and that 'end' the production of such a populace as he describes? How can he say that liberal education 'aims' at this practical result when by definition it must be pursued for its own sake?

The confusion is real and the fault is certainly Newman's. But except for a few sentences in the seventh discourse his argument is in fact consistent. It is on these few sentences, however, that Dwight Culler pounces in his influential and generally admirable study. He quotes what he calls the 'rather grudging conclusion' to the discourse, that ' "if . . . a practical end must be assigned to a University course, I say it is that of training good members of society" '. Here, argues Culler, Newman has done 'what Bentham said that every opponent of the utilitarian philosophy must do, he has combatted the principle of utility with reasons drawn "from that very principle itself" '. Newman has assigned a utilitarian end to university education even though 'the whole burden of the fifth discourse was that one must not, that liberal knowledge is its own end'.[1]

There would be no point in trying to clear Newman of the responsibility for a rhetorical confusion which he has certainly created; and to call the confusion rhetorical is not to say that it is not real. But when a thinker of Newman's stature constructs a superb argument with considerable compression and economy it seems hasty to claim that he has utterly reversed himself and in fact fallen prey to an antagonistic school of thought on the rather ambiguous evidence of a few incongruous sentences. To accept Culler's point as he makes it seems to me to claim that what is perhaps the most valuable assertion of *The Idea of a University* is ultimately and irreversibly contradicted by its author.

Newman in fact anticipated the difficulty so clearly and so often throughout the discourses that it is a matter of surprise as

[1] *The Imperial Intellect*, p. 222.

well as regret that he allowed the confusion to remain. Even in
the fifth discourse itself he remarks of liberal knowledge that
'further advantages accrue to us and redound to others by its
profession, over and above what it is in itself'. The whole burden
of the fifth discourse is not that one must not expect social benefits
from a liberal education. The whole burden of the fifth discourse
is the freedom of the university from *domination* by utilitarian
aims and methods. It does not therefore argue that such education will take place without benefit to society. Liberal knowledge is that 'which stands on its own pretensions, which is
independent of sequel, expects no complement, refuses to be
informed (as it is called) by any end, or absorbed into any art, in
order duly to present itself to our contemplation'.[1] Liberal
knowledge is independent of, not irrelevant to, the improvement of society.

Newman actually takes considerable care to emphasize the
special value to society of a university conducted without reference to immediate social objectives. In his introduction he speaks of
the familiar, partially educated person who speaks idly and long
on subjects of which he knows nothing: 'I am referring to an
evil which is forced upon us in every railway carriage, in every
coffee-room or *table-d'hôte*, in every mixed company.' The
university will correct this evil without shaping itself to do so,
by imparting to the student a respect for order and method which
will lead him to feel 'nothing but impatience and disgust at the
random theories and imposing sophistries and dashing paradoxes,
which carry away half-formed and superficial intellects'.[2]

Throughout the discourses Newman distinguishes between
shaping an education to meet the needs of society and establishing

---

[1] *The Idea of a University*, pp. 92, 95–6. The italics, as in all quotations throughout
this study, are the original author's, not mine. In the eighth discourse Newman
seems again aware of a possible confusion in his argument, and he attempts to correct it by a summary: 'Such, I said, was that Knowledge, which deserves to be
sought for its own sake, even though it promised no ulterior advantage. But,
when I had got as far as this, I went farther, and observed that, from the nature
of the case, what was so good in itself could not but have a number of external
uses, though it did not promise them, simply because it *was* good; and that it was
necessarily the source of benefits to society, great and diversified in proportion
to its own intrinsic excellence' (p. 160).   [2] Ibid., pp. xxxiv, xxxvi.

an independent university which benefits society by cultivating the individual intellects of its members. In the former the controlling considerations are broadly conceived social needs and education is shaped and corrected on a utilitarian calculus. In Newman's ideal university liberal knowledge must be studied and taught as good in itself, but it does not lack a point of reference. 'Utility may be made the end of education, in two respects: either as regards the individual educated, or the community at large.'[1] A liberal education has this in common with Newman's vision of Christianity, that it approaches its object not in the first place through the community at large, the institutional structure of society, but in the first place by its effect on, by its transformation of, the individual mind.

Why, for example, must liberal education refuse to be informed by any end outside itself? Because, for Newman, as education becomes more and more dominated by ends determined outside the university it loses its freedom, its variety, its comprehensiveness, and, above all, its vision of unity. When a university has lost these qualities it loses as well the power to impart them. 'I only say that Knowledge, in proportion as it tends more and more to be particular, ceases to be Knowledge.'[2] As knowledge becomes more and more specialized, more practical, it helps us to exercise more control over the reality which surrounds us, but as individuals become more specialized they lose the unique internal balance which only a liberal education provides.

The way in which it affects the mind of the student determines for Newman the structure of his university education. For this reason he does not think of liberal knowledge as a collection of facts and theories about the physical and human worlds but as 'an acquired illumination', 'a habit', an 'inward endowment'. He regrets that the English language does not possess 'some definite word to express, simply and generally, intellectual proficiency or perfection, such as "health", as used with reference to the animal frame, and "virtue", with reference to our moral nature'.[3] It has been suggested that what Newman needs is

---

[1] *The Idea of a University*, p. 142.   [2] Ibid., pp. 99–100.
[3] Ibid., pp. 100, 110.

Matthew Arnold's term 'Culture',[1] but in the absence of such a word he calls the 'perfection or virtue of the intellect by the name of philosophy, philosophical knowledge, enlargement of mind, or illumination'. It is a condition of being, 'something individual and permanent', rather than a process. 'When, then, we speak of the communication of Knowledge as being Education, we thereby imply that Knowledge is a state or condition of mind.' And this state of mind seems to Newman 'an object as intelligible as the cultivation of virtue, while, at the same time, it is absolutely distinct from it'.[2]

Enlargement of mind takes place not so much by the reception of previous unknown facts,

but in the mind's energetic and simultaneous action upon and towards and among those new ideas, which are rushing in upon it. It is the action of a formative power, reducing to order and meaning the matter of our acquirements; it is a making the objects of our knowledge subjectively our own, or, to use a familiar word, it is a digestion of what we receive, into the substance of our previous state of thought; and without this no enlargement is said to follow.

As always, Newman sees the educated mind as active, ordering, driving towards conclusions, reconciling antinomies, and relating what was unknown to what is known. Like the Illative Sense, the philosophic mind is personal and contemplative rather than public and expressive. Its fullness is realized only by itself, and yet 'to have even a portion of this illuminative reason and true philosophy is the highest state to which nature can aspire in the way of intellect'.[3]

At the end of his eighth discourse Newman shows us how a mind possessed of this 'true philosophy' manifests itself in ordinary social life. This is his celebrated portrait of a gentleman, his

---

[1] Raymond Williams, *Culture and Society, 1780–1950* (London, 1958), pp. 115–16, 127–8.

[2] *The Idea of a University*, pp. 111, 101, 108. Newman gives as his aim, 'to open the mind, to correct it, to refine it, to enable it to know, and to digest, master, rule, and use its knowledge, to give it power over its own faculties, application, flexibility, method, critical exactness, sagacity, resource, address, eloquent expression' (ibid., p. 108).

[3] Ibid., pp. 118–19, 122.

ideal product of his ideal university, representing in social behaviour the effects of 'acquired illumination'.

And the first thing we notice about the gentleman is his
sweetness and flexibility, his willingness, almost his need to shape
his actions to the circumstances and personalities among which he
finds himself. His perfect mental balance does not take the form
of an imperturbable and stoic indifference, but of a complete and
generous attentiveness and interest. He is 'tender', 'gentle',
'merciful', 'patient, forbearing, and resigned'. But when the
situation demands he can be 'as simple as he is forcible, and as
brief, as he is decisive'. He 'throws himself into the minds of his
opponents', he 'respects piety and devotion', he possesses 'the
gentleness and effeminacy of feeling, which is the attendant on
civilization'.[1]

The passivity of the gentleman, a quality which has been often
noticed and criticized, is not a passivity of indifference or scepticism, but what may be called a passivity of assent. Newman's
gentleman accepts without protest the universal conditions of
human life: 'he submits to pain, because it is inevitable, to bereave-
ment, because it is irreparable, and to death because it is his
destiny'.[2] His stillness in the face of these conditions does not
represent an absence of sensibility but a high achievement of the
intellect, a quiescence almost Socratic, which comes not from
ignorance but from penetration, not from obtusity but from
comprehension. And this penetration and comprehension make
it impossible for the gentleman, even if he is not a Christian, to be
an enemy of religion. There is more than a hint that his acquiescence in conditions he cannot alter precludes, to say the least, any
note of defiance in his attitude towards their dispensation.

The gentleman manifests the virtues of a liberal education, but
of course these are not the highest virtues in Newman's scale of
values, nor does the gentleman represent his ultimate ideal of
human character.[3] His sweetness, his impulse to assent, makes the

---

[1] *The Idea of a University*, pp. 185–6.   [2] Ibid., p. 186.

[3] For the gentleman's limitations see William E. Buckler, 'Newman's "Apologia" as Human Experience', *Thought*, xxxix (1964), pp. 78–9; C. F. Harrold,
John Henry Newman, pp. 113–17; and James Collins (ed.), *Philosophical Readings*

gentleman sympathetic to Christianity but it does not necessarily make him that very particular and, for Newman, not always refined being, a Christian.

In Newman's philosophy of mind a liberal education, though it enables its possessor to handle most subject matters with propriety and discipline and most social situations with grace and economy, remains nevertheless liable to those epistemological limitations characteristic of all human endeavour not informed by Christian dogma. This point can perhaps be best illustrated by the following passage from *The Idea of a University*, a passage in which Newman at once celebrates and qualifies the range of liberal knowledge:

That prefection of the Intellect, which is the result of Education, and its *beau ideal*, to be imparted to individuals in their respective measures, is the clear, calm, accurate vision and comprehension of all things, as far as the finite mind can embrace them, each in its place, and with its own characteristics upon it. It is almost prophetic from its knowledge of history; it is almost heart-searching from its knowledge of human nature; it has almost supernatural charity from its freedom from littleness and prejudice; it has almost the repose of faith, because nothing can startle it; it has almost the beauty and harmony of heavenly contemplation, so intimate is it with the eternal order of things and the music of the spheres.[1]

Newman said in 1852 that *The Idea of a University* was one of his two most perfect works artistically.[2] The repetition of 'almost' in this passage, the tolling of a philosophical knell, consigns the highest aims of a liberal education to what is at best a kind of spiritual hopefulness, characteristic of the gentleman himself, reserving the true perceptive power, the transcendent vision, for those whose minds are informed by Christian truth. Years later, in *The Grammar of Assent*, Newman speaks kindly of 'what is called, with a special appositeness, a gentleman's knowledge'.

in *Cardinal Newman* (Chicago, 1961), Section xix, n. 2, p. 421; but also John R. Griffin, 'In Defence of Newman's "Gentleman"', *Dublin Review*, ccxxxix (1965), 245–54.
[1] *The Idea of a University*, p. 123.
[2] The other is *The Present Position of Catholics*. See *Letters and Diaries*, xv. 226.

But he observes that 'it is never more than the furniture of the mind, as I have called it; it never is thoroughly assimilated with it.'[1]

LIBERAL KNOWLEDGE AND CHRISTIANITY: BEYOND THE SECULAR IDEAL

'If we pursue liberal knowledge as a kind of mental gymnastic, a mere exercise of the mind', asks Dwight Culler, 'are we not in danger of sacrificing the power which knowledge has of placing us in communion with reality?' He goes on to give what is certainly the right answer to his question, that liberal knowledge offers the intellect a perception of 'the rational character of reality' as well as providing the means to its own enlargement.[2] In other words, as David DeLaura puts it in his fine comparative study, 'the task of the critical intelligence, for Arnold, is "to see the object as in itself it really is"; for Newman, university training teaches the individual "to see things as they are"'.[3] For Newman the marriage of the philosophic mind to its subject-matter is indeed the exercise of a power, a power of perception which has been celebrated by philosophers and poets from Plato to Wordsworth as a virtue in itself, perhaps the greatest of virtues and the greatest of powers. When Newman celebrates it, however, his readers, especially Platonic or Wordsworthian readers, must guard themselves against the assumption that his admiration is simple or unqualified. Before beginning a close examination of what it means in Newman's philosophy of mind to 'see things as they are', we might look more closely at the way in which liberal knowledge is imparted by his ideal university.

In *The Idea of a University* Newman splendidly projects the growth of mental powers in the student, but the only subject-matter he treats with sustained enthusiasm is theology. The general effect of a careful reading of the work, I think, is to reduce one's sense of the external importance of what is being taught.

---

[1] *The Grammar of Assent*, p. 42.   [2] *The Imperial Intellect*, pp. 216, 219.
[3] David J. DeLaura, 'Matthew Arnold and John Henry Newman: The "Oxford Sentiment" and the Religion of the future', *Texas Studies in Literature and Language*, vi (Supplement 1965), 625.

I suspect—though it is impossible to prove—that Newman carefully shaped the lectures so that they would have this effect. For if the arts and sciences are viewed primarily as exercises for the development of the student's mental powers, then the importance within the university of their external reality, the objective truth of their discoveries, maxims, and principles, is lowered. Students do not attend a university to learn specific truths, or a number of mere facts, but to receive mental culture. A student may in a course in geology hear claims which appear to conflict with assertions in Genesis. But if he and his teachers regard geology not primarily as providing a description of reality but primarily as a mental discipline, much of the force of its apparent conflict with Genesis is deflected. Geology, as a branch of liberal knowledge, is studied 'for its own sake', for the sake, that is, of its enlarging effect upon the student's mind. We do not study geology for what it tells us about our poor place in the universe, not so that we act upon what we learn, certainly not so that we equate it with that other sort of knowledge which in Newman's view comes to us not from the professor but from the priest, not in the lecture-hall but in the church, and which we properly receive not for its own sake, for the enlargement of our minds, but for the glory of God and the salvation of our souls.

It may be said of Newman that he regards knowledge as dangerous when it becomes utilitarian. Knowledge becomes more than the 'furniture of the mind' when we begin to act upon it, when we exercise it towards some end external to itself, when, in order to act, we must assume and depend upon its truth. Obviously Newman holds that the most useful knowledge a man can possess is a knowledge of Catholic doctrine. If the Catholic is devout he will not regard Revelation as liberal knowledge, but, as we have seen in the discussion of *The Tamworth Reading Room*, will act upon it as the means of his salvation.

Partly because Catholic doctrine must be viewed as useful knowledge, or at least because to regard it primarily as an exercise for the enlargement of the mind approaches dangerously near to a merely subjective religion, Newman had great difficulty in finding the proper place for theology in his circle of sciences. In a letter of 1852, after writing his first lecture, he announces that he will 'treat the whole subject, not on the assumption of Catholicism, but in the way of reasoning, and as men of all religions may do'. A few months later, sensing the Irish hostility to a university constructed in 'the way of reasoning', Newman sent John Dalgairns one of the several introductions he drafted for *The Idea of a University*. In the accompanying letter Newman admits that he fears '*perplexing* men, and making them suspect something by a laboured Introduction'. The object of a university is to teach 'all knowledge' and since the 'subject matter of *faith* comes into the idea of "all knowledge"' a university must teach the faith.[1] By this neat syllogism he appears to mean that theology will be taught but will not dominate or control the circle of the sciences. In his original fifth discourse he suggests that since the Catholic creed is philosophically true a university which is not Catholic must be hostile to philosophy. But on the way to making this point he gives the impression that the secular disciplines will be indirectly dominated, if not immediately controlled, by the pervasive influence of the Church. After his resignation from the university, Newman omitted his original Discourse V from the edition of 1859, thus removing a confusion and preserving at once the intellectual freedom, the 'liberal' or autonomous quality of his idea of education.[2] He realized that to govern the other sciences with theology, to teach students primarily those subjects and facts which would benefit them spiritually, would give a utilitarian quality to the entire educational process.

In addition, to make theology queen of the sciences would be to court the danger of rebellion. Perhaps Newman feared that once theology began to claim a special power over and intimacy with truth, other disciplines might insist that they too were not primarily exercises for mental enlargement, but capable of presenting truths which must be acted upon, which deserve to influence other sciences, and which affect theology herself.

---

[1] *Letters and Diaries*, xv. 67, 134.

[2] See Harrold's preface to *The Idea of a University*, p. viii. After 1859, and in most available editions, the fifth stands as the discourse defining liberal knowledge, discussed as such in the preceding section.

In order to take a place in the circle of sciences, each discipline must offer, as its epistemological credentials, a unique approach to reality. In illustration of this point Newman argues that theology can demand a place among the sciences only if God is more than nature. If He is not, then physical science may claim to be the measure of reality; it may assume that the phenomena it deals with comprehend God:

If the Supreme Being is powerful or skilful, just so far forth as the telescope shows power, and the microscope shows skill, if His moral law is to be ascertained simply by the physical processes of the animal frame, or His will gathered from the immediate issues of human affairs, if His Essence is just as high and deep and broad and long as the universe, and no more; if this be the fact, then will I confess that there is no specific science about God, that theology is but a name, and a protest in its behalf a hypocrisy. Then is He but coincident with the laws of the universe; then is He but a function, or correlative, or subjective reflection and mental impression, of each phenomenon of the material or moral world, as it flits before us. Then, pious as it is to think of Him, while the pageant of experiment or abstract reasoning passes by, still, such piety is nothing more than a poetry of thought or an ornament of language, and has not even an infinitesimal influence upon philosophy or science, of which it is rather the parasitical production.[1]

But physical science does not comprehend the nature of God. In one of his 'Occasional Lectures' delivered to the university, Newman maintains that of the three great subjects of the human reason, God, nature, and man, theology is the study of God, literature of man, and science of nature. Theology excepted, literature and science together 'nearly constitute the subject-matter of Liberal Education'. Of 'the two injuries, which Revealed Truth sustains', literature subserves its corruption and science its exclusion.[2]

As has already been observed, Newman asserts that 'Revelation and Physical Science cannot really come into collision'. But I am now concerned with his intention in *The Idea of a University* to separate the various disciplines so that they do not usurp each other's proper function in imparting philosophical knowledge.

[1] Ibid., pp. 34–5.   [2] Ibid., p. 194.

Just as Newman fears that reasoning can undermine the habit of assent in the individual mind by addressing itself to questions it is quite unsuited to answer, so in the structure of his liberal education he wishes to limit the exercise of scientific investigation, in which reason is master, to the study of nature. Newman sees that to certain questions both science and theology could provide an answer and that these answers would appear to conflict. He gives an example of such a question in his ninth discourse: a 'philosopher' or scientist asks the cause of certain volcanoes and 'is impatient at being told it is "the divine vengeance"'. The theologian asks the cause of the overthrow of the guilty cities 'and is preposterously referred to the volcanic action still visible in their neighbourhood'. Newman goes on to point out that 'The inquiry into final causes for the moment passes over the existence of established laws; the inquiry into physical, passes over for the moment the existence of God. In other words, physical science is in a certain sense atheistic, for the very reason it is not theology.'[1]

A problem of causality clearly lies at the heart of Newman's sense of the limitations of science. In my second chapter I discussed his awareness of the faults, shortcomings, and failures characteristic of all rational calculi or 'economies' in connection with his view of the epistemological limitations of the human mind. When we examine Newman's conception of the role of physical science, however, we must eventually go beyond his idea of the human mind and examine certain of his assumptions as to the relation of spiritual reality to physical.

In the sermon which became famous in the Kingsley controversy, 'Wisdom and Innocence' (1843), Newman speaks of the resistance men have developed to the idea of Providential interposition in the affairs of the world.[2] Such men resemble the scientist who dismissed the idea that the *cause* of the destruction of the guilty cities was divine vengeance. In the third discourse of *The Idea of a University* Newman creates an important extended analogy to illustrate the effect of omitting theology from the university curriculum. He supposes that a system of scientific

---

[1] *The Idea of a University*, pp. 314, 196.
[2] *Sermons on Subjects of the Day*, p. 307.

education is being organized which cannot take account of the
agency of man in the material universe. Only physical and
mechanical causes will be treated: 'volition is a forbidden subject'. A prospectus is put out containing a list of sciences to be
taught and explaining the omission of 'the mind and its powers'.
The prospectus explains that after long and anxious thought it
has been deemed impracticable to include in the list of lectures
the 'Philosophy of mind'. Although 'hitherto intelligence and
volition were accounted real powers', the professor in this supposed educational endeavour cannot take account of them. When
a stone flies from a hand, the will of the thrower is not a 'motive
principle' in his science. 'He ascribes every work, every external
act of man, to the innate force or soul of the physical universe.'
Moral action must be regarded merely as part of the physical
universe. The professor examines the domestic arrangements of
a private family, its clothing, furniture, food:

what would become of them, he asks, but for the laws of physical
nature? Those laws are the causes of our carpets, our furniture, our
travelling and our social intercourse. Firm stitches have a natural
power, in proportion to the toughness of the material adopted, to keep
together separate portions of cloth; sofas and chairs could not turn up-
side down, even if they would; and it is a property of caloric to relax
the fibres of animal matter, acting through water in one way, through
oil in another, and this is the whole mystery of the most elaborate
cuisine.[1]

The significance of the analogy is obvious. Exclude the study
of God from the circle of the sciences and your education must
be absurdly limited. Let the scientist or philosopher insist that
material phenomena rest *exclusively* upon physical causes, then
Newman tells him, '*Ne sutor ultra crepidam*: he is making his
particular craft usurp and occupy the universe.' But readers
familiar with Newman's later work will realize that his choice
of an analogy, the omission of human will from the study of
nature, is highly significant. In terms of the analogy, human
volition as an agency in the natural world resembles the exercise

---

[1] *The Idea of a University*, pp. 49–51.

of God's will in the temporal universe. Physical science, in Newman's opinion, can explain neither human volition nor divine will. The Hindus believed that the earth stands upon a tortoise, but the physicist does not ask by what external influence the universe is sustained. Of physical science Newman writes: 'With matter it began, with matter it will end; it will never trespass into the province of mind.'[1]

But what becomes of this assertion if there is no fundamental distinction between the laws which bind matter and those by which the mind functions? Newman's position assumes that mind and matter move on different principles. Writing in 1869 to Charles Meynall, who was helping him with the theology of the *Grammar of Assent*, Newman asks, 'Am I right in thinking that you wish me to infer matter as a *cause* from phenomena as an *effect*, from *my own view* of cause and effect. But in *my own view* cause is *Will*; how can matter be *Will*?'[2]

The question suggests that Newman did not completely grasp, or else rejected, the arguments on the freedom of the will in Mill's *Logic*, which he possessed in the edition of 1851. Mill asserts that 'to my apprehension, a volition is not an efficient, but simply a physical cause. Our will causes our bodily actions in the same sense, and in no other, in which cold causes ice, or a spark causes an explosion of gunpowder.' He refuses to grant that 'our consciousness of volition contains in itself any *a priori* knowledge that the muscular motion will follow'. Men conceive of volition as the only source of action from an illusory but 'spontaneous tendency of the intellect to account to itself for all cases of causation by assimilating them to the intentional acts of voluntary agents like itself'. The strength of this theory, however, does not arise from rational proof but 'in its affinity to an obstinate tendency of the infancy of the human mind'.[3]

---

[1] *The Idea of a University*, pp. 53, 312.
[2] *Philosophical Readings in Cardinal Newman*, pp. 119-200.
[3] J. S. Mill, *A System of Logic*, 3rd edition (London, 1851), i. 361, 362, 365-6. In a note among the Birmingham papers Newman comments: 'Mill denies (vol. i, p. 360) that volition and its effect is more than an instance of physical antecedent and consequent, as fire warming. But whether it *ought* or not to do nothing more than give birth to the latter idea, the question is whether in fact it does not

Newman makes precisely the assumption which Mill attacks, but instead of rejecting that 'spontaneous tendency of the intellect' and 'the obstinate tendency of the infancy of the human mind' as irrelevant, he employs them as proofs. That causation must be will, Newman argues in the *Grammar*, we infer analogically from what we know of ourselves. The infant early perceives the connection between willing and doing, so that the notion of causation is one of the first lessons of experience. And the child does not ascribe this process to unconscious physical objects, but limits it to 'agents possessed of intelligence and will'. Thus children beat the ground after falling; they imply that what has hurt them has, like them, intelligence. Similarly, the force of this analogical reasoning may be seen 'wherever the world is young' in the primitive attribution of the movements and changes of nature to the will of hidden agents.[1]

But, Newman continues, as man grows more sophisticated he achieves another view of the physical universe; our analogical reasoning causes another and more serious error. Because we always will before we act, we discover invariable antecedents and consequents. Eventually we begin to think of the former as causes of the latter even when intelligence and volition are lacking. We 'confuse causation with order'. This is an error because nothing in our experience supports it. Cause must be 'effective will', for we have no true experience of any other source. Natural laws are not causes; they are not even experiences; they are 'more or less probable hypotheses'. Even the most accurate law is not a cause, but a description. Laws do not alter only so long as the will which governs them, which *causes* the sequence of events they describe, does not alter.[2]

suggest to the mind the idea of power and causation. Would he deny that we *had* the idea of efficient causation? How would *he* say that we got it?'

[1] *Grammar of Assent*, p. 51. The analogy between human will and God's will, which Newman considers a pregnant one, suggests the interrelation between his psychology and his theology. One reason for my constant use of the rather difficult word 'epistemology' is that its significance includes the necessary vertical range, from the depths of the human unconscious to the sublimity of divine volition, the range, in fact, of Newman's speculations on the nature of *mind*.

[2] Ibid., pp. 52–5. Newman summarizes this argument in a letter to William Froude in 1879. He writes that he sees no ground in reason or experience on which

When Wilfred Ward visited Newman in 1885, the old man amused himself and his guest by speaking of the connection between miracles and volition. Newman picked up a paper knife and pushed his ink-stand with it, claiming that by an exercise of his will he had interfered with the laws of nature. If one believes in the existence of God it is little enough to grant, he went on, that He can do what man can do, 'and yet, so far as we know, a miracle amounts to no more than this'. Wilfred Ward pointed out that, according to the 'phenomenist school', Newman's very act of will is due to physical conditions in his brain and that by moving the ink-stand he was merely conforming to the laws of nature, not interfering with them. Newman seemed a trifle irritated and said, according to Ward, 'I only contend that what man can do God can do'.[1]

Ward wished to suggest to Newman that his sensation of free choice or volition may be illusory and that, to use Mill's phrase, volition may be merely a 'physical cause'. Newman's impatience, however, does not mean that he was ignorant of the argument, or had not tried to counter it. In a letter to R. H. Hutton in 1872 he explains again his dislike of abstract categories and analysis, this time in connection with the freedom of the will. 'Proof in concrete matter does not lie, so to say, on one line, as the stages of a racecourse, as it *does* in abstract, but is made up of momenta converging from various directions, the joint force of which no analytical expression can represent.' Taken in its fullness, each 'moment', each reality or experience is unique and cannot be categorized for use in abstract analysis. 'Nor is this the only case in which logic or science move in a different medium from the living mind. Mr. Mill aims at showing there can be no real freedom of the will, but he does so on a mere logical analysis

to base the common conclusion that the laws of nature are invariable and uniform. Nor can laws be causes, but are only formulae under which large orderings of phenomena are represented (Ward, ii. 587). However, Newman had long known that in assuming the existence of natural laws, scientists agree that 'the great agencies in the material system are invisible, and that what is visible is deceptive' ('Faith and Experience', 1838, *Sermons on Subjects of the Day*, p. 65).

[1] Ward, ii. 494–5.

of the antecedents of its action.'[1] Thus Newman argues for the
freedom of the will by asserting the uniqueness of reality, its
irreducibility to category. Freedom of the will depends, according
to this argument, upon the mind's ability to grasp this uniqueness and to treat it with originality. To grant that the mind
possesses this power is to make nonsense of a logical analysis of
thought aimed at disproving the freedom of the will.

And this strength of perception is what Newman's university
ideally enables its students to enlarge: 'The philosophy of an
imperial intellect, for such I am considering a University to be, is
based, not so much on simplification as on discrimination.' The
university recognizes that each reality or experience must be
finally regarded as peculiar to itself and that the 'constituent
parts' of the universe 'admit indeed of comparison and adjust-
ment, but not of fusion'. For this reason the 'true representative'
of a university 'defines rather than analyses', viewing each object
as clearly as he can, denying none of its reality simply in order to
place it in an abstract category or in order to use it in abstract
analysis. 'He takes things as they are; he submits to them all, as
far as they go.'[2] The perceptive power which comes with liberal
knowledge frees the mind from the dullness of abstract patterns
and enables it to respond with originality to realities correspond-
ingly original.

All this is not to suggest that Newman's argument for the
freedom of the will contains no difficulties or confusions, just as
Mill's opposing theories do. What is of primary interest here,
however, is the relation of Newman's defence of free will to his
conception of a liberal education. Liberal knowledge heightens
the student's ability not so much to reason but to perceive.
Newman had believed for some time that 'Anyone can reason;
only disciplined, educated, formed minds can perceive'.[3] But if
this is granted, how is it that the effect upon Newman's student

[1] Quoted in Boekraad and Tristram, *The Argument from Conscience*, pp. 196–7.
The reference could be either to J. S. Mill's *Logic* or to his father's doctrine of
association.

[2] 'Christianity and Scientific Investigation' (1855), *The Idea of a University*,
p. 337.

[3] Letter of 1843, Mozley, ii. 409–10.

of defining rather than analysing, of discriminating rather than simplifying, is not a sense of disorder and fragmentation but of order and unity? Why is it that the student does not graduate with a sense of a multitude of unrelated perceptions?

The student receives his impression of unity because ultimately, at its source, existence for Newman is unified. Each perception, each reality when grasped in its fullness, points back to its origin, to God. As Newman argues in the *Grammar*, since we have no experience of causation other than 'effective will', by means of analogy we can detect will operating through all of nature:

> The agency then which has kept up and keeps up the general laws of nature, energizing at once in Sirius and on the earth, and on the earth in its primary period as well as in the nineteenth century, must be Mind, and nothing else, and Mind at least as wide and as enduring in its living action, as the immeasurable ages and spaces of the universe on which that agency has left its traces.[1]

The magnificent sentence was written nearly twenty years after the first university discourses, but it was nevertheless his belief in a transcendent Mind governing the universe which gave Newman confidence in the ultimate unity of knowledge, a unity not unlike Bacon's *philosophia prima*, the trunk from which the branches of knowledge spring.[2] Like Bacon's, Newman's mind has an urgent drive towards wholeness, towards the idea of unity. When, however, Newman uses the word 'idea' in *The Idea of a University*, he wishes to denote a vast, often apparently heterogeneous complex. The idea comprehends the organization and transmission of 'all' knowledge, and like the essential unity of Christian doctrine, the 'idea' in the *Essay on Development*, the unity of all knowledge cannot be apprehended directly by any individual mind. The subject-matter of liberal knowledge includes every variety and aspect of existence from the 'Divine

[1] *Grammar of Assent*, p. 56. No doubt Newman here employs ideas closely related to the argument from design, which he rejects as a convincing proof of God's existence. But he simply infers the presence of 'Mind' in nature and not such divine attributes as justice or mercy.

[2] For an excellent discussion of Newman's debt to Bacon see Culler, *The Imperial Intellect*, pp. 173–88.

Essence' down to our own emotions, from 'the most solemn appointments of the Lord' down to 'the accident of the hour'.

Now, is it not wonderful that, with all its capabilities, the human mind cannot take in this whole vast fact at a single glance, or gain possession of it at once. Like a short-sighted reader, its eye pores closely, and travels slowly, over the awful volume which lies open for its inspection. Or again, as we deal with some huge structure of many parts and sides, the mind goes round about it, noting down, first one thing, then another, as it best may, and viewing it under different aspects, by way of making progress towards mastering the whole. So by degrees and by circuitous advances does it rise aloft and subject to itself a knowledge of that universe into which it has been born. These various partial views or abstractions, by means of which the mind looks out upon its object, are called sciences.[1]

From various glimpses of existence, glimpses given from the different viewpoints of the various sciences, the mind of the student begins to reflect the unity of creation. He gains some insight into the architecture of the universe, social and spiritual as well as physical. 'Not to know the relative disposition of things is the state of slaves or children; to have mapped out the Universe is the boast, or at least the ambition, of philosophy.'[2] But from their increasing specialization, their narrowing prospect, most men have lost 'a philosophical comprehensiveness, and orderly expansiveness, an elastic constructiveness' because they have lost the idea of unity:

An idea, a view, an indivisible object, which does not admit of more or less, a form, which cannot coalesce with anything else, an intellectual principle, expanding into a consistent harmonious whole,—in short, Mind, in the true sense of the word,—they are, forsooth, too practical to lose time in such reveries![3]

[1] *The Idea of a University*, p. 41. It is interesting to compare this passage with the more complicated one from the *Essay on Development* in which Newman argues that 'all the aspects of an idea are capable of coalition, and of a resolution into the object to which it belongs; and the *primâ facie* dissimilitude of its aspects becomes, when explained, an argument for its substantiveness and integrity, and their multiplicity for its originality and power' (p. 32). See also *The Idea of a University*, p. 368.   [2] Ibid., p. 100.

[3] Ibid., p. 393. This passage comes from the original fifth discourse which was omitted from the 1859 edition.

Clearly Newman's idea of Mind is almost synonymous with his idea of unity. Both are religious; and his intention of imparting this idea of unity and this idea of mind in a university education, despite what seem to be his claims to the contrary, cannot be viewed as strictly secular. The 'philosophical knowledge' or enlargement of mind which he expects a liberal education to impart reflects his vision of existence as essentially unified by Mind, the transcendent Will, or God.

In a letter to W. G. Ward in 1859, Newman writes of the intimate analogy between divine faith, faith granted by God, and human faith, faith reached by the human mind's free exercise. Using the relationship of divine faith to human faith as an analogy, Newman goes on to indicate how the 'enlargement of mind', the 'philosophical knowledge' of a university education, might vastly transcend the claims he made on the gentleman's behalf:

Human faith lies *in* the intellect as well as Divine faith; but the former is created there by previous acts of mere human reason, the latter is the creation of supernatural grace. Why then may there not be a 'Divine *philosophy*' or largeness and comprehensiveness of mind on all objects Divine and human, proceeding from grace and begotten of a spiritual taste or connaturality with their true worth and real place in God's sight, as well as a Divine faith? And how will it not be analogous or parallel to intellectual philosophy, as Divine faith is parallel to human faith? and how will it fail to react upon sanctity and charity, and exalt them . . . ?[1]

It is not necessary to attribute to *The Idea of a University* a pedagogical aim which its author specifically denies, an intention to prejudice the students of the university in favour of the truth of Christianity. At the same time we can recognize the implied inference that if enlargement of mind enables one to apprehend truth in its many forms and in the unity behind the forms, and if Christianity is true and its Author the Source of that unity, then the recipients of a liberal education may well find Christianity congenial. In the letter to Ward, Newman writes of 'Divine *philosophy*' as deriving from a 'spiritual taste', by which he appears

[1] Ward, i. 638.

to mean the ability to ascertain the place and worth in God's sight of objects of study. We may observe in passing that if one wished to establish a university which would be pleasing to God, a 'divine philosophy' would be of considerable value in setting up and administering a curriculum.

Shaped by a liberal education, then, the student's mind in its measure reflects the essential unity of existence. Philosophical knowledge is at least analogous to that divine philosophy which seeks to understand the aspects of existence, the various sciences, in relation to God's intention, His Will in the universe, His Mind. This is not to say that a liberal education aims at this divine philosophy. Newman allows that his gentleman could be a 'mere philosopher'. Still, the perception of unity in creation must move the perceiver towards a religious position. Conversely, the specialist who, for example, refuses to allow the agency of effective volition in the material world blinds himself to the apprehension of unity and moves in the direction of atheism.

To relate the discussion briefly to Catholic doctrine, primarily for the sake of clarification, let us ask what Newman would have made of Augustine's definition of charity in relation to his ideal of liberal education:

I call 'charity' the motion of the soul toward the enjoyment of God for His own sake, and the enjoyment of one's self and one's neighbor for the sake of God; but 'cupidity' is a motion of the soul toward the enjoyment of one's self, one's neighbor, or any corporal thing for the sake of something other than God.[1]

How, if liberal knowledge is its own end, does it escape the charge of 'cupidity?' Even granting what is certainly true, that Newman distinctly insists that in order to be morally and religiously as well as intellectually complete a man must have dogmatic Christian knowledge in addition to liberal knowledge, how can the pursuit of knowledge for its own sake be justified to an Augustinian, or to those Roman Catholics who in 1852 objected,

[1] St. Augustine, *On Christian Doctrine*, trans. D. W. Robertson, Jr. (Indianapolis and New York, 1958), p. 88.

and to those who still object, to what became known as the 'philosophy of severance?'

After Newman omitted his original fifth discourse from the 1859 edition of *The Idea of a University*, his justification, which is that liberal education is a temporal ideal, perhaps a secular answer to liberalism, may well make Augustinians uncomfortable. But in his letter to Ward and in the omitted discourse we have seen that the ideal was not, in his mind, divorced from religion, that he tends to assume that as the mind reflects the unity of existence it must be moving towards a religious position. In a cancelled introduction to *The Idea of a University*, Newman reacts to an assertion made by Joseph Gordon that a Catholic university cannot be a temporal ideal, that its primary purpose must be to educate men for God. The introduction states as the author's intention,

1. That he does not profess to treat *here* of the *indirect effects* of University Education
2. These are *religious*.
3. He proposes to treat of them in their place.
4. But he is speaking of the *direct end* of a University.
5. This end is *Knowledge*, in a large sense of the word, or cultivation of mind, as such.[1]

In seeking to impart an idea of unity, the indirect effect of university education, Newman divorced liberal knowledge from any end outside itself, from knowledge cultivated 'either for secular objects or for eternal'. Indeed, Newman argues, 'For all its friends, or its enemies, may say, I insist upon it, that it is as real a mistake to burden it with virtue or religion as with the mechanical arts.'[2] He clearly saw that a university conducted primarily for moral or theological objects would lose its variety and comprehensiveness and with them the apprehension of unity.

All of Newman's philosophy of mind points towards this religious idea of unity. We are familiar with his conviction that the human mind is made for truth, and that through the

[1] *Letters and Diaries*, xv. 130-1.
[2] *The Idea of a University*, pp. 102, 106.

perception of different aspects of truth the mind can apprehend the unity of an idea. Let one approach to truth, such as physical science, or one method of perceiving it, such as reason, claim complete and exclusive validity and the mind begins to err, to alienate itself from the multifarious unity of existence. But give the mind the opportunity for real catholicity in its education, an education which comprehends the validity of all experience, experience of love and fear as of reason and logic, and the mind begins to reflect the essential unity of creation and its source. The university of Newman's vision leads its students to that quiescence he called liberal knowledge, knowledge which, like the ultimate unity it reflects, is its own end.

In *The Tamworth Reading Room*, then, Newman argues that secular education cannot equip its students with virtue. No adequate morality, he insists, can be inferred by science from the physical universe; and literature, the history of the natural man, tends to induce a moral passivity because it arouses emotions without providing a field for action.

Nevertheless, Newman believes that a liberal education can provide society with refined and cultured citizens, citizens for whom he saw a special need in the Roman Catholic community. Liberal education is not, however, the source of useful religious or economic information; it functions free from immediate religious and social objectives. A liberal education leads directly neither to salvation nor to social progress. To the extent that the intellectual life in a university is uninformed by Christian dogma, liberal education bears an affinity to liberalism. But because liberal knowledge is pursued for its own sake and the subjects studied are to be regarded primarily as exercises for the enlargement of mind, the danger that a single science will attempt to dominate the university is obviated. The circle of sciences in Newman's university are intended to have a collective action on the minds of its students. Philosophical knowledge, the aim of the university curriculum, is neither revealed truth nor a body of scientific fact but a state of mind, a state of mind which possessed by its citizens must raise the cultural tone of society. In this a university education acts analogously to Christianity, approaching its objects through the individual mind rather than through the structure of society.

But unlike religious teaching, liberal education aims at producing a condition of mind which is its own end. Each science, Newman thought, should provide an approach to the ultimate unity of existence, enabling the mind to perceive truth in the only way it can, through various aspects of the whole. The mind informed by the study of these aspects or sciences, none of which can consider itself complete or exclusive, finally reflects in its degree the unity which informs them all, and, given this essentially religious apprehension, transcends the social ideal.

CHAPTER FIVE

Conversion: Newman's Philosophy of Mind in his Novels and Autobiography

It is in thee, my mind, that I measure times. Interrupt me not, that is, interrupt not thyself with the tumults of thy impressions. In thee I measure times; the impression, which things as they pass by cause in thee, remains even when they are gone; this it is which still present, I measure, not the things which pass by to make this impression. This I measure, when I measure times.

(ST. AUGUSTINE, *Confessions*, translated by E. B. Pusey)

Loss and Gain, Callista, and the *Apologia pro Vita Sua* each represent in a different context, but with a basic similarity of pattern, the process of conversion. Newman's profound interest in the psychology of belief engaged him in a variety of attempts to discover how convictions and alliances are altered. His philosophy of mind therefore provides an important approach—I think the most important approach—to the interpretation of these more dramatic and personal works.

With the novels and the carefully structured *Apologia,* however, the problems of interpretation are complicated and enriched by their very drama and personality. Questions of aesthetics arise which so far I have considered only indirectly. In fact, the virtues of aesthetic appeal, the power which beauty in its various forms exercises over the mind, is a theme central to the three books. Callista abandons the lucidity and elegance of her Greek paganism, her Hellenic intellectual universe, to suffer a revolting martyrdom. Charles Reding and John Henry Newman leave their gentle friends and good families, perhaps most reluctantly of all their beloved Oxford, to seek the comparative obscurity and monotony of a Roman Catholic priesthood. Each of the converts resists an aesthetic appeal which seems to be largely on the side of the position he gives up. When he has learned to hold his own against the arguments of the establishment and has faced separation from his friends and family, the convert's trial consists in setting himself against the beauty, order, and sweetness of the life he is leaving.

A potential convert, for Newman, is someone seeking the truth, or, more exactly, the authority which can transmit the truth to him. Charles Reding and Callista eventually recognize that the aesthetic appeals of Anglicanism and Hellenism in no way derive from the sanctity of their authority. In Newman's epistemology the perception of beauty and the realisation of religious truth are disparate intellectual actions. We have seen in *The Idea of a University* that he sharply distinguishes adherence to dogma from liberal knowledge. A knowledge of dogma is spiritually useful but liberal knowledge is pursued for its own sake. A university, Newman warns in his ninth discourse, may grow antagonistic to dogma because liberal knowledge has a tendency to impress us with 'a mere philosophical theory of life and conduct, in the place of Revelation'. He goes on to make his basic distinction between the two types of knowledge, a distinction dramatized in both his novels: 'Truth has two attributes—beauty and power; and while Useful Knowledge is the possession of truth as powerful, Liberal Knowledge is the apprehension of it as beautiful.' The sense of order and propriety, the cultivation of what was called taste, can make the mind impatient with miracle and mystery, with the severe and the terrible, and 'a perception of the Beautiful becomes the substitute for faith'.[1]

In place of the difficult dogmas of Christianity, which at points seem so awkward to a cultivated imagination, Newman observes that men of taste tend to develop a 'Religion of Philosophy'. Even a pious man can become tainted with it. Newman quotes Burke's famous lamentation on the passing of the spirit of chivalry:

'It is gone,' cries Mr. Burke; 'that sensibility of principle, that chastity of honour, which felt a stain like a wound; which inspired courage,

[1] *The Idea of a University*, pp. 192–3.

while it mitigated ferocity; which ennobled whatever it touched, and under which *vice lost half its evil by losing all its grossness.*' In the last clause of this beautiful sentence we have too apt an illustration of the ethical temperament of a civilized age. It is detection, not the sin, which is the crime; private life is sacred, and inquiry into it is intolerable; and decency is virtue.[1]

And we know that even Newman's celebrated portrait of a gentleman does not represent his ideal of human conduct, but the ideal ethical character of a cultivated intellect, intellect operating without direct reference to religious principle. The gentleman may be found within the church and without it. If he is not a Christian, his religion, like Burke's sense of chivalry, 'is the embodiment of those ideas of the sublime, majestic, and beautiful, without which there can be no large philosophy'.[2]

But Newman knew from the reactions to his own conversion that the world does not lightly forgive the abandonment of its social and aesthetic achievements. Members of the nineteenth-century establishment are apt to be astonished at the choice made by converts to Roman Catholicism:

Here is a lady of birth; she might be useful at home, she might marry well, she might be an ornament to society, she might give her countenance to religious objects, and she has perversely left us all; she has cut off her hair, and put on a coarse garment, and is washing the feet of the poor. There is a man of name and ability, who has thrown himself out of his sphere of influence and secular position, and he chooses a place where no one knows his worth; and he is teaching little children their catechism.[3]

The same judgement was made of the primitive Christians by their pagan contemporaries. Newman quotes Plutarch: 'What men like best are festivals, banquets at the temples, initiations, orgies, votive prayers, and adorations. But the superstitious wishes indeed, but is unable to rejoice. He is crowned and turns pale; he sacrifices and is in fear; he prays with a quivering voice, and burns incense with trembling hands.'[4] These are the observations of a reasonable man, of a philosopher and artist; and yet

---

[1] Ibid., pp. 178–9.   [2] Ibid., p. 186.

[3] *Discourses to Mixed Congregations*, p. 313.

[4] *Essay on Development*, pp. 210–11.

those despised superstitious possess the emotional readiness for assent which Newman defends, while Plutarch represents that lucid reasonableness which in religion he deplores.

In *The Idea of a University* Newman quotes Gibbon's account of the death of Julian wherein the emperor calmly reproves his mourners for their tears and hastens his own end by arguing with the philosophers Priscus and Maximus on the nature of the soul. Of this Socratic example of philosophic dignity and courage at the ultimate moment Newman appreciatively but ironically remarks:

> Such, Gentlemen, is the final exhibition of the Religion of Reason: in the insensibility of conscience, in the ignorance of the very idea of sin, in the contemplation of his own moral consistency, in the simple absence of fear, in the cloudless self-confidence, in the serene self-possession, in the cold self-satisfaction, we recognize the mere philosopher.[1]

All 'mere' philosophies, those which reject as superstitious the severe, the terrible, the mysterious in religion for the sake of the elegant and pleasurable, suffer in Newman's writings. His Christianity is the reverse of fastidious. The very teachings of Jesus seem to him to have been delivered almost without regard for our love of the beautiful, for our sense of order, or even for our need of lucid explanation. 'Now I would say that the greater part of our Lord's teaching is *not* clear—and where it is clearest, it is most startling to the imagination. Perhaps the clearest doctrine of all laid down is that of eternal punishment. (Is this doctrine to be received as a sole dogmatic truth, like some promontory coming clear out of a thick sea of fog?)'[2] The simile is a striking one. The doctrine did indeed prove something of a promontory for many of Newman's contemporaries and continues to trouble some of ours. There is no doubt that Newman's vision of the devout mind includes among its attributes the ability, even the need, to admit doctrines so disagreeable in their representation and significance as to create even in the orthodox a sense of revulsion.

---

[1] *The Idea of a University*, pp. 173-4.   [2] *Letters and Diaries*, xiv. 181.

Nor is such difficulty mitigated by the legend and history of the early church. At the end of his great analysis of religious belief in the *Grammar of Assent*, a work generally spare and direct, Newman gives accounts of the deaths of various martyrs in order to show the strength of Christian faith. He insists upon the peculiarly grotesque quality of their suffering. The slave Blandina is roasted in a red-hot chair and exposed in a net to a bull. Another, Potomiaena, is boiled in pitch. 'When Barulas, a child of seven years old, was scourged to blood for repeating his catechism before the heathen judge—viz. "There is but one God, and Jesus Christ is true God"—his mother encouraged him to persevere, chiding him for asking for some drink.' How are we, orthodox or mere philosophers, supposed to react to this? Newman tells us: 'Call such conduct madness, if you will, or magic; but do not mock us by ascribing it in such mere children to simple desire of immortality, or to any ecclesiastical organization.'[1]

THE NOVELS

The opposition between the apparent grotesque irrationality of Primitive Christianity and the reasonable appeals of art and nature forms the central theme of Newman's second novel. *Callista* begins with a description of the richness of the countryside and the magnificence of the architecture around the city of Sicca in Proconsular Africa. The landscape is a garden or a vineyard, decorated with radiant villas and temples. Nature has given her best and man has made himself comfortable with it. The chief deity is the goddess Astarte who takes upon herself the three characters of Urania, Juno, and Aphrodite and whose manifestations in human state are respectively the philosopher, the statesman, and what Newman rather obliquely calls the vulgar. The young are urged, '"do not be out of tune with nature, nor clash with the great system of the universe"'. Life, for those who have the means to live, is luxurious and easy, conditions which Newman illustrates with some skilful strokes in the early chapters: 'A pause occurred in the conversation as one or Jucundus's

[1] *Grammar of Assent*, pp. 365–9.

slaves entered with fresh wine, larger goblets, and a vase of snow from the Atlas.'[1]

Christianity, however, has been allowed to degenerate through the laxity of corrupt bishops and through the decline of virtue in their congregations. Third-century Sicca has had its religious opportunity and has neglected to take it. Punishment arrives in the form of a plague of locusts, whose destruction of city and land is superbly described. They are a 'visitation', an 'instrument of divine power'.[2] They destroy the richness and beauty which men did not know how to value as a gift, which they took for its own sake rather than for the sake of the Giver.

More difficult to appreciate is the analogous destruction of Callista's personal beauty, which Newman carries out with particular emphasis. She is an exquisite sculptress of exquisite pagan images, who improvises poetry and acts with brilliance passages from the great drama of her native Greece. Her beauty, however, serves as a temptation to the young Christian Agellius who rationalizes his way to contemplating marriage with a pagan. The fault is his and she rejects him, an act which reconfirms his faith and which forms a step on the way to her conversion.

Nevertheless, as Callista draws closer to Christianity her physical loveliness fades. We as readers watch the deterioration primarily through the eyes of Caecilius Cyprianus, Bishop of Carthage, who is what Newman would call the 'human means' of her conversion. It is when he first sees her that we first feel her beauty in its fullest impressiveness:

It was the calm of Greek sculpture; it imaged a soul nourished upon the visions of genius, and subdued and attuned by the power of a strong will. There was no appearance of timidity in her manner; very little of modesty. The evening sun gleamed across her amber robe, and lit it up till it glowed like fire, as if she were invested in the marriage *flammeum*, and was to be claimed that evening as the bride of her own bright god of day.[3]

---

[1] *Callista*, ch. i, p. 9; ch. v, p. 50. *Callista* was completed in 1855, *Loss and Gain* in 1848.
[2] *Callista*, ch. xv, pp. 168, 170.   [3] Ibid., ch. xix, p. 213.

The language, not markedly demure by the standards of Victorian fiction, shows, I think, that Newman understood what he was willing to sacrifice. And sacrificed it is, for when Caecilius next finds Callista she is imprisoned on a charge of Christianity. She begs him to make her formally a Christian, and in a passage which is not easy to enjoy Newman gives us the bishop's reaction:

'Sit down calmly,' he said again; 'I am not refusing you, but I wish to know about you.' He could hardly keep from tears, of pain, or of joy, or of both, when he saw the great change which trial had wrought in her. What touched him most was the utter disappearance of that majesty of mien, which once was hers, a gift, so beautiful, so unsuitable to fallen man. There was instead of it a frank humility, a simplicity without concealment, an unresisting meekness, which seemed as if it would enable her, if trampled on, to smile and to kiss the feet that insulted her. She had lost every vestige of what the world worships under the titles of proper pride and self-respect. Callista was now living, not in the thought of herself, but of Another.

'God has been very good to you,' he continued. . . .[1]

The conflict between temporal and Christian grace is disturbingly represented. The destruction of Callista's beauty is the smashing of an idol. So Agellius had adored it, and her employer Jucundus had called her the 'divine Callista'. To her friends her temporal refinement was her highest self. 'This embellishment of the exterior', writes Newman in *The Idea of a University*, 'is almost the beginning and the end of philosophical morality. This is why it aims at being modest rather than humble; this is how it can be proud at the very time that it is unassuming. To humility indeed it does not even aspire.'[2] Gradually Callista's mortal gifts cease to manifest her essential being as she is transformed by her

---

[1] Ibid., ch. xxxi, p. 345. In a sermon called 'Affliction, a School of Comfort' (1834), Newman makes a similar argument: 'Sometimes we look with pleasure upon those who have never been afflicted. We look with a smile of interest upon the smooth brow and open countenance, and our hearts thrill within us at the ready laugh or the piercing glance. There is a buoyancy and freshness of mind in those who have never suffered, which, beautiful as it is, is perhaps scarcely suitable and safe in sinful man' (*Parochial and Plain Sermons*, v. 305).

[2] *The Idea of a University*, p. 181.

inward perception of Christ, the divine Object correlative of her deepest desires and fears.

If *Callista* were a conventional religious novel, a delicately sensuous account of a lovely saint, primitive or nineteenth-century, the conclusion would have to celebrate the pleasures of conversion and even martyrdom would have its notorious appeal. Callista does achieve inner peace, but Newman will not allow the imputation of romantic motives. She neither submits to the lion nor embraces the stake. Instead she is scornfully thrust into a reeking prison and, after a trial effectively described in the form of an official report, dropped into the *barathrum*, which, Newman explains, 'was nothing short of the public cesspool'. ' "Black as Orcus" ', amends one of her guards. Strapped to the rack, calling upon her ' "Lord and Love" ', she expires at the first turn of the wheels. ' "Spit in her face" ', advises an executioner.[1] And it is only Callista's corpse which glows mysteriously before the bewildered crowd and her vision which works wonders.

Callista's conversion, like that of Charles Reding in *Loss and Gain* and like Newman's own, is a gradual process. But unlike Charles or Newman himself Callista appears from the beginning possessed of perhaps as much experience in love as skill in sculpture. Newman plainly hints at her adventures in Greece: ' "Time was," ' she remarks, ' "it gratified my conceit and my feelings to have hangers on. Indeed, without them, how should we have had means to come here?" ' After her rejection of Agellius she muses, ' "And they thought to persuade her to spend herself upon him, as she had spent herself upon others." ' Only after her death do her features assume 'an expression of childlike innocence and heavenly peace'. After these suggestions it comes as something of a shock to learn late in the novel that she 'had not yet seen eighteen summers'.[2]

It is interesting that Newman, with his conviction on the virtue of celibacy, should give his heroine what is sometimes called a 'past'. In fact he takes pains to give Callista every ex-

---

[1] *Callista*, ch. xxxiii, p. 365; ch. xxxiv, pp. 366, 369.
[2] Ibid., ch. x, pp. 116–17; ch. xi, p. 132; ch. xxxv, p. 372; ch. xxix, p. 323.

perience of temporal pleasure—success, art, love—so that her rejection of the world will be conclusive.

Indeed, when we first see her she already feels a growing awareness of the hollowness of her present life. She tells her brother that ' "there's a weariness in all things" '. She broods about death, demonstrating a classical talent for aphorism: ' "The young have to fear more than the old have to mourn over. The future outweighs the past. Life is not so sweet as death is bitter." ' In Greece she worshipped the sun, ' "but somehow I worship nothing now. I am weary." ' Africa is devoid of joy. ' "And the race of man", she continued, "is worse than all." ' ' "If I were a Christian," ' she thinks, ' "life would be more bearable." ' [1]

When Agellius proposes marriage to Callista another phase of her conversion begins. He, as a Christian, recognizes a sympathy between them which leads him to hope that God has created them for each other. Callista violently reproaches him for not speaking for his God, for using God 'as a means to an end'.[2] She contrasts Agellius with a dead Christian slave of hers named Chione, who lived only for Christ. As he leaves her, Agellius repents his selfishness and asserts that, whatever she may think of his own inconsistency, the Christian God is indeed the Object she seeks.

During an attempt to save Agellius from the Christian-hunting rabble, Callista is arrested and charged with Christianity. She denies the charge regretfully but refuses to sacrifice to Jupiter, recognizing the error but not yet seeing the truth. During this most painful phase her bewildered brother brings the celebrated and shallow Polemo to dissuade her from her obstinacy. This philosopher makes the mistake of appealing to her beauty and intellectual refinement. He says he is Socrates visiting Aspasia. He points out that to burn incense on the altar of Jupiter is nothing more than a pledge of loyalty to the Roman government—analogous, we may suppose, to subscribing to the Thirty-nine Articles in order to obtain an Oxford degree. If Callista is not yet a Christian, Polemo reasonably demands, why will she not perform an act devoid of any but civil significance? But Callista's natural religious first principles prove too strong for such a sophism. She

---

[1] Ibid., ch. x, pp. 117–21.   [2] Ibid., ch. xi, p. 129.

says she will not make Caesar her god and asks the philosopher if the 'invisible Monitor' whose voice she recognizes within her will not one day judge them all. Polemo leaves in fury and fear, and his parting words reveal his devotion to the pursuit of truth only as beauty, what Newman calls the religion of philosophy: '"Poor, blind, hapless, perverse spirit—I separate myself from you for ever! Desert, if you will, the majestic, bright, beneficent traditions of your fore-fathers, and live in this frightful superstition! Farewell!"'[1]

Callista now reads the Gospel of St. Luke which Caecilius has given her. In the idea of Christ she recognizes all that was lacking in her desultory heathenism and her conversion is effected. She recognizes that by responding to conscience rather than taste she can indeed escape from the tedium of the self and the horror of spiritual isolation which Agellius's brother Juba experiences. It is the dictates of the conscience, Newman writes elsewhere, 'which *carry the mind out of itself and beyond itself, which* imply a tribunal in future, and reward and punishment which are so special. The notion of a future judgement is thus involved in the feeling of Conscience.' Notions of the beautiful and the ugly, on the other hand, are 'attended by no sanction'.[2] And so Callista comes to understand. Before her imprisonment she rejected the dogma of an 'eternal Tartarus' because her 'mind revolts from the notion'. After reading St. Luke she says she has chosen between heaven and hell.[3]

Newman's principle of the opposition of truth as beauty to truth as power is not calculated to increase his dedication as a novelist. His almost exclusively didactic motives for writing lie evident on every page. Worldly beauty may indeed fade before the truths of Christian dogma, but perhaps the novel is not the best place to prove it. Unless, as in Thackeray or Dickens, the attractions of the world, the gorgeousness of transitory pleasures, the temptations of the flesh are given a certain rein, a certain life of their own, and the moral judgement is held for a time sub-

---

[1] *Callista*, ch. xxviii, p. 316.
[2] Quoted by Boekraad and Tristram, *The Argument from Conscience*, pp. 118–19.
[3] *Callista*, ch. xix, p. 220; ch. xxxi, p. 346.

servient to the art itself, the work is not apt to be highly valued by our current critical standards. No one, I hope, would place *Callista* or *Loss and Gain* among the best novels of the century; but they can reveal aspects of Newman's thought which come to us elsewhere only indirectly or in the abstract.

Newman's characters, for example, have been especially criticized. For most readers they lack life, or depth, or richness; they seem flat, two-dimensional, wooden. By Jamesean or even Dickensian standards indeed they are. But Newman never intended to make his characters full of the unexpected possibilities of an Isabel Archer or even of a Mrs. Micawber. Nor on the other hand are they fixed in their positions like the speakers in a dialogue. Instead they represent certain intellectual attitudes or temperaments, what our jargon calls psychological types, and as such they provide interesting concrete manifestations of Newman's philosophy of mind.

When we examine the simpler characters in *Callista* we see that they are third-century prototypes of Victorian temperaments. Cornelius, a civil servant of some rank, thinks and talks of nothing but Rome. In his exaggerated praise of her virtues, in his blindness to her faults, and above all in his inability to recognize the value of any other race or way of life he anticipates Dickens's Podsnap who believes the customs of England to be divinely ordered. Jucundus, benevolent uncle to Agellius, is a man of the establishment, clinging to his comfortable gods because he is used to them and because they are sanctioned by the state. '"All is vanity,"' he observes, '"but eating and drinking."'[1] He tries to save Agellius from Christianity by promoting the union with Callista, but his descriptions of the various pagan marriage ceremonies horrify the young Christian. Callista's brother, Aristo, represents the average intelligent young Greek or Englishman—self-seeking, pleasant, briefly compassionate—whose gods are art, laughter, and the sun. Away from all these moves Callista while from their fixed positions they do their trivial best to hold her back.

But one other character besides Callista shows what may be called a genuine development. This is Juba, whose arrogant self-esteem

[1] Ibid., ch. vi, p. 62.

contrasts with the sweet rude humility of his brother Agellius. Juba represents the proud independence of the natural man, a scoffer and cynic who scorns with equal fervour the black magic of his mother, the witch Gurta, the hedonistic polytheism of his uncle, Jucundus, and the rough Christian first principles which motivate Agellius. Newman reserves for this atheistic flaunting of private judgement the worst fate of any of his characters. Juba's nemesis arrives when his mother Gurta revenges herself for his mockery by hurling some unknown but hideous beast at his face. 'The blow seemed to act on Juba as a shock to his nervous system, both from its violence and its strangeness.' Possessed, Juba runs madly away, a voice pursuing him: ' "You cannot escape from yourself." '[1]

In several of his early sermons Newman made use of the idea that the irreverent, sceptical, self-reliant individual is so constituted in mind and temperament that he would be unhappy in heaven. Juba is Newman's characterization of such a man. Like Milton's Satan he carries his own hell within him. The blasphemies he shrieks in his exile are involuntary and fill him with horror. On the brow of a hill just as dawn breaks he sees below him a valley of fruit trees, flowers, rich fields. A river flows through this Eden and flocks and herds graze on the slopes. But Juba's mind is a waste land:

Juba stood and gazed till the sun rose opposite to him, envying, repining, hating, like Satan looking in upon Paradise. The wild mountains, or the locust-smitten track would have better suited the tumult of his mind. It would have been a relief to him to have retreated from so fair a scene, and to have retraced his steps, but he was not his own master, and was hurried on. Sorely against his determined strong resolve and will, crying out and protesting and shuddering, the youth was forced along into the fullness of beauty and blessing with which he was so little in tune. With rage and terror he recognized that he had no part in his own movements, but was a mere slave.[2]

Juba's independence of mind, that unrestrained indulgence of reason and private judgement which in one form or another

---

[1] *Callista*, ch. xxiii, pp. 264, 265.   [2] Ibid., ch. xxiv, pp. 269–70.

Newman attacked throughout his life, has utimately made the sceptic the slave of his own nature. He has become alienated from God and from a creation which without God is incomprehensible. Helped by Caecilius his frenzy gives way to a state of quiet idiocy. By an act of grace, the martyred Callista appears to him in a dream, restoring his mind so that he can request baptism and die a Christian. Newman insists upon the last didactic irony by neatly transforming the novel's most relentless scoffer into a manifestation of God's transcendent mercy.

In *Loss and Gain*, which is closer to the *Apologia* in action and scene, the characters again represent states or attitudes of mind, ultimately praised or rejected depending upon their relation to dogmatic Christianity. In this novel set in Oxford the types are more subtly connected with their time, and the range of religious positions is not so great as in *Callista*. What *Loss and Gain* lacks in range, however, it makes up in subtlety. Instead of the simple contrast of pagan with Christian habits of mind we have the range of Christian movements in England. Instead of an atheist we have a liberal, instead of a pagan hedonist an Anglican of the eighteenth-century stamp, instead of Greek philosophers Oxford dons, and instead of a saint a priest. Judged by their reality and depth as credible personalities they are failures; but judged as representations of religious positions and attitudes in Tractarian Oxford not a word is wasted in their delineation.

As in *Callista*, each of these variants is embodied in a character whose position remains fixed while the protagonist develops and changes. After Charles has learned to accept the authority and doctrine of Roman Catholicism and just before his conversion, a Mr. Batts confronts him with the programme of a certain 'Truth Society', a programme opposing everything Charles has learned in relation to dogma. The Society holds that objective truth may not exist but that the aim of life is the search for it, that 'as Catholicism begins with faith, so Protestantism ends with inquiry'. The Emperor Julian, according to Mr. Batts, may be justified for his rejection of Christianity because he believed what *he* thought truth.[1]

---

[1] *Loss and Gain*, Pt. III, ch. viii, pp. 405, 404.

Mr. Batts and the others who visit Charles near the novel's end represent a kind of burlesque of the anti-dogmatic convictions and personalities which confront him at Oxford. Early in the novel Charles listens while Freeborn, an Evangelical, clumsily advocates justification by faith; but because he has rejected dogma and with dogma all strict definition, he cannot explain what faith is or what its objects are. Freeborn can only insist that theology constitutes a vast mistake, that one must have a right state of heart for true faith. He finds himself unable to provide the substance for a conviction. His religion amounts to mere personal feeling.

Mr. Vincent, the tutor, is more devious. His characteristic donnish banter has been admirably caught:

'Take some more tea, Mr. Reding; it won't hurt your nerves. I am rather choice in my tea; this comes overland through Russia; the sea-air destroys the flavour of our common tea. Talking of air, Mr. Tenby, I think you are a chemist. Have you paid attention to the recent experiments on the composition and resolution of air? Not? I am surprised at it; they are well worth your most serious consideration. It is now pretty well ascertained that inhaling gases is the cure for all kinds of disease. . . .'

This, if not quite innocent, seems harmless enough. The trouble with Mr. Vincent is that he cannot be serious on serious subjects. His levity prevents him from aligning himself with any party. He considers '"that all errors are counterfeits of truth. Clever men say true things, Mr. Reding, true in their substance, but", sinking his voice to a whisper, "they go *too far*."' The absurdity of Vincent's equivocation is evident in the advice he gives Charles on how to respond to the sermons of a Dr. Brownside, an all-religions-are-one rationalist who argues that dogmas are mere modes or forms of expression: '"I would advise you, then, to accept the *good* which his sermons offer, without committing yourself to the *bad*. That, depend upon it, Mr. Reding, is the golden though the obvious rule in these matters."' When Charles asks Vincent to be specific on points of doctrine he evades the question by urging the young man to read nothing but dead authors, for '"dead authors are safe"'.[1]

---

[1] *Loss and Gain*, Pt. I, ch. x, pp. 77, 81-3.

Among others who try to influence Charles are Campbell and Carlton, intelligent, sincere Anglicans, good Christians in every sense except that they lack the impulse to move towards the Roman Church. Charles leaves them with regretful love. Mr. Malcolm, like Jucundus in *Callista*, fails with all his paternal kindness to persuade Charles to give up his intention and, like Jucundus, he feels in his equally confused way a deep disappointment. The characterization of Willis reminds one of Hurrell Froude, especially as Froude appears in the *Apologia*. Willis is the precursor of Charles, a natural assenter whose sufferings mar his youth and beauty. Bateman, a bewildered Anglo-Catholic, tries to adopt or revive the forms of the Roman Church in a hollow official establishment, redecorating parish churches in a Catholic fashion but without Roman Catholic substance.

In *Loss and Gain* some of Newman's most cutting satire attacks the insincerity of those who pretend to follow the Anglo-Catholic precepts of the Tractarians, but who are really exploiting the movement for the sake of fashion and variety. Such a man is White, a contemporary of Charles who eventually abandons his Catholic views for the sake of establishment support in a good living. Early in the novel, after a party where he has shocked Bateman with his pretences of radical Catholicism, White together with Willis accompanies two sisters to their home, in the process making the young ladies late for their Anglican service. The four blithely indulge in the fantasy of a Catholic Oxford, peopled by monks and nuns, administered at the highest level by the pope. White observes that even the heads of houses will have to go to confession. ' "All?" asked Miss Bolton; "you don't mean converts confess? I thought it was only old Catholics." There was a little pause.'[1]

As well there might be. When the handsome prospective 'nun and monk' bid each other a respectful goodbye one is prepared to see them next with 'Love in their eyes, joy in their voice, and affluence in their gait and bearing'. Poor Charles, about to leave Oxford forever, sickens at the sight of sensations so remote from his own heart-broken loneliness. He hears the bride compare a

[1] Ibid., Pt. I, ch. viii, p. 58.

drawing of St. John the Baptist with ' "little Angelina Primrose" ' for ' "the hair is just like hers" '. What the lady really wants is a book, but she has forgotten the title. Her husband suggests one emblematic of his own compromise, 'Modified Celibacy'.[1]

More impressive than the vagaries of Bateman and White are the arguments of Charles's closest associate, Sheffield. Sheffield is a rationalist, a liberal in his habit of mind. Lucid, respectable, charming, he lacks the first principles of religion: 'he had no perceptible need within him of that vision of the Unseen which is the Christian's life. He was unblemished in his character, exemplary in his conduct; but he was content with what the perishable world gave him.'[2] Sheffield inquires into everything and yet scoffs at all conclusions. His intellect is primarily critical and iconoclastic rather than assenting and constructive.

In his milder way a forerunner of Juba in *Callista*, Sheffield particularly enjoys exposing shams, hypocrisies, inconsistencies. He ridicules the Oxford academic dress as ' "mere outside, and nothing else" '. Charles disagrees: ' "this is a great place, and should have a dress" '. But Sheffield goes on throughout the novel to apply his notion of 'outside without inside' to Anglican religious observances. He points out that a Roman Catholic priest can offer sacrifice without a congregation, but that the Anglican service is 'Common Prayer' and requires an audience. Still on this theme a few pages later he says ' "I fall in with this Bateman, and he talks to me of rood-lofts without roods, and piscinae without water, and

---

[1] *Loss and Gain*, Pt. III, ch. ii, pp. 349–51. White also suggests 'The Catholic Parsonage', 'The English Church Older than the Roman', 'Anglicanism of the Early Martyrs', and 'Confessions of a Pervert', all of which are intended to suggest what Newman now sees as the contradictions within Anglo-Catholicism. White's list includes as well 'Lays of the Apostles', meant of course to suggest the *Lyra Apostolica* to which Newman was the chief contributor, and 'Eustace Beville', which refers to Miss E. F. S. Harris's novel published anonymously under the title *From Oxford to Rome*. This last professed sympathy to those who, like its protagonist 'Eustace B.', were captivated by the Oxford Movement. But Miss Harris saw conversion to the Roman Church as their logical and soul-shattering destiny. Newman probably had *From Oxford to Rome* in mind when he stated in the Advertisement to the Sixth Edition that a novel 'wantonly and preposterously fanciful' in its representation of Tractarian views provided the stimulus for writing *Loss and Gain* (p. ix).
[2] Ibid., Pt. II, ch. ix, p. 230.

niches without images, and candlesticks without lights, and masses without Popery; till I feel, with Shakespeare, that 'all the world's a stage' "'. The effect of Sheffield's remarks and Bateman's absurdities is to suggest to Charles that Anglo-Catholicism may be form without content, a ceremony uninformed by spiritual reality. Again Sheffield shocks Charles by telling a parable of a little negro boy who steals into his master's closet and is later seen parading about, naked as usual, except for a cocked hat and a pair of white kid gloves. He is the Anglican Church in its schismatical garb. Thus when Sheffield accuses him of being on the road to Rome Charles lightly but significantly responds, ' "Well, if I am, you have put me on it . . . for you are ever talking against shams, and laughing at King Charles and Laud, Bateman, White, roodlofts, and piscinas." '[1]

In Charles, whose sensibility contrasts directly with Sheffield's, we have a Christian forerunner of Newman's gentleman in *The Idea of a University*, a forerunner whose own antecedents go far back in Newman's experience. When Newman won the Trinity scholarship in 1818 his mother gave him an edition of Bacon's works. One passage marked in pencil has particular relevance to Charles's character. Bacon is arguing that academics can become interested not only in providing solutions to problems but in maintaining existing doubts. An interested party may in fact wish to leave a problem unsolved even when a solution has been discovered, 'whereas the true use of wit is to render doubtful things certain, and not certain ones doubtful'.[2] ' "Well, I honour the man who builds up," said Reding, "and I despise the man who breaks down." '[3]

But Charles soon learns that love, the impulse to assent, and humility are not enough. Like Callista, he feels a growing dissatisfaction with his life, a sense like hers that it is action without meaning, form without content. His college suspends him on suspicion of Romanist tendencies just as Callista is imprisoned before her actual conversion. At home when Charles's sister

---

[1] Ibid., Pt. I, ch. ii, pp. 9–10, 13; ch. iv, p. 23; ch. vii, p. 52; ch. xiv, pp. 118–19.
[2] Bacon, *Works* (London, 1815), vi. 100. This is Newman's copy and may be seen at the Oratory in Birmingham. [3] *Loss and Gain*, Pt. I, ch. xiv, p. 121.

Mary notices his melancholy Charles tells her, '"I suppose it is coming out of shadows into realities"'.[1] As Charles is forced to leave his family, his gentlemanly associates, his exquisite Oxford, he too learns that religious truth is very different from the philosophical apprehension of truth as beauty.

Callista's conversion takes place because she recognizes in Christianity an unmistakable correlative of her psychic being. Charles, however, is born a Christian with 'an habitual sense of Divine Presence'. The fundamental development which he undergoes is towards an understanding of dogma. He gradually abandons his hopeful view that there exists some good in everything and some truth in every conviction. He loses respect for persons who hold what Sheffield calls a 'sham', even though their belief may be sincere. He perceives that it is 'not respectable in any great question to hold false opinions'. He begins his search for an authority, an authority which has the power to provide what Sheffield calls the 'inside', the reality which informs and vivifies the visible outside. 'Thus the principle of dogmatism gradually became an essential element in Charles's religious views.'[2]

The hollowness, not the hypocrisy, of the Anglican position is the main theme of *Loss and Gain* and Newman plays many variations upon it. This is the significance of the discussions on Gregorian music and Gothic architecture. In other words, does the English Church have essential unity? Poor Bateman wears a cassock with a tail-coat over it, manifesting in his costume the incongruity of his religious attitudes. Charles constantly sees Anglicans in argument over the nature of their religion. Is the English Church one with the Roman? Are the Rubrics and the Calendar binding? Should one fast on Friday? '"What, not fast on Friday!" cried Bateman; "we always did so most rigidly at Oxford." "It does you credit," answered Campbell; "but I am of Cambridge."'[3] But where, one is meant to smile at the classic line and wonder, is the English Church?

---

[1] *Loss and Gain*, Pt. II, ch. xii, p. 255. Charles's phrase anticipates the epitaph which Newman chose for himself: ' EX UMBRIS ET IMAGINIBUS IN VERITATEM.'

[2] Ibid., Pt. II, ch. ix, pp. 230–1; Pt. I, ch. ix, p. 66.

[3] Ibid., Pt. II, ch. xviii, p. 300.

In Charles's flight from the anomalies of Anglicanism Newman strikes a definite autobiographical note. We have seen how before his conversion he gradually lost confidence in his *via media*, how he came to see the English Church as corrupted within by that rationalistic spirit of which the ultimate extension is atheism. That Sheffield's attacks unintentionally drive Charles towards Roman Catholicism is relevant to William Buckler's observation that the *Apologia* represents Newman's flight from liberalism rather than his positive attraction to the Roman Church.[1] As potential converts, both John Henry Newman and his fictional Charles Reding protest that they have never known Roman Catholics or their form of worship. Both embrace Roman Catholicism as the only alternative to a position which they have come to see as—to use a favourite word of Newman's—unreal.

THE *APOLOGIA*

Imputations of dishonesty, of having been a secret Catholic during his Anglican life, of being an insincere one after 1845, had surrounded Newman since before his conversion. He acknowledges in the preface to the *Apologia* that he had long had a 'tacit understanding' with himself to take advantage of any open challenge delivered by a 'person of name' to plead his cause before the world. His chance came with Kingsley's famous charge:

Truth, for its own sake, had never been a virtue with the Roman clergy. Father Newman informs us that it need not, and on the whole ought not to be; that cunning is the weapon which Heaven has given to the saints wherewith to withstand the brute male force of the wicked world which marries and is given in marriage.[2]

Newman could not have had a more propitious opening. Not only was this the precise imputation from which he desired to

[1] 'Newman's "Apologia" as Human Experience', *Thought*, xxxix (1964), 82–3.
[2] *Apologia*, pp. 2, 341. Martin J. Svaglic's new edition (cited throughout this study) contains the relevant portion of Kingsley's review, the Kingsley–Newman correspondence, Kingsley's pamphlet *What, Then, Does Dr. Newman Mean?*, and the revisions made in the first (1864) for the second (1865) edition of the *Apologia*.

clear himself, but also the one which his deepest intellectual interests most fitted him to refute. As J. A. Froude observes, 'Kingsley, in truth, entirely misunderstood Newman's character. Newman's whole life had been a struggle for truth.'[1] Kingsley made his first mistake when he allowed himself to accuse an honest man of having no regard for truth; but he compounded his error when, in the pamphlet which followed Newman's publication of their correspondence, he suggested that Newman did not know what truth was. *What, Then, Does Dr. Newman Mean?* alternately accuses Newman of having lost sight of the meaning of truth and hints—despite its author's pretence of giving up the charge of conscious dishonesty—that Father Newman may have ' "wisdom" enough of that serpentine type which is his professed idea'.[2] Unfortunately for Kingsley, Newman's honesty was to be defended by one of the most acute epistemologists of his generation, an adversary to whom questions of equivocation and opinion, sincerity and conviction were far from unfamiliar.

In a sense Newman years before had created the Kingsley—surely the worst of possible Kingsleys—who figured in the controversy. 'Mr Kingsley has read me from beginning to end in the fashion in which the hypothetical Russian read Blackstone; not, I repeat, from malice, but because of his intellectual build.'[3] The hypothetical Russian we recognize as Newman's own creation in *The Present Position of Catholics* who in a parody of English anti-Roman sentiment is made to show his countrymen that English tyranny, among other atrocities, asserts the immortality of the king. We can recognize shades of Newman's Kingsley as well in the Cornelius of *Callista*, and the head of Charles's college in *Loss and Gain*: ' "You will corrupt their minds, sir," he said,—"you will corrupt their minds. . . . You will introduce them, sir, to some subtle Jesuit—to some subtle Jesuit, Mr. Reding." '[4] It is precisely this provinciality of intellect, this

---

[1] J. A. Froude, 'The Oxford Counter-Reformation', *Short Studies*, 4 vols. (London, 1883), iv, p. 326. It was Froude's own *History of England* that Kingsley was reviewing for Macmillan.   [2] *Apologia*, p. 381.
[3] Ibid., p. 387.   [4] *Loss and Gain*, Pt. II, ch. x, p. 241.

absurd insularity, which Newman captures in his portrayal of Kingsley: 'He appears to be so constituted as to have no notion of what goes on in minds very different from his own, and moreover to be stone blind to his ignorance.'[1] The tone is that of a competent collector engaged in identifying a specimen of some inferior order; and if Newman's characterization does less than justice to an Englishman whose broad career reveals a generous heart, one cannot help feeling that at least the author of *What, Then, Does Dr. Newman Mean?* stands defined.

But without wishing to defend Kingsley's role in the controversy (as is sometimes sentimentally attempted) and leaving the motives for his disingenuousness to his competent biographers,[2] there is no doubt that in the confrontation of Newman and Kingsley we find a contrast of sensibilities, of what Newman would call 'first principles', which is of greater interest than the resolution of the particular controversy. From this larger viewpoint Kingsley's bewilderment does not seem contemptible. He was dealing with a man who possessed the highest kind of dialectical intelligence, a psychologist of the first rank, a reasoner who could meet J. S. Mill on his own ground, and yet one who could affirm that the relics of St. Philip 'raised up from death or almost death, two young women and one child',[3] that 'St. Francis Xavier turned salt water into fresh for five hundred travellers; St. Raymond was transported over the sea on his cloak; St. Andrew shone brightly in the dark; St. Scholastica gained by her prayers a pouring rain; St. Paul was fed by ravens; and St. Frances saw her guardian Angel'.[4]

In offering affirmations of this sort Newman usually makes two major qualifications: that Catholic doctrine does not depend upon the validity of such accounts any more than the British Constitution depends upon the legends surrounding the Tower of London, and that he reserves the possibility that such 'miracles'

[1] *Apologia*, p. 387.
[2] Kingsley's distrust and anger had general and personal sources of a sexual nature. See R. B. Martin, *The Dust of Combat* (London, 1959), pp. 238–41; and Una Pope-Hennessy, *Canon Charles Kingsley* (London, 1948), pp. 22–3.
[3] *Letters and Diaries*, xiii. 400.
[4] *The Present Position of Catholics*, p. 300.

are produced by unknown laws of nature. Although these qualifications greatly modify the quality of Newman's credulity, his expressions of assent to these improbable reports are very striking and remain, I think, a disheartening extravagance.

Newman had long known that his somewhat impulsive veneration of religious personalities and objects seemed unbalanced to most of his educated contemporaries, and he had constructed a kind of reply to their attacks. Bateman in *Loss and Gain* conducts a long and, for the Anglican side, disastrous discussion with the Roman Catholic convert Willis on the subject of relics. Bateman points out that in a particular Roman Basilica the head of St. Paul is venerated. Other Roman Catholics, however, believe that St. Paul's head was discovered under his own church. At least one of these groups must be carrying on a species of idolatry. Willis replies that since both heads as relics preserved by Christians must have belonged to martyrs, it is not a question of false veneration but of a minor error in identification.[1] A true Catholic sensibility, Newman suggests elsewhere, comprehends such excesses as part of the human condition:

Why, then, should He, the Great Father, who once walked the earth, look sternly on the unavoidable mistakes of His own subjects and children in their devotion to Him and His? Even granting they mistake some cases in particular, from the infirmity of human nature, and the contingencies of evidence, and fancy there is or has been a miracle here or there when there is not;—though a tradition, attached to a picture, or to a shrine, or to a well, be very doubtful;—though one relic be sometimes mistaken for another, and St. Theodore stands for St. Eugenius, or St. Agathocles;—still, once take into account our First Principle, that He is likely to continue miracles among us, which is as good as the Protestant's [that He is not], and I do not see why He should feel much displeasure with us on account of this error, or should cease to work wonders in our behalf.[2]

---

[1] *Loss and Gain*, Pt. II, ch. xix, pp. 317–23.

[2] *The Present Position of Catholics*, pp. 310–11. Also quoted in the first edition of the *Apologia* (p. 435 in our text). Newman distinguishes between Protestant and Catholic first principles on the continuance of miracles: 'Both they and we start with the miracles of the Apostles; and then their first principle or presumption against our miracles is this, "What God did once, He is *not* likely to do again";

As Newman suggests, such toleration of factual error, the expression of broad, urbane, almost witty charity derived from Catholic first principles or basic habits of mind or what I have called sensibility was quite beyond Kingsley's reach.

If Newman's rather abrupt characterization of Kingsley came easily to his hand, his representation of himself did not. Its immense success cost him acute suffering, and in fact one of his most effective roles is that of the sufferer who must expose his secret self. Kingsley's attack has made Newman perform on himself a 'cruel operation, the ripping up of old griefs, and the venturing again upon the "infandum dolorem" of years, in which the stars of this lower heaven were one by one going out'. We see him gradually more and more alone as he gives up one by one the friends who love him. Finally the suffering Newman writing in 1864 puts the suffering Newman of twenty years earlier before us with the poignant misquotation of Pascal's 'on mourra seul' as the more personal 'Je mourrai seul'.[1]

But Newman in pain is only one of the self-portraits in the *Apologia*. Kingsley's characterization is that of simple if barbarous insularity, but he suffers more from the implicit comparison with Newman than from the characterization itself. The variety and richness of Newman's mind and life, conveyed superbly by prose of the greatest flexibility and range, contrasts with what the *Apologia* represents as Kingsley's unexplained savagery. We see the Newman whose sentimental devotion to Trinity College wakes a response in all who love places, we are offered almost as a kind of penance the anti-Roman Newman who must later eat his words, we notice the accuracy of what may be called the scholarly Newman who is always assembling letters and quoting

while our first principle or presumption for our miracles is this: "What God did once, He *is* likely to do again." They say, It cannot be supposed He will work *many* miracles; we, It cannot be supposed He will work *few*.' Newman goes on to ask that if you had seen a miracle once, 'would it not . . . predispose you to listen to a new report?' (*Apologia*, pp. 432–3). Newman is again quoting himself from *The Present Position of Catholics*, pp. 301–7.

[1] *Apologia*, pp. 90, 197, and n. 197. 10 on page 560. In this discussion of Newman's self-representation I am generally indebted to Walter E. Houghton's *The Art of Newman's 'Apologia'* (New Haven, 1945).

notes in the preparation of his autobiography, we find the Newman who talks too much, who becomes too proud of his own
subtlety, and, finally, the ironic or tragic Newman caught in
the dialectic of his own assertions and the victim of his own
researches.

Most frequently of all, however, we have the English Newman.
The author of the *Apologia* exploited his knowledge of the English
mind not only in his representation of Kingsley but in creating a
favourable impression of himself. This he does with admirable
restraint, neither vying with Kingsley in bluffness not ingratia-
ting himself with flattering humility. The English Newman is
largely the work of a fine indignant colloquial prose: 'Am I
alone, of Englishmen, not to have the privilege to go where I
will, no questions asked?' he demands of the public journals.
After resigning his living he found no fault with the liberals,
for 'they had beaten me on a fair field'. The bishops, however,
seem to lack this English sense of fair play, for they, 'to borrow a
Scriptural image from Walter Scott had "seethed the kid in his
mother's milk"'.[1]

Readers who know Newman's letters, especially those of his
maturity, are aware that this straight-talking colloquial style is
not a mask but a natural medium for his thoughts. But even if
he could boldly show the public that he was not the super-subtle
sophist of Kingsley's nightmare nor the effeminate, debauched
Jesuit of *Punch's* cartoons, the basic task remained. He had to
represent to his Anglican readers his conversion to Roman
Catholicism in such a way as not to rearouse suspicion. He
achieved this by again being tough, tough about the historical
and theological claims to authority of the Anglican and Roman
Churches (Anglicanism is the 'half-wayhouse' on the road to
Rome), tough about the severity of Roman Catholic claims
('the right of inflicting spiritual punishment, of cutting off from
the ordinary channels of the divine life, and of simply excom-
municating, those who refuse to submit themselves to its formal
declarations'), and, above all, tough about the mind itself ('the
energy of the human intellect "does from opposition grow"; it

[1] *Apologia*, pp. 158, 193.

thrives and is joyous, with a tough elastic strength, under the terrible blows of the divinely-fashioned weapon, and is never so much itself as when it has lately been overthrown').[1] This, Newman declares, is what I believe and what Roman Catholics accept; *you* are not being asked to agree.

One of the major ethical premises of the *Apologia* is that one has the right to one's position, to the fruit of one's knowledge, even to one's private judgement. But is not this premise in some sense inconsistent with the book's brilliant defence of dogma and authority? Newman's answer, as has been suggested in an earlier chapter, refers to the nature of the subject-matter upon which judgement is exercised. The proper sphere for private judgement is the search for authority, for the church which has the power to transmit divine truth. Charles in *Loss and Gain* finally has to learn 'that we used our private judgement to find the Church, and then in all matters of faith the Church superseded it'.[2] And in the *Apologia* Newman's repeated insistence that he must go by reason rather than feeling seems strange until we recognize that in his philosophy of mind the search for authority is the appropriate field for the exercise of private judgement. The fact, for Newman, was 'that the Church in which I found myself had no claim on me, except on condition of its being a portion of the One Catholic Communion, and that that condition must ever be borne in mind as a practical matter, and had to be distinctly proved'.[3]

If we approach the *Apologia* as an account of a man's search for God we are bound to be disappointed: faith in God had possessed Newman almost from the beginning. His great auto-biography concerns a less momentous but no less profound pil-grimage. Broadly speaking, it shows us a man seeking not faith in God but a source of information about God, a means of drawing nearer, a medium of communion. For this reason its intellectual centre, its highest source of abstract interest, is neither essentially theological nor deeply psychological. Instead the *Apologia* provides us with a kind of personal epistemology in which the

---

[1] Ibid., pp. 185, 224, 225. [2] *Loss and Gain*, Pt. I, ch xv, p. 126.
[3] *Apologia*, p. 139.

inquirer attempts to discover not spiritual truth but the voice which can utter it.

'I was on a journey.'[1] Like the novels the *Apologia* represents the convert surrounded by friends, many of whom maintain a static religious identity while he moves. Pusey and Keble, like Campbell and Carlton in *Loss and Gain*, are intelligent, sincere Anglicans, good Christians in every sense except the divinely granted impulse to move towards what Newman believes to be the true Catholicism. Whately is the liberal, the rationalist whose personal kindness must not be permitted to blind the convert to the danger of the principles he espouses. Hurrell Froude, perhaps the most interesting of all, represents the assenter, the natural Catholic mind which seeks and embraces the widest available range of genuine religious experience.[2]

Away from these friends Newman moves not only through the exercise of his reason upon questions of authority, of the catholicity and apostolicity of the English Church, but in response to the convergence of events and influences. Throughout the *Apologia* we find hints that its author is being led, guided through the maze of controversy and history by a divine hand. Before the Mediterranean trip with the Froudes, 'I naturally was led to think that some inward changes, as well as some larger course of action, were coming upon me'. During his illness in Sicily he says '"I shall not die, for I have not sinned against light"' and is unable quite to tell us what he means. He admits that his vehement feelings were perhaps necessary for the original impetus of the Tractarian Movement but that once it had begun 'the special need of me was over'. Hurrell Froude's choice of a motto, the

---

[1] *Apologia*, p. 112.

[2] 'Mr. Rose said of him with quiet humour, that "he did not seem to be afraid of inferences." It was simply the truth; Froude had that strong hold of first principles, and that keen perception of their value, that he was comparatively indifferent to the revolutionary action which would attend on their application to a given state of things' (*Apologia*, p. 46). That is, Froude was an assenter rather than a reasoner. Church writes that Froude made Keble's ideas aggressive, public, and active (*The Oxford Movement*, London, 1892, pp. 31–2). Froude perhaps personified the principles of the Oxford Movement for Newman. For the specific practices and doctrines which Newman learned from Hurrell Froude see *Apologia*, pp. 33–5; and Middleton, *Newman at Oxford*, pp. 65–6.

words of Achilles, '"You shall know the difference, now that I am back again"', ring in the *Apologia* with a sense of Newman's own destiny. The echo from St. Augustine, '"*securus judicat orbis terrarum*"', which frightened Newman in 1839, makes him feel that the 'heavens had opened and closed again'.[1]

The sense of destiny, of being led by a divine will, is appropriate to the dramatic structure of the *Apologia*. Though, of course, the autobiography cannot be called a tragedy, yet elements of tragic irony are present. We see a Newman led, at times almost blindly, towards the agony of separation from his Church by means of his own desire to reach the true authority. Permitted first to make fierce accusations against the Roman Church, he is later forced to retract and taste the bitterness of his retractions. Desperately trying to support the Anglican position he must watch the *via media* retreat on two fronts under the antithetic attacks of liberalism and Roman Catholicism while his own church rejects his Catholic interpretation of the Articles and dissipates the strength of its claim to apostolic succession. Finally the Primitive Church convicts Anglicanism of schism by historical analogy. As in classical tragedy divinity and destiny have trapped the protagonist in the machinations of his own attempts to escape. At last the tragic irony blends with a pattern of Christian hope as Newman finds himself on his 'death-bed' in the English Church where he awaits rebirth in Roman Catholicism.

'From the time that I became a Catholic, of course I have no further history of my religious opinions to narrate.'[2] In the last chapter of the *Apologia*, '*Position of My Mind since 1845*', Newman shows himself at rest. He has not himself been transformed—'No one', he once observed, 'is *changed* here'[3]—but he has found his authority and it has put him in communion with the eternal. This communion enables him to live not without pain but without the uncertainty which most gave him pain. He seems like Charles at the end of *Loss and Gain*, 'so happy in the Present, that he had

---

[1] *Apologia*, pp. 41, 43, 44, 42, 110, 111. See also George Levine, 'The Prose of the *Apologia Pro Vita Sua*', *VNL*, no. 27 (Spring, 1965), pp. 5–8.

[2] *Apologia*, p. 214.

[3] 'Remarks on the Covenant of Grace' (1828?), Birmingham papers.

no thoughts either for the Past or the Future'.[1] And this sense of peace, in Newman's philosophy of mind, provides a strong proof that he has indeed found the source of truth; for we have seen that he believed the mind to be made for truth, to rest in truth as it cannot rest in falsehood.[2]

Once he has shown us a Newman at rest in Roman Catholicism, the author of the *Apologia* finds himself free to attempt a broad intellectual justification of the Catholic Church and its claims to authority. In so doing, however, he gives us as well hints of meanings which the writing of autobiography has for him, hints suggesting that biography, which here is the religious history of a living mind, must carry implications which go beyond those of fictional representations of character.

In a sermon called 'The Immortality of the Soul' (1833), Newman points out that the infant child believes himself to be a part of the world as a branch is part of a tree. He has no notion of his separate existence. As we grow aware of our separateness from the rest of the visible world we gain a sense of autonomy and consequently of responsibility for our actions. This sense of separation and consequent responsibility ultimately leads to a kind of spiritual awareness and, according to Newman, we perceive that the world is alien to our true religious being. We

are weaned from the love of it, till at length it floats before our eyes merely as some idle veil, which, notwithstanding its many tints, cannot hide the view of what is beyond it;—and we begin, by degrees, to perceive that there are but two beings in the whole universe, our own soul, and the God who made it.[3]

The sermon recalls vividly the familiar passage in the *Apologia* where Newman describes his conversion to serious Christianity at the age of fifteen, when he rested 'in the thought of two and two only absolute and luminously self-evident beings, myself and my Creator'.[4]

Despite his emphasis on external religion Newman maintained a deep confidence in the validity of this perception. The individual mind is for him always closer to God than to any external

[1] *Loss and Gain*, Pt. III, ch. xi, p. 432.   [2] *Grammar of Assent*, p. 167.
[3] *Parochial and Plain Sermons*, I, 18–20.   [4] *Apologia*, p. 18.

temporal object. In a manuscript of 1859, written when he was preoccupied by ideas which later led to the *Grammar of Assent*, Newman constructs a brief argument for the existence of God based by analogy on the sensation of consciousness in the individual: 'all I ask you to allow is *this*—that it is *true* that I *am*—or that my consciousness that I am represents the fact external to my consciousness (viz.) of my existence'. From a fact of which he has experience, his consciousness, he infers a fact which he does not directly experience, his existence. But if this essentially Cartesian argument is permitted, then he can infer the existence of God from the existence of conscience. 'Therefore the idea is not absurd that as from "sentio" I infer the existence of myself, so from "conscientiam habeo" I infer the existence of God, and again from the phenomena of sense I have the existence of matter.'[1]

Clearly there are immense difficulties with the substance of this argument. One might urge, for example, that consciousness and one's own existence are rather more intimately related than one's own experience of conscience and the existence of God. But Newman is interested chiefly in the form of argument and so are we. The important point here is that in this form of argument, as elsewhere in Newman's writings, an examination of mental phenomena leads him to realities outside the individual mind. And the example is especially relevant to the present discussion because here the mind infers God from a recognition of its own nature, so that God and self are the two existences immediate to the intellect.

'Ward thinks I hold that moral obligation is because there is a God. But I hold just the reverse, viz. there is a God, because there is moral obligation.'[2] Newman's religious thought is based upon

---

[1] *Philosophical Readings in Cardinal Newman*, pp. 190–6. Obviously Newman conceives of consciousness as a reflexive power: 'consciousness seems to me to imply a reflex act, viz. that of being aware that you apprehend. "Conscius" has "sibi" understood' (note of 9 May 1857 in the Birmingham papers). Newman is not implying that consciousness can exist without objects for its exercise, 'objects being a sine qua non, but not a guarantee of self reflection, . . . i.e. personality' (note of 3 April 1860, ibid.). Presumably most of these 'objects' must be brought to the consciousness by means of the senses.

[2] Quoted by Boekraad and Tristram, *The Argument from Conscience*, p. 103.

his study of the mind. Because the mind is most surely conscious of itself, the tracing of his own intellectual development in the *Apologia* had great religious and even theological significance for him. As Boekraad and Tristram put it, 'The best argument for God's existence is . . . part and parcel of our own existence. In the deepest recesses of our own reality we find the elements which go to make up the argument, once they are brought out and realized. The argument for God's existence par excellence is thus nothing else than: "a realization of what we are"'. They go on to quote Newman's remark about someone who had accused him of scepticism: '"I can only suppose that he contrasts philosophical with personal . . . I do not understand the distinction."'[1]

In tracing the development of his own mind Newman embarks upon a theological as well as a personal odyssey. He offers us the history of his own religious opinions, but this properly understood is nothing less than the history of the action of God's will and guidance upon his intellectual development. Introspection and the perception of divinity are almost simultaneous or synonymous acts. As B. M. G. Reardon puts it:

> His claim is that the nature and implications of the moral consciousness itself are at once and essentially religious. The simplest moral act refers us to a personal God, not merely inferentially, but concretely, as a matter of psychological fact. For when the dictates of conscience—feelings whether of satisfaction or remorse—are examined, one finds that the thought of God is actually inseparable from it. Conscience is thus 'a connecting principle between the creature and his creator'. We apprehend the divine *in* our moral experience.[2]

The *Apologia* shows us a man discovering God's will in his own moral experience. It is this which gives the book that claim to a significance transcending the history of an individual which sympathetic readers find in it. And in a sense this claim derives from a breathtaking egocentricity: 'If I am asked why I believe in a God, I answer that it is because I believe in myself.' At the beginning of his great defence of Roman Catholicism in the

[1] *The Argument from Conscience*, pp. 57, 64–5.
[2] 'Newman and the Psychology of Belief', *Church Quarterly Review*, clviii (1957), 321–2.

Apologia's last chapter he strikes the note again: 'If I looked into a mirror, and did not see my face, I should have the sort of feeling which actually comes upon me, when I look into this living busy world, and see no reflection of its Creator.'[1] The analogy is characteristically more than a comparison. It suggests that God and the self are still together, self-evident, in glorious league against the indifference, the ultimate irrelevance of the world.

And yet the *Apologia's* egocentricity, which is at once the most justifiable egoism and the most radical self-denial, does not prevent this history of Newman's mind from containing a momentous implication for other minds. There is for Newman but one source of truth. He was led to it in his individual way. But he *was* led to it, *led* by a guidance he believes to be divine. To what end, the book seems to ask, would such guidance have been granted him but so that he could perceive the truth? Or, as Jonathan Robinson puts the question, 'Why is it that the *Apologia*, being an account of a personal approach to truth, can be said to be of relevance to anyone but Newman himself—I mean beyond the immediate purpose of showing that he was not a liar?' His answer is Newman's: 'truth is not personal in the sense of being peculiar to the individual who discovers it'.[2]

But the character of the individual who discovers and assents bears directly on whether or not we accept his assertions as truth: 'our criterion of truth', Newman writes in the *Grammar*, 'is not so much the manipulation of propositions, as the intellectual and moral character of the person maintaining them, and the ultimate silent effect of his arguments or conclusions upon our minds'.[3] From what we have seen of Newman's belief in the presence of

---

[1] *Apologia*, pp. 180, 216. 'Not talking of myself makes me seem unreal—as if I were but a book or a system' (note of 1851, quoted by Boekraad and Tristram in *The Argument from Conscience*, p. 65). The structure of the *Apologia* is broadly based upon the changing states of Newman's mind in his progress towards his church: see Robert Colby, 'The Structure of Newman's *Apologia pro Vita Sua* in Relation to his Theory of Assent', *Dublin Review*, ccxxvii (1953), 142.

[2] 'The *Apologia* and the *Grammar of Assent*', *Newman's Apologia: A Classic Reconsidered*, V. P. Blehl, S.J., and F. X. Connolly (eds.) (New York, 1964), p. 162.

[3] *Grammar of Assent*, p. 230. Robinson goes on to use these words as well but forgets to indicate that he is quoting.

God's voice in the conscience, taken with his analogy between human volition and divine will, we can perhaps apply this point to Newman's autobiography and agree that his development represents in his own eyes a kind of proof of the existence of God and the truth of Catholicism.

An example may clarify this point. Throughout his career Newman defended the validity, the *reasonableness*, of a firm assent to dogma even when it presents logical difficulties or is mysterious. We know that in the *Apologia* he first takes care to clear himself of the charges of insincerity and sophistry, to represent himself as thoroughly English but deprived by prejudice of privacy and fair play, and yet an Englishman with a special mission and living under special spiritual influences. Then, with his character thus established, he claims that he easily received those additional articles of faith to which as a Roman Catholic he was bound to subscribe. 'Ten thousand difficulties do not make one doubt, as I understand the subject; difficulty and doubt are incommensurate.' He did not believe the doctrine of transubstantiation until he joined the Roman Church. He believed it as soon as he believed that the authority asserting it was the true one. 'It is difficult, impossible, to imagine, I grant;—but how is it difficult to believe?'[1]

Newman's psychological basis for this argument, as we know, is that assent is an absolute state of mind. Difficulties inhere in evidences. Men have rational difficulties with evidences without doubting. In the *Grammar of Assent* he will make a careful distinction between assent and inference. But in the *Apologia* the force of Newman's contention is not the force of abstract argument but of personal appeal and trust: I have shown you what I am, and I accept this as truth; 'but if *I* had no difficulty, why may not another have no difficulty also? why may not a hundred? a thousand?'[2] Indeed, perhaps the doctrine is true. The effect upon the reader of witnessing Newman's individual assent, the assent of a sincere and dedicated Englishman, is to suggest that the doctrine itself may have greater validity than he had supposed, a validity evinced by the character of the assenter. The history of a

---

[1] *Apologia*, pp. 214, 215.   [2] Ibid., pp. 227–8.

religious mind becomes an argument for the objective truth of doctrines to which that mind assents. By making his claim personal, Newman succeeds in making it universal.

Kingsley had asked what Newman meant: 'his very question is about my *meaning* ... about that living intelligence, by which I write, and argue, and act'.[1] The *Apologia* in the widest sense treats its author's life as a sacrament. Newman's *meaning* is that God is, that He is just and then merciful, and that His Church is Catholic.

The following is from a private note of 7 November 1877:

> Do you love, my dear Self, or don't you, your active abidance time past in the Church of England? E.g. you have a photograph of Trinity Chapel before your eyes daily, and you love to look at it. Yes and it is in a great measure an abstract—yet it is not the Church of England that I love—but it is that very assemblage, in its individuals concrete, which I remember so well—the times and places, the scenes, occurrences— my own thoughts, feelings and acts. I look at that communion table, and recollect with what feelings I went up to it in November 1817 for my first communion—how I was in mourning for the Princess Charlotte, and had silk black gloves—and the glove would not come off when I had to receive the Bread, and I had to tear it off and spoiled it in my flurry.[2]

If we understand the basic movement of the *Apologia* then we understand Newman's love of the moment in the chapel at Trinity College. The silk glove is spoiled indeed, but in the act of communion.

Newman's two novels may best be understood as dramatizations of the process of conversion, each character and each discussion embodying or illuminating a religious attitude or difficulty. In *Loss and Gain* and *Callista*, as in the *Apologia*, the convert moves away from his original apprehension of truth as beauty, away from friends and family, away from poetry and 'mere philosophy', away from Greece or Oxford, towards the acceptance of truth as power, towards dogmatic Christianity. But the

---

[1] Ibid., p. 12.
[2] Birmingham papers.

Apologia differs from the novels in representing the search for the source of spiritual truth by a living, actual mind, a mind which its author believes has been created to perceive the truth and which is protected from resting in falsehood by a love of God. For Newman, when such a mind has embraced a doctrine as true it provides a kind of proof of its validity, transcending in the very act of assent the personal meanings inherent in an *Apologia pro Vita Sua.*

INDEX

i

PRINTED IN GREAT BRITAIN
AT THE UNIVERSITY PRESS, OXFORD
BY VIVIAN RIDLER
PRINTER TO THE UNIVERSITY